WHAT ON EARTH
IS GOING ON?

TOM BAIRD
and ARTHUR HOUSE

What on Earth is Going On?

A Crash Course
in Current Affairs

FOURTH ESTATE • *London*

This edition produced for The Book People Ltd,
Parc Menai, Bangor LL57 4FB

First published in Great Britain in 2009 by
Fourth Estate
An imprint of HarperCollins*Publishers*
77–85 Fulham Palace Road
London W6 8JB
www.4thestate.co.uk

Visit our authors' blog: www.fifthestate.co.uk

A catalogue record for this book is
available from the British Library

ISBN 978-0-00-785932-0

Typeset in Minion by G&M Designs Limited,
Raunds, Northamptonshire

Printed in Great Britain by Clays Ltd, St Ives plc

Mixed Sources

Product group from well-managed
forests and other controlled sources
www.fsc.org Cert no. SW-COC-1806
© 1996 Forest Stewardship Council

FSC is a non-profit international organisation established to promote the
responsible management of the world's forests. Products carrying the FSC
label are independently certified to assure consumers that they come
from forests that are managed to meet the social, economic and
ecological needs of present or future generations.

Find out more about HarperCollins and the environment at
www.harpercollins.co.uk/green

INTRODUCTION

We wrote this book with a shared conviction that a) most people's knowledge of current affairs is a lot worse than they would like to admit, b) it wouldn't hurt to start filling in the gaps, and c) while many of these issues are dauntingly complex, they would nevertheless benefit from a clear and concise introduction.

Keeping up with the news is an interminably tall order. The media deluge us with so much content each day that by the time we've digested the headlines, a new day arrives and we have to start all over again. It's not surprising that many of us choose to stick our heads in the sand and avoid it completely.

But that's not the only alternative. The media would have us believe that events of earth-shattering importance happen every single day and that only by remaining glued to the 24-hour news cycle can we have any hope of keeping ourselves informed. Of course this isn't true. Just as important as keeping up-to-date is understanding the root causes behind issues, and gaining some perspective on how they have developed over time.

Our hope is that *What on Earth is Going On?* will help achieve this. It is a book for the bedside table, the morning commute or the downstairs loo, where it can be consulted by the confused dinner party guest who has taken refuge from the conversation next door. We hope that they will rejoin the table having flushed away some of their ignorance, and feeling all the better for it.

TOM BAIRD *and* ARTHUR HOUSE, *August 2009*

LIST OF ENTRIES

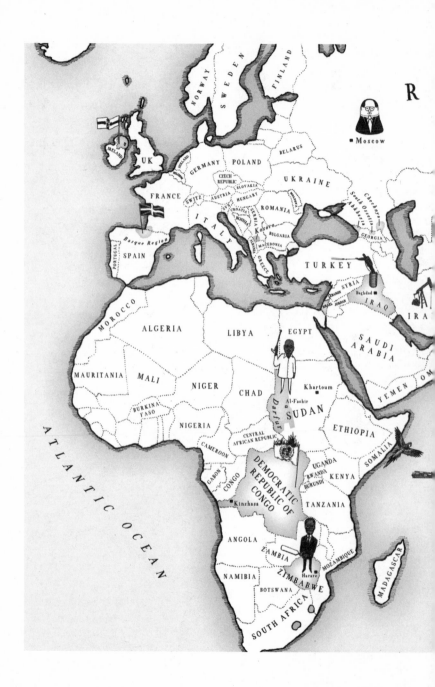

Afghanistan

Some basic facts
Afghanistan is one of the world's poorest countries, the result of decades of war and political instability which have hindered its development and crippled its economy. Its literacy rates are among the lowest in the world (51% for men and 21% for women) and average life expectancy is only 43. Afghanistan's extensive natural resources (which include copper, gold, iron ore, gemstones, petroleum and natural gas) remain largely untapped. Instead, much of the country's revenue comes from cultivating poppies, which are used to produce 95% of the world's heroin. The population of around 32 million is almost entirely Muslim (roughly 80% Sunni, 20% Shi'a – see **Islam**), but ethnically diverse and multilingual. The most common language is Persian, spoken by around 80% of the population, followed by Pashto, the language of the Pashtun people, who dominate the southern lowlands of the country and constitute its largest ethnic group (42% of the population; groups dominating the centre and northern regions include Tajiks (27%), Hazaras (9%) and Uzbeks (9%)). Afghans usually place their loyalties with their tribe or local clan leader. This, combined with the mountainous and rugged terrain of much of the country, limits the power of state government (the current president Hamid Karzai's nickname is the 'Mayor of Kabul').

Has it always been a war-torn country?
Afghanistan's importance as a focal point for trade and migration between East and West has seen it possessed and conquered by a host of peoples throughout history, including Arabs, Persians, Turks, Macedonians, Mongols and Mughals. In

the 19th century the country was of key strategic importance in the 'Great Game' between Russia and the British empire; after several Anglo-Afghan wars, it fell into British hands before regaining independence in 1919. Sixty years later, Afghanistan once again became the pawn in a struggle between two superpowers, this time the Cold War adversaries: the USSR and the USA.

What happened?

In 1979 the CIA began funding the Mujahedeen, an Islamist group composed of diverse factions and local warlords who opposed the communist secular government. The Soviet Red Army intervened to support the government, and were dragged into a decade-long war against the US-sponsored Mujahedeen that Soviet premier Mikhail Gorbachev referred to as a 'bleeding wound'. Eventually the dogged resistance and guerrilla tactics of the Mujahedeen forced the Soviets to pull out in 1989. The US lost interest in Afghanistan after the collapse of the USSR, and the country entered a volatile period in which the Mujahedeen ousted the communist government and took control of the capital, Kabul, in 1992. During the ensuing 'reign of chaos' a new Islamist group, the Taleban, arose in opposition.

Who are the Taleban?

The Taleban (literally 'students') are a strictly religious Sunni movement drawn mainly from the Pashtun ethnic group. They originated in the madrassas (Islamic schools) of the southern city of Kandahar under the leadership of Mullah Omar, a one-eyed veteran of the Soviet war. The Taleban started making war on the Mujahedeen with the intention of restoring stability to Afghanistan and implementing Sharia law (see **Islam**). When they stormed Kabul in late 1996 they were greeted as heroes and bringers of peace, but they soon imposed an austere religious regime which required that all 'modern distractions' from the teachings of Islam were banned. These included music, TV, card playing, dancing, high heels, kite-flying, football and even paper bags. Women were forced to go completely covered in the street, and were not allowed jobs, being expected to stay at home instead. In 1996 the Taleban provided a safe haven in Afghanistan for Osama bin Laden and his fellow al-Qaeda members (see **Al-Qaeda**). Several of these, including bin Laden, already had contacts in the Taleban (having fought with them in Afghanistan against the Soviets) and shared their fundamentalist beliefs.

What happened after 9/11?

A month after the attacks, on 7 October 2001, George W. Bush launched Operation Enduring Freedom in response to the Taleban's refusal to surrender bin Laden. This was an offensive launched with the UK which aimed to capture bin Laden, destroy al-Qaeda, and remove the Taleban regime. With the help of the Northern Alliance (former Mujahedeen militias also known as the United Islamic Front), the Taleban were successfully expelled from Kabul and Kandahar in November 2001. An interim government under Hamid Karzai, made up mainly of Northern Alliance members, was set up in early 2002. The US and UK military were joined by the ISAF (International Security Assistance Force) established in December 2001 and deployed under the approval of the UN Security Council. Led by NATO since 2003, this now consists of over 58,000 troops from 42 different countries, of which 26,000 are American and 8,000 British. The coalition also began training a new Afghan National Army to help fight the insurgents, which by mid-2009 numbered 86,000.

How successful have the coalition forces been?

Although eight years have passed since the US/ISAF invasion, bin Laden is still alive and al-Qaeda are functioning to some extent in the tribal areas beyond the Pakistan border, where multiple Islamist groups have made their bases and training camps. Despite being ousted from power in 2001, the Taleban regrouped and fought back with a new insurgency from 2003–5 which was particularly prevalent in their heartland, namely the southern provinces of Helmand and Kandahar as well as central Oruzgan. Having emerged as a distinctly Afghan movement, the Taleban's ranks have swelled in the last few years due to Pakistani recruits joining the cause in the name of jihad (see **Islam**). Although the Taleban forces are estimated at only 10,000, their guerrilla tactics (and terrorist methods including suicide bombing) are extremely hard for conventional armies to counter, and the coalition forces face similar difficulties to those experienced by the Soviet army in the 1980s. Their success will depend not on military victories but on winning the 'hearts and minds' of the people, stamping out heroin production (the Taleban briefly banned poppy cultivation in 2000 but since the 2001 invasion it has been their main source of funding), and co-operating with Pakistan to rid its tribal areas of Taleban, al-Qaeda and other Islamist militant groups.

In March 2009 Barack Obama laid out his plans for a 'comprehensive strategy' for Afghanistan and Pakistan. This involved establishing a 'trilateral dialogue' between the US and these two countries, sending in more troops in the short term to root out 'high-level terrorist targets', and channelling financial and infrastructural resources to the area that had previously been going to Iraq. Obama's policy is a hybrid of focused counter-terrorism and broader counter-insurgency, and some commentators doubt its ability to achieve both aims.

What other problems face Afghanistan?
A ruined economy and infrastructure, a weak government, an unpopular president, a corrupt police force, widespread human rights abuses (particularly against women and girls) and a poor education system.

'We'll smoke 'em out of their holes.'

GEORGE W. BUSH, *15 September 2001*

'We are not in Afghanistan to control that country or to dictate its future. We are in Afghanistan to confront a common enemy that threatens the United States, our friends and allies, and the people of Afghanistan and Pakistan who have suffered the most at the hands of violent extremists.'

BARACK OBAMA, *27 March 2009*

Aid

What is aid?
Aid (also called international aid or foreign aid) is the voluntary transfer of resources from one country to another. Aid may be bilateral, given directly from one country to another, or multilateral, dispensed via international organisations such as the World Bank, IMF (see **World Bank/IMF**) and European Development Fund, or via charities or NGOs (non-governmental organisations) such as Oxfam, ActionAid or Médecins Sans Frontières. Most types of aid fall into two categories: humanitarian aid and development aid.

What is humanitarian aid?
This is emergency aid supplied to alleviate suffering in the immediate aftermath of a war or a natural disaster. It often involves the provision of food, medicine, transport, temporary housing (e.g. refugee camps) and logistical support (management of the flow of supplies and information).

What is development aid?
Development aid (or development assistance) is a much bigger sector than humanitarian aid, requiring far more money, as it focuses on helping extremely poor countries develop economically and socially in the long term. This can involve improving infrastructure, building schools and medical centres, providing clean water supplies, tackling the effects of climate change in vulnerable countries (see **Climate Change**), enabling access to anti-retroviral drugs, setting up microfinance initiatives (see **Microfinance**), providing financial grants, loans, or debt forgiveness grants, and donating skills and expertise in

many different areas. In the long run, development schemes aim to help poor countries become self-sufficient, well governed, safe and economically prosperous.

Which countries supply the most aid?

The world's principal aid donors are the 22 rich DAC (Development Assistance Committee) states of the OECD (Organisation for Economic Co-operation and Development). Of these, the USA, Germany, France and UK give the most aid in real terms, but as a percentage of Gross National Product (GNP) they give less than the 0.7% demanded by the UN in order to meet the Millennium Development Goals. In fact, most DAC countries are lagging behind on an average of 0.47% of GNP – the only countries doing better than the 0.7% target, and therefore the most generous donors in relative terms, are Sweden, Luxembourg, Denmark, Norway and the Netherlands. In 2005, wealthy countries pledged to step up their aid donations at the G8 summit at Gleneagles, and also agreed to write off US$40 billion worth of debt owed by 18 HIPC (Highly Indebted Poor Countries) to the World Bank, IMF and African Development Fund. Since then the UK has made good on its commitments to increase aid, and this looks set to continue despite the economic crisis, with Alistair Darling's 2009 Budget pledging to deliver 0.6% of GNP by 2010–11 and reach the UN target of 0.7% in 2013.

What are the Millennium Development Goals?

These are a set of eight international development goals to be met by 2015 which grew out of the United Nations Millennium Declaration signed in September 2000. All 192 UN member countries and over 23 international organisations agreed to meet these ambitious goals, which were: eradicating extreme poverty and hunger (halving the number of people that live on less than a dollar a day); ensuring all children receive primary education; eliminating gender disparity at all educational levels; reducing by two-thirds the mortality rate of children under five; improving maternal health; halting and reversing the spread of AIDS, malaria and other diseases (and ensuring universal access to AIDS treatment by 2010); ensuring environmental sustainability and establishing a global partnership for development. Progress towards meeting these goals has been steady in Asia and South America, but sub-Saharan Africa is falling well short and some of its countries are unlikely to meet any of them. Despite a falling number of armed conflicts, Africa is still rife with disease, poverty and weak governance and remains the biggest focus and challenge for development programmes today.

How does the UK government spend its aid budget?
This is handled by DFID (the Department for International Development), a branch of the government with its own Secretary of State (currently Douglas Alexander MP). In 2007/8, 57% of DFID's programme was spent on bilateral aid, both development and humanitarian – the largest recipients of bilateral development assistance were India, Ethiopia and Tanzania, whereas the largest humanitarian aid channels were to the Sudan, the Democratic Republic of Congo and Iraq (see **Darfur**, **Congo** and **Iraq**); roughly 10% of bilateral assistance went to UK Civil Society Organisations such as the British Red Cross, VSO (Voluntary Services Overseas) and Oxfam; 38% of DFID's programme went on multilateral aid, chiefly to the European Commission's Development Fund, followed by the World Bank and the United Nations.

How effective is aid?

There are plenty of success stories that testify to the effectiveness of aid in saving the lives of poor people, particularly those suffering from diseases; for example in Morocco, cases of blinding trachoma – a bacterial eye infection – have fallen 75% since 1999 thanks to a massive donation of antibiotics from a pharmaceutical company; in China, a World Bank loan financed a tuberculosis project which is now saving an estimated 30,000 lives per year; and in Uganda and Malawi, anti-retroviral drugs issued by the Global Fund to Fight AIDS, TB and Malaria have kept hundreds of thousands of HIV/AIDS sufferers alive since 2001 who would otherwise have died. However, there are many cases where aid has not reached its intended target, or has been hampered by poor planning, corrupt governments in recipient countries or war. In 2007, the fighting in southern Afghanistan made it too dangerous for DFID to deliver much-needed food aid to thousands of starving people, which only increased local support for the Taleban insurgents. Beyond the effectiveness of delivering food or medicine, the effectiveness of development aid is difficult to measure and is a matter of some controversy.

Why?

On the face of it, richer countries helping poorer countries seems like a straightforwardly good thing. And it is true that if all aid were suddenly to stop, millions of people around the world would suffer as a result. However, there is an ongoing debate surrounding the long-term effects of aid on developing countries. It often centres on the fact that aid is seldom given for purely altruistic reasons, but usually comes with strings attached. Aid programmes were started in earnest during the Cold War by the USA/NATO and the Soviet Union as a way of fostering alliances with weaker countries and influencing their politics with capitalist or communist ideology. Since the collapse of communism, the World Bank and the IMF have been accused of being run (at least in part) by people with vested business interests who use aid programmes to open up new opportunities for global capitalism in developing countries. Some say this sort of 'neo-colonialism' leads to exploitation and benefits the corporations more than the countries concerned, whereas others argue that aid creates a dependence on the donor countries, and that increased trade is instead the key to sustainable development – hence the slogan 'trade not aid'. The OECD estimates that 58% of all foreign aid is 'tied aid' – consisting of bilateral agreements in which money has to be spent in the donor country, thereby increasing the donor country's exports and exerting its political influence over the recipient country. Tied aid is also less efficient than 'untied' aid, increasing costs for the recipient country by around 20%, much of which is spent on paying the high wages of international consultants. Aid has also been criticised for sustaining weak or corrupt governments; with a steady stream of unearned revenue at their disposal, they do not need to rely on the taxes of their citizens, who thus lose the ability to hold them accountable. Alternatively, it might allow such governments to free up funds to spend on potentially dubious areas such as defence, while the essential needs of their people are left to aid programmes.

'Millions in Africa are poorer today because of aid; misery and poverty have not ended but have increased.'
DAMBISA MOYO, *Zambian economist and author of* Dead Aid

'Development assistance based on proven technologies and directed at measurable and practical needs – increased food production, disease control, safe water and sanitation, schoolrooms and clinics, roads, power grids, Internet connectivity, and the like – has a distinguished record of success.'

JEFFREY D. SACHS, *American economist,*
Special Advisor to UN Secretary-General Ban Ki-moon and
author of Common Wealth *and* The End of Poverty

Al-Qaeda

What is it?
Al-Qaeda (meaning 'the Base') is an international Sunni
Islamist movement founded in 1988 by the Saudi Arabian
Osama bin Laden. Since 1992 it has carried out terrorist attacks
on civilian and military targets across the world in an extreme
interpretation of jihad (see **Islam**), the Islamic doctrine of holy
struggle. Most devastatingly, it was responsible for the attacks

on the World Trade Center and Pentagon on 11 September 2001, which claimed around 3,000 lives and injured 6,300.

How is it run?

The command structure and operational methods of al-Qaeda are a matter of some debate. Al-Qaeda has been known to operate cells (small groups of clandestine agents) in Western cities and to have local networks across the Muslim world (in Iraq and North Africa, for example). However, the extent to which these regional representatives are controlled by the central leadership is disputed; some claim that al-Qaeda is a coherent militant organisation, while others see it as a loosely defined concept, with a few core members providing ideology and inspiration for followers around the world. Despite this uncertainty, the 'destruction of al-Qaeda' was a key aim of George W. Bush's 'War on Terror' and the US invasion of Afghanistan following the 9/11 attacks. What is left of al-Qaeda today is unclear, but its leaders are believed to be hiding in Pakistan's tribal areas next to the Afghan border, where several other jihadi groups are based. Al-Qaeda is known to share training camps with these groups, such as the Pakistani-based Lashkar-e-Taiba, as well as fostering contacts with other militant Islamist movements such as the South-East Asian Jemaah Islamiyah.

What are al-Qaeda's aims and beliefs?

Al-Qaeda aims to remove foreign, especially Western, influence from Muslim countries and establish a new Caliphate (an Islamic empire based on Sharia law – see Islam) across the Muslim world. Bin Laden and his followers are thought to be heavily influenced by the writings of Sayyid Qutb, a mid-20th-century Egyptian Islamist intellectual who

---

Apart from 9/11, which other attacks have been attributed to al-Qaeda?

1992: Hotel bombings in Aden, Yemen (2 killed, 7 injured)

1993: First World Trade Center bombing, New York, USA (6 killed, 1,042 injured)

1998: US Embassy bombings in Nairobi, Kenya (212 killed, around 4,000 injured) and Dar-es-Salaam, Tanzania (11 killed, 85 injured)

2000: Attack on the USS *Cole*, Aden harbour, Yemen (19 killed, 39 injured)

2003: Truck bombings in Istanbul, Turkey (57 killed, 700 injured)

2003–6: Attacks in Iraq on UN, US and Shi'ite targets by Abu Musab al-Zarqawi's 'al-Qaeda in Iraq' (thousands killed and injured)

2007: Car bombings in Algiers, Algeria (roughly 90 killed, 350 injured)

2008: Danish Embassy bombings in Islamabad, Pakistan (6 killed, 24 injured)

---

advocated offensive jihad to rid the world of non-Muslim influences. He also declared that any Muslim not living under Sharia law is automatically an apostate (i.e. guilty of renouncing their faith), a crime punishable by death. This idea has been used by al-Qaeda to justify the killing of fellow Muslims. Bin Laden has been quoted as saying that Afghanistan under the Taleban regime of 1996–2001 was the 'only Islamic country' in the world.

What are its roots?
Whilst fighting against the Soviets in Afghanistan in 1984 for the CIA-funded Mujahedeen (see **Afghanistan**), Osama bin Laden co-founded the Maktab al-Khidamat ('Services Office'), an organisation which raised funds and recruited foreign jihadis, or 'Afghan Arabs', for the war effort. In 1988 bin Laden split from Maktab al-Khidamat, taking with him a loyal following; this was the core of what would later become known as al-Qaeda. After the Soviet defeat in Afghanistan, bin Laden directed his jihad towards American targets. His fervent anti-American stance has been well known since 1990, when he publicly denounced his own country, Saudi Arabia, for allowing US forces on to its soil in order to repel Saddam Hussein's invasion of Kuwait. From 1992–6 bin Laden and al-Qaeda operated out of Khartoum, the Sudanese capital, where they were joined by members of EIJ (Egyptian Islamic Jihad). EIJ's leader Ayman al-Zawahiri subsequently became deputy leader of al-Qaeda. In 1996 bin Laden and al-Zawahiri were expelled from Sudan and granted a safe haven by the Taleban regime in the mountains of Afghanistan, which became al-Qaeda's new headquarters. In 1998 bin Laden, al-Zawahiri and three others (as the 'World Islamic Front for Combat Against the Jews and Crusaders') issued a fatwa calling for the deaths of Americans and their allies, despite the fact that they did not possess the necessary Islamic qualifications to do so.

How is it funded?
Bin Laden is extremely rich himself, having been born into a prominent Saudi family, and he has close ties with wealthy Islamist sympathisers across the Muslim world. Funds are channelled to al-Qaeda from a variety of sources, including hawalas (small money-brokering operations), Islamic charities,

fake companies, lightly regulated banking centres (e.g. Dubai and Liechtenstein) and commodities such as Angolan diamonds or Afghan opium, which can be transported easily and traded for cash or weapons. Identifying the sources of funding for al-Qaeda and other Islamic militant groups is a major aspect of counter-terrorism operations against them.

'We love death. The US loves life. That is the difference between us two.'

OSAMA BIN LADEN, *November 2001*

Banking

What do commercial banks do?
Commercial banks, which include high street banks and building societies, operate a fairly simple business model: they borrow money from depositors (those who open an account at the bank and deposit money in it) at low rates of interest, and make a profit by lending it out at higher rates of interest. The sorts of loans offered by banks vary, and include business loans,

overdrafts, career-development loans, and mortgages (in which building societies specialise). Banks must keep hold of a certain amount of money (the 'cash reserve ratio', set by the government) in case depositors wish to withdraw their money. It is vital that banks manage their risk well; some of their riskier loans may default, so banks must set their rates of interest carefully to allow for this and still remain profitable.

What do investment banks do?
Broadly speaking, investment banks help raise capital for clients by investing their money (corporate finance), manage company takeovers (mergers and acquisitions) and trade securities in the global markets. Securities are financial products that are tied to the value of an underlying asset (see **Stocks and Bonds** and **Hedge Funds**). Investment banks can structure and sell new and complex types of security, including CDOs (Collateralised Debt Obligations); these contain slices of different debts of varying risk, some of which may be 'mortgage-backed' (see **Credit Crunch**). Investment banks also seek to profit from trading in the foreign exchange markets and insure other people's bonds against default by issuing Credit Default Swaps. Investment banks do a lot of lending and borrowing between themselves, lending to each other at a rate of interest known as the LIBOR (London Interbank Offered Rate), which is adjusted on a daily basis.

What was the Glass-Steagall Act?
This was legislation passed in 1933 to separate commercial and investment banking practices in the US. It was introduced after the Wall Street Crash to regulate the banking system and to protect depositors' money from the riskier practices of investment banking. The Glass-Steagall Act was repealed in

1999, allowing for the creation of 'universal' banks (e.g. Bank of America), which engaged in both commercial and investment operations. Some financial commentators have recently claimed that this deregulation was one cause of the credit crunch, as it allowed former commercial banks such as Citigroup to trade in risky sub-prime mortgage-backed securities and CDOs. In 1999 Citigroup was the largest bank in the US by asset size, but in November 2008 it had to be rescued by a massive US Government bailout having lost vast amounts of money as a result of its sub-prime exposure.

What does the Bank of England do?

The Bank of England is the UK's central bank, providing banking services both to the government and to the banking system. Its job is to maintain financial and monetary stability in the UK economy ('financial' relates to finance, which is the commercial activity of providing funds and capital, whereas 'monetary' refers to the amount of money in circulation, its rate of growth and interest rates). The Bank of England issues banknotes, acts as 'lender of last resort' for the other banks, and controls the UK's gold and foreign exchange reserves. The Bank became independent from the government (which had nationalised it in 1946) in 1997, since when it has been responsible for setting UK interest rates. Its Monetary Policy Committee adjusts interest rates to keep inflation in line with the Chancellor's annual inflation target stated in the Budget, which is based on the Consumer Price Index.

How do interest rates affect inflation?

Inflation is a general increase in prices across the economy. It is estimated with either the Retail Price Index (RPI) or the Consumer Price Index (CPI), which are calculated by adding together the prices of a selection of goods and services (exactly which ones differ in each index). Inflation occurs when demand (the amount of money being spent in the economy) exceeds supply (the goods and services produced by the economy); this creates competition for goods and services, which pushes prices up. A small amount of inflation is normal in a growing economy, but the Bank of England adjusts interest rates to ensure inflation remains low and stable in order to achieve price stability.

Interest rates control the price of borrowing and the value of saving – if they are low, borrowing is cheap and saving is not especially worthwhile, but when they are high, borrowing is expensive and saving more worthwhile. Adjusting interest rates therefore influences consumers' spending habits, and controls the demand for goods and services – if demand far exceeds supply, interest rates can be raised to discourage spending and lower demand, whereas if supply exceeds demand (which could cause a general lowering of prices known as deflation), or demand is lower than usual (for example during a recession), interest rates can be lowered to encourage spending. In January 2009, to encourage spending to combat the recession brought on by the credit crunch, the Bank lowered interest rates to 1.5% – the lowest in the Bank's 315-year history – then lowered them again in February, to 1%, and then again, in March, to 0.5%.

'It is well enough that people of the nation do not understand our banking and monetary system, for if they did, I believe there would be a revolution before tomorrow morning.'

HENRY FORD, *US car tycoon*

Basque Country/ETA

Where is it?

The Basque Country is a rugged and beautiful region of northern Spain and south-western France that straddles the Pyrenees and borders the Bay of Biscay. It is made up of seven provinces – four in Spain and three in France – and is a popular tourist destination that includes cities such as Bilbao and Pamplona, and the seaside resorts of Biarritz and San Sebastián. The Basque people are one of Europe's most ancient ethnic groups, and they have fought hard to hold on to their culture and land over the centuries. Their language, Euskara, is one of the oldest in the continent, and isn't related to any other. The French Basque region (Pays Basque) has mostly avoided the violent struggle for independence associated with its Spanish equivalent (País Vasco).

How is Spain governed?

Compared to most other nations in Western Europe, Spain is remarkable for its decentralised system of government. The 1978 Constitution, which marked the return to democracy following Francisco Franco's fascist dictatorship, allowed Spain's local regions to become 'autonomous communities' with their own government and parliament, ruling themselves with differing degrees of independence from the central government in Madrid. There are now 17 of these autonomous communities, including Andalusia in the south, Catalonia in the north-east and the Basque Country in the north (this is composed of three of the four Spanish Basque provinces, while the remaining province, Navarre, is a separate autonomous community). The Basque Country currently enjoys the highest

level of autonomy, with education and tax collection among the
responsibilities of the region's parliament.

How did the Spanish Civil War affect the Basque Country?
During the 1936–9 Spanish Civil War the Basque people sided
with the republican government against the nationalist forces of
General Franco. Franco was the latest in a long line of threats to
the Basque Country, which had in its troubled history held off
Romans, Vikings, Visigoths and Moors. When Franco came to
power in 1939 he sought retribution, and punished the region
for its resistance by banning its language and neglecting its
economy. It was during Franco's reign that the group ETA
appeared in 1959, and it has remained active ever since.

What is ETA?
ETA stands for *Euskadi Ta Azkatasuna* ('Basque Homeland and
Freedom'). It is a separatist organisation calling for complete
independence in all seven provinces of the Basque region in
both Spain and France. Spain, the European Union and the US
all regard the group as a terrorist organisation, and since
forming it has been responsible for killing over 800 people.
Police, politicians and the general public have all been victims of
ETA's violent campaign – for example, police chief Melitón
Manzanas was murdered in 1968; Spanish Prime Minister Luis
Carrero Blanco was assassinated in 1973; and a car bomb set off
by ETA killed an American tourist in 1985. ETA's political wing,
Herri Batasuna ('Unity of the People'), was formed in 1978 in
reaction to the new Spanish constitution, and fostered close
links with the Irish republican party Sinn Féin.

What did the Spanish government do?

In the 1980s, Felipe Gonzalez's government made a botched attempt at combating ETA by setting up Anti-Terrorist Liberation Groups (GAL); essentially these were mercenaries charged with assassinating key members of the separatist organisation. However, 10 of the 28 people killed by the GAL between 1983–7 turned out to have nothing to do with ETA, which led to the jailing of some of those who had set up the death squads.

Does ETA have public support?

There was strong support for ETA in the Basque provinces during Franco's reign and into the 1980s: more than half of those surveyed in a poll there in 1979 felt ETA's militants were 'patriots' or 'idealists'. However, in general, support for ETA has waned since the Franco years as the group sought civilian rather than military targets and its actions became increasingly bloody. In 1997, 6 million Spaniards protested against ETA's killing of a young local councillor from the Basque region.

Recently ETA's strength has been sapped further; its political wing was banned in 2003, and, despite broken ceasefires and continued car-bomb attacks on politicians, judges and journalists, the Spanish government – under the leadership of José Luis Rodriguez Zapatero since 2004 – seems to be winning the battle against the organisation. ETA's military commander Garikoitz Aspiazu Rubina and suspected leader Javier López Peña were both caught in 2008; in all some 750 suspected members of the organisation have been detained since 2000. In March 2009, ETA suffered another big blow when 29 years of nationalist domination in the Basque Country came to an end as the Basque Nationalist Party failed to muster a majority in the region's elections. This paved the way for the Socialist Party and Popular Party to create an informal coalition. They strongly support the Basque Country remaining part of Spain, and have promised to boost funding to combat ETA.

Guernica

The Spanish artist Pablo Picasso painted his iconic image of Guernica, a town in the Basque Country, after more than one and a half thousand people were killed when bombs were dropped by the Luftwaffe in 1937, in the first major air raid specifically aimed at killing civilians.

Basquetball

The second-largest Basque city of Vitoria-Gasteiz is home to one of Europe's top basketball clubs, Tau Ceramica. In addition, the Basque people have produced a number of star sportsmen over the years, including the footballers Xabi Alonso, Mikel Arteta, Didier Deschamps, Bixente Lizarazu; rugby players Serge Blanco and Imanol Harinordoquy; cyclist Miguel Indurain and golfer José María Olazábal.

Blogging

What is a blog?

A blog is a page or site on the internet which is updated with material, usually on a regular basis, by a single writer ('blogger'). Bloggers can post anything from breaking news to essays, opinions and diaries, often including photos and links to other websites.

What do bloggers write about?

Bloggers write about anything, from what they ate for supper to who they believe is going to win the next general election. Some see blogs as a quick and easy way to communicate their thoughts to a wide audience, but others may simply write in order to clear their thoughts – an online diary. One unifying factor about the majority of blogs is that they are, to varying degrees, personal: 'A blog is a personal diary. A daily pulpit. A collaborative space. A political soapbox. A breaking-news outlet. A collection of links. Your own private thoughts. Memos to the world.' (Blogger.com)

Are they popular?

Absolutely. Blogging has become a global phenomenon. There are no conclusive statistics on how many blogs there are, but certainly well over 100 million. The popularity of blogs varies enormously, with some attracting few or no visits while others are highly influential and command big readerships.

Who came up with the term?

In 1997 Jorn Barger – an American whose blogs vary from essays on artificial intelligence to James Joyce – came up with the term 'web log' when he began logging a daily list of links to websites he had visited. 'Web log' was shortened to 'blog' by Peter Merholz, a prolific blogger himself, in 1999. However, blogs were in existence before they were given these names. Justin Hall is seen as a pioneer – he began back in 1994 while an intern at *Wired* magazine. He posted just shy of 5,000 pages worth of entries in 11 years before throwing in the towel.

Dirty laundry

Airing your thoughts on the internet means that anyone might stumble across them, including your employer. In 2004 flight attendant Ellen Simonetti was initially suspended and then fired from her job at the American airline Delta because of photos posted on her blog 'Queen of Sky', in which she wrote about the adventures of an anonymous air hostess. One of the photos showed her dressed in uniform, with the company logo visible, which prompted the airline to take action. Similarly, Catherine Sanderson was sacked in 2006 from her secretarial job when her boss stumbled upon her popular blog, 'Petite Anglaise', about her life as a Brit in Paris. Although she never named her employers, they claimed that the photos of her on the site identified her, and therefore the firm. Sanderson won a groundbreaking case in which she sued the company for wrongful dismissal and has since written a book, also called *Petite Anglaise*.

Sleazy does it

Matt Drudge (www.drudgereport.com) is one of America's best-known bloggers. In 1998 the one-time maverick, who now commands great respect, broke the news that the magazine *Newsweek* had decided against running a story on President Bill Clinton's liaison with a White House intern from 1995–7. The following day he revealed her name: Monica Lewinsky. His story was published on a Saturday, and was seized upon by other websites, but it was not until the Wednesday that it appeared in the newspapers.

Diplomatic own goal

Arsenal fan David Miliband, who is also the UK's Foreign
Secretary, got into hot water in 2008 when he aired frustrations
on his blog about the Champions' League quarter-final in which
his team lost 4–2 to Liverpool and bowed out of the
tournament. The comments in his blog, which is part of the
Foreign Office's website, included criticism of Swiss defender
Philippe Senderos, who apparently 'left half of north London
cursing that he was ever let into the country'. An attaché at the
Swiss Embassy responded that although the defender may not
have had his best game, that was 'not a reason for a diplomatic
incident between two friendly nations'.

Burma

Where is it?
Burma is the largest country in mainland South-East Asia,
situated between Bangladesh and Thailand on the Bay of
Bengal. It sits on plentiful natural resources, including precious
stones, gas and oil, which neighbouring giants China and India
are keen to get their hands on. However, rather than benefiting
from these resources, the people of this once prosperous
country have lived in poverty for decades under a corrupt and
authoritarian military regime.

What happened after Burma became independent?
Burma gained its independence from the British Empire in
1948, and after a period of instability General Ne Win seized
power in a military coup in 1962. Ne Win quickly set about
introducing the 'Burmese Way to Socialism', a 28-point
manifesto which nationalised all industry and trade, devastated
the economy and isolated Burma from the international
community. Since military rule began, political opposition has
been consistently shackled and human rights have been abused.
Ne Win remained president until 1981, but clung on to his role
as Chairman until he finally resigned in 1988. Internal
bickering among the military leaders then caused the
constitution to be annulled, and a re-shuffled military regime
emerged which called itself the State Law and Order
Restoration Council, later renamed the State Peace and
Development Council. They remain in charge under General
Than Shwe, head of state since 1992.

What's in a name?

In 1989, the new military junta changed Burma's name to Myanmar, in an attempt to rid the country of its colonial ties. However, the country's democratic movement continue to use Burma on the basis that it is not legitimate for an unelected regime to change a country's name. While some countries, including Britain, the US and Canada, continue to refer to Burma, others such as China, Germany and Japan have adopted Myanmar. The United Nations also recognises Myanmar.

Is there any opposition from within?

Yes. In the face of this oppressive regime, Aung San Suu Kyi has consistently campaigned for democracy, her efforts winning her the Nobel Peace Prize in 1991. Her father is a national hero, having led the Anti-Fascist People's Freedom League to fight with the British against Japanese occupation in 1945. After studying and living in the UK, Kyi returned to her homeland in 1988, though for much of the time since then she has lived under house arrest. The National League for Democracy, which she leads, won the last elections – held in 1990 – with 392 out of 492 seats, but the military's grip on the country continued unabated.

Have the Burmese people protested against the regime?

Yes. In 1988, prompted by Ne Win's resignation, hundreds of thousands of demonstrators called for an end to the regime. The military reaction resulted in the deaths of around 3,000 people. In 2007, against the backdrop of rising fuel prices, Burma's monks protested after the military broke up a peaceful rally. As the number of protesting monks grew, so did images of them flooding the streets. Their courage in openly demonstrating against the junta, captured in newspapers, on

George Orwell, the novelist whose works include *Nineteen Eighty-Four* and *Animal Farm*, served in the Indian Imperial Police in Burma during colonial rule. The country also provided the inspiration for his first novel, *Burmese Days* (1934).

television and on the internet, dramatically focused the world's attention on the country's oppressive regime. Since then the monks have paid a heavy price, with jail sentences of up to 65 years being handed down to some of the protest's chief instigators.

Cyclone Nargis
Burma is no stranger to natural disasters. Since 1900 there have been around 15 cyclones, 5 earthquakes and 13 floods. In May 2008, 130,000 people died in Cyclone Nargis, which also left hundreds of thousands homeless. In the aftermath of the cyclone, Burma's government were criticised for their handling of the crisis and stubbornness in refusing to accept international aid. One bizarre twist was the arrest of a popular Burmese comedian, Zarganar, who had rallied a group of around 400 volunteers to deliver essential aid to remote areas.

Sly saves the day
In the fourth *Rambo* film (2008), which boasts more on-screen deaths (262) than any of the other films in the franchise, Vietnam veteran John Rambo, played by Sylvester Stallone, once again saves the day. While enjoying a simple and secluded life capturing snakes for a living in Thailand, Sly's peace is disturbed by a group of Christian human rights missionaries

who appeal for him to ferry them on a dangerous trip upriver into Burma. Sly reluctantly agrees and, after running into all kinds of trouble, ends up defeating the Burmese army. When speaking to reporters about the film, Stallone confronted the Burmese junta: 'If they think this movie is a fantasy, I welcome the opportunity to let me come over there and walk around the country without armed guards following me every inch of the way.'

CERN

What does it stand for?

Conseil Européen pour la Recherche Nucléaire, or the European Organisation for Nuclear Research. When it was founded in 1954, the cutting edge of theoretical physics was concerned with investigating the nucleus of the atom, hence the word 'nuclear' in the title. Today CERN's research focuses on the sub-atomic particles at a much deeper level than the nucleus; for this reason

it is sometimes also referred to as the European Laboratory for Particle Physics. CERN makes a strong claim to be the greatest experiment ever undertaken by humankind, remarkable for its scale, number of scientists and countries involved, technological expertise and sheer ambition.

Where is it?

CERN's research centres are spread across a number of sites in France and Switzerland. Its flagship site is the Large Hadron Collider (LHC) near Geneva, a gigantic particle accelerator which spans the Swiss–French border at a depth of 100 metres underground. The main component of the LHC is a 27 km ring of superconducting magnets, each chilled to −271°C, around which trillions of charged subatomic particles – either lead ions or hadrons (bundles of quarks) – are accelerated in opposite directions in a near-perfect vacuum. When they have reached 99.99999999% of the speed of light the particles are collided, generating temperatures 100,000 times hotter than the sun's core and recreating the conditions in the thousandths of a nanosecond following the Big Bang.

There are 10,000 scientists and engineers from 100 different countries working on the LHC, and six separate experiment teams analysing the data from these collisions, each of them focusing on different particles with their own set of specialised equipment. The LHC took 13 years to build and cost around £4.5 billion, and was officially switched on on 10 September 2008, sending its first particle beams successfully around the circuit. Unfortunately, an electrical fault only nine days later caused a helium leak and damage to some of the magnets, requiring lengthy repairs and delaying the atom-busting action until mid-2009.

What's the point of it?

In short, the CERN scientists are trying to discover more about the basic building blocks of the universe. Theoretical physicist Dr Subodh Patil uses this culinary analogy to explain it in layman's terms: 'Imagine you have some really exquisite quiche and you want to find the recipe, except that the person who made it won't tell you a thing. So you throw it around the room against other stuff, like fruit or custard pies, and hope that the crap that flies out gives you some hint of the fine herbs and spices used.' Over the past few decades, the Standard Model of particle physics has been developed to explain many of the observable features and interactions of the universe. It identifies twelve types of sub-atomic particle out of which all matter is made; six quarks (the up, down, charm, strange, top and bottom quark) and six leptons (the ϵ-neutrino, electron, μ-neutrino, muon, τ-neutrino and tau particle). It also recognises the effects of three fundamental forces (the strong, weak and electromagnetic forces) on these particles, resulting from the exchange of force carrier particles called bosons (gluons, photons and W and Z bosons).

However, the Standard Model is incomplete, because it fails to reconcile the theory of general relativity (Einstein's theory of gravity, which phrases gravity as nothing more than the effects of matter and energy curving spacetime to make us feel gravitational forces) with quantum theory, which is used to describe goings-on at a sub-atomic level. Recreating the conditions just after the Big Bang should give scientists a more coherent idea about the universe's workings as well as providing insights into such mysteries as: the origins of mass (why some particles weigh more than others, and why some particles seem to have no mass at all), the nature of antimatter, dark matter, dark energy and the 'primordial soup' that the universe consisted of immediately after the Big Bang (quark-gluon plasma, apparently), and whether multiple dimensions exist beyond the four that we currently know about.

What is the Higgs boson?
The so-called 'God particle' is a force-carrier particle theorised by English physicist Peter Higgs to explain why matter has mass. His theory supposes that all particles had no mass immediately after the Big Bang, but an invisible force field (the 'Higgs field') condensed as the universe cooled, and any matter that interacted with it was given a mass via the Higgs boson. This, however, may be completely wrong, and if they can't find this elusive particle at CERN (or at Fermilab, a rival American particle accelerator trying to beat them to it) the boffins will have to come up with a different theory altogether.

What is antimatter?
Antimatter was first proposed by physicist Paul Dirac in 1928. For each particle of matter that exists, there exists a corresponding particle of antimatter, with the same mass but the opposite electric charge. This idea was confirmed in 1932 when positrons (antiparticles to electrons) were found to be naturally occurring in cosmic rays, and since then anti-particles have been produced in labs (including the first anti-atom at CERN in 1995). Because matter and antimatter annihilate when they come together, and the Big Bang produced equal amounts of each, scientists don't understand why any matter still exists, or, if the antimatter's somehow disappeared, where it's all gone.

What are dark matter and dark energy?
It turns out that the majority of the universe consists of these invisible and poorly understood substances. According to the

latest observations, dark matter accounts for 22% of it, and although it cannot be seen its density can be measured because it has a gravitational field which bends light. Dark energy makes up around 74% of the universe, is evenly distributed through space and time and has a repulsive effect on the universe as a whole, which accelerates its expansion. The remaining 4% of the universe is made of matter – 3.6% of which is intergalactic gas, leaving 0.4% for the stars, planets, etc.

Is the Large Hadron Collider going to destroy the world?
No. As Brian Cox – formerly the keyboardist with pop band D:Ream and now a professor at the University of Manchester – put it eloquently last year, 'anyone who thinks the LHC is going to destroy the world is a twat'. Despite this and many other assurances to the contrary from the scientific community, some people still think it might. One group, which included a few scientists (but no particle physicists), lodged a lawsuit at the European Court of Human Rights in September 2008, claiming that CERN had not properly considered the danger to human life that the experiment posed. They feared that the collisions in the LHC could create a microscopic black hole which would grow uncontrollably and suck the earth inside out within four years. Earlier in the year two Americans pursued a similar claim at a federal court in Hawaii, worrying not only about black holes but also about the possibility of the LHC emitting 'strangelets', hypothetical objects made of up, down and strange quarks which might turn the entire planet into a dense lump of homogenous 'strange matter'. Both of these lawsuits were dismissed.

A modest proposal

In 1989, Englishman and CERN employee Tim Berners-Lee drafted a document entitled 'Information Management: A Proposal'. His supervisor's response to it was 'vague, but exciting', and he gave Berners-Lee the go-ahead to develop his idea. A year later the World Wide Web was born.

Chechnya

Where is it?

Chechnya is a republic in Russia located in the Caucasus, a mountainous region seen as part of a natural border between Europe and Asia. This area is also home to Armenia, Azerbaijan and Georgia, as well as other Russian republics including North Ossetia and Ingushetia. The majority of Chechens are Muslim and traditionally owe allegiance to their local clan (*teip*) or group of clans (*tukkhum*).

Struggle for independence

After long and fierce resistance, Chechnya became part of Russia's expanding empire in the late 1850s, but periodic fighting persisted. It enjoyed fleeting independence between 1917 and 1922 when Russia was experiencing its own civil strife. But in 1922 the Union of Soviet Socialist Republics (USSR – see **Russia**) was formed, and within it, the Chechen Autonomous Region. Fourteen years later, when the regions were being re-jigged, it became the Chechen-Ingush Autonomous Soviet Socialist Republic (ASSR), twinned with what is now Chechnya's neighbouring Russian republic, Ingushetia. The population of the Chechen-Ingush ASSR were brutally punished by Joseph Stalin for their continued insurgence; in 1944 he deported the entire population to Siberia and Central Asia on the groundless accusation that they had collaborated with the Nazis. They remained there until 1957 when the next Russian president, Nikita Khrushchev, ordered their return. The deportation caused devastating loss of life. The Chechen-Ingush ASSR lasted over thirty more years until the USSR collapsed in 1991.

What happened after the USSR fell?

A group of politicians calling themselves the National Congress
of the Chechen People, led by Dzhokhar Dudayev, declared
independence for Chechnya. Initially Moscow didn't react, but
in 1994, troops were sent in to sort out the defiant region and
ensure that other republics in the region didn't follow
Chechnya's example and break away. After some initial gains,
the incompetent Russian federal military were forced to pull out
in 1996 after dogged guerrilla resistance by the separatist forces
led by Aslan Maskhadov. The First Chechen War claimed the
lives of up to 100,000 civilians and roughly 15,000 soldiers as
well as injuring hundreds of thousands more. A ceasefire
agreement, the Khasav-Yurt Accord, was signed in August 1996,
giving Chechnya a significant degree of autonomy but not
complete independence. In January 1997 Russia recognised the
government led by Aslan Maskhadov, who had won the
presidential election.

And then?

Over the next few years tensions once again escalated.
Maskhadov's government in the capital Grozny was opposed by
extremist Wahhabi Muslim factions who began to take over
more and more areas of the country. The introduction of Sharia
law (see **Islam**) in February 1999 did nothing to appease these
groups, and in August an extremist rebel army, led by Shamil
Basayev and Saudi Arabian mercenary Ibn al-Khattab invaded
neighbouring Dagestan in an effort to establish a separate
Islamic state, which would cover part of Chechnya and
Dagestan. Vladimir Putin, the Russian Prime Minister at the
time, quelled this uprising quickly.

In September, bombs were set off in different areas of Russia,
causing around 300 deaths. While critics, including former

Russian spy Alexander Litvinenko – who was poisoned in London in November 2006 – have accused Russia's Federal Security Services of co-ordinating the bombings, Russian officials pointed the finger at Chechen rebels. As a result, soldiers were sent in on the pretext of fighting future terrorism and the Second Chechen War got under way, with Putin declaring Maskhadov's government illegitimate and Russia striving again to claim authority over the restless region. Thousands more military and civilian casualties ensued, and hundreds of thousands were displaced. Grozny fell back into Russian hands in February 2000, and three years later was pronounced the 'most destroyed city on earth' by the United Nations.

What happened at Beslan school?

On 1 September 2004 Chechen separatists took over School No.1 in Beslan, a small city of 40,000 people in North Ossetia, which shares a small part of its border with Chechnya. The group stormed the school, held over 1,000 adults and children hostage, and began rigging bombs everywhere from the ceiling to the walls, and even in basketball hoops. The hostages, who were confined to the cramped gym, were refused food and water; many drank their own urine to avoid total dehydration, and removed their clothes because of the heat. After a few days of extreme tension, Russian special forces entered the school after hearing explosions. Over 330 hostages were killed during this siege, of which 186 were children, and at least 700 were injured. Of the 32 separatists involved, 31 were killed and the sole survivor was handed a life sentence for his involvement. The Chechen warlord Shamil Basayev later claimed to have been the mastermind behind the siege. He was killed in July 2006, apparently by Russian special forces.

Journalist silenced

Russia maintains a tight grip on journalists reporting on the ongoing troubles in Chechnya. This clampdown began in earnest during the Second Chechen War after extensive coverage of the previous conflict had exposed Russia's heavy-handedness to the world. Anna Politkovskaya was an investigative journalist dedicated to exposing human rights abuses on the part of both Russian and Chechen troops, and her extensive writing, which includes the books *Dirty War: a Russian Reporter in Chechnya* and *Putin's Russia*, made her numerous enemies. Politkovskaya was shot and killed in the lift of her Moscow apartment block in October 2006, having previously received death threats and survived attempts on her life. Three men who stood trial for their involvement in the murder were acquitted in February 2009, while the murder suspect is on the run and is thought to have fled the country.

What does the future hold?

Recent elections in Chechnya were criticised by foreign observers for being neither free nor fair – in December 2007 the United Russia party won 99% of the vote. The current president of the Chechen Republic is the young, bullish and bearded Ramzan Kadyrov, who is backed by Putin and has a reputation for his tough stance against rebels. He is the son of the first president of the Russian-backed republic, Akhmad Kadyrov, who was assassinated in 2004 after only seven months in office. From 2000–9 fighting continued sporadically between rebel insurgents and the Kadyrovtsy, a militia loyal to both Kadyrovs that has been widely accused of kidnappings, torture and human rights abuses. With an administration loyal to Russia now in charge, the rebels are contained at the time of writing – Russia's 'counter-terrorism operation' against the separatists

officially came to an end in April 2009 – but uncertainty
remains over the long-term stability of the region.

> 'The people have already determined Chechnya's status at the
> referendum – it is a unit of the Russian Federation. Its political
> status is not to be discussed any more.'

AKHMAD KADYROV, August 2003

Civil Liberties

What are they?

Civil liberties are freedoms to exercise one's rights as guaranteed by the laws of one's country, or rights which protect the individual from interference or abuse by the government. Civil liberties and human rights are two sides of the same coin – civil liberties is used in the context of a government's relationship with its citizens, whereas human rights refers more to the fundamental rights that we all share, regardless of our country. Many countries have their own interpretation of civil liberties written into their constitution: the best known of these is the Bill of Rights, which are the first ten amendments of the US Constitution. This guarantees the American people several important freedoms and securities, including the right to 'keep and bear Arms' (Second Amendment) and protection from 'unreasonable searches and seizures' (Fourth Amendment). The *Déclaration des Droits de l'Homme et du Citoyen* (Declaration of the Rights of Man and the Citizen), adopted in 1789 during the French Revolution, is another key civil liberties document; in addition to forming the basis for the French Constitution, it was a forerunner of international human rights documents.

What civil liberties do we have in the UK?

The right to a fair trial, the right to privacy, *habeas corpus* (the right not to be imprisoned by the state without charge or reason), freedom of speech and freedom to protest: all of these are in the famous British tradition of civil liberties, gained over centuries of hard-won reform rather than violent revolution. Documents such as Magna Carta (1215), the Great Reform Acts (1832 & 1867) and the Representation of the People Act (1918) represent important steps on the way to 'freedom under law' and our modern political system, a parliamentary democracy that is the envy of many other countries of the world. However, despite this strong tradition, we have no single written constitution that specifies exactly what our civil liberties are; and because of parliamentary sovereignty, which incorporates Acts of Parliament into the constitution as they are passed, our civil liberties are not fixed, but subject to change. In recent years, and particularly since the 9/11 attacks of 2001, the Labour government has passed a swathe of legislation in the name of security that has led to widespread criticism of what many see as the erosion of civil liberties in this country. The Liberal Democrats and campaign groups such as Liberty and NO2ID have been particularly vocal in their condemnation of these measures.

Stop and Search

Section 44 of the Terrorism Act (2000) allows police officers to stop and search anyone for 'articles of a kind which could be used in connection with terrorism', whereas previously they needed to have 'reasonable grounds' for doing so. This was introduced as an anti-terrorism measure but has been applied in other contexts, such as with protesters at anti-war, anti-capitalist and anti-nuclear demonstrations. In 2007–8 a total of 117,278 people in England and Wales were stopped and searched under this legislation, the vast majority of these searches occurring in London. Fewer than 0.1% led to arrest for terrorism offences (let alone charges or convictions). As well as being overused, the Act has also caused social tensions, with black and Asian people four times more likely to be stopped and searched than white people. If you are subject to a random stop-and-search, remember that you are under no obligation to divulge any personal details to the police.

Freedom to protest
Sections 132–8 of the 2005 Serious Organised Crime and Police Act (SOCPA) introduced several measures that have interfered with the right to peacefully protest, including banning unauthorised protests within 1 km of parliament and placing restrictions on those that are authorised. This was widely viewed as a way of ousting the anti-Iraq war protester Brian Haw from his five-year 'peace camp' in Parliament Square. A High Court hearing in the same year ruled that SOCPA did not apply to Haw as his protest predated the legislation, but the Home Office won an appeal in 2006 that overturned this ruling. After further legal battling, Haw was allowed to stay but with various restrictions placed upon his protest, including limited use of his loudspeaker and a greatly reduced protest area. Maya Evans and Milan Rai were the first people to be convicted under SOCPA in 2005, for standing at the Cenotaph on Whitehall and reading out the names of UK soldiers and civilians killed in the war in Iraq. Two parliamentary committees (the Joint Committee on the Draft Constitutional Renewal Bill and the Joint Committee on Human Rights) have recommended that sections 132–8 of SOCPA be repealed, but at the time of writing the government has done nothing about this.

Freedom of speech
An extension of the Terrorism Act in 2006 outlawed the 'glorification' of terrorism, even if no intent to commit terrorist acts is involved. Some civil liberties campaign groups such as Liberty fear that silencing political extremists or dissenters by limiting their freedom of speech could make the country a more dangerous place by forcing their activities underground.

Habeas Corpus

As part of Tony Blair's post-9/11 measures to combat terrorism in the UK, the amount of time suspects could be held without charge in police custody was increased from 14 to 28 days, the longest in Western Europe. In 2008 Gordon Brown tried to extend this to 42 days – this was narrowly passed in the Commons but emphatically rejected by the Lords later in the year. Shadow Home Secretary David Davis resigned in protest over this issue, saying that it threatened to undermine *habeas corpus*, the right not to be imprisoned without charge or reason established by Magna Carta. The limit remains at 28 days.

The right to a fair trial

The 2005 Prevention of Terrorism Act allowed the government to place control orders on terrorism suspects in cases where there was insufficient evidence to prosecute them, for example when intelligence against the suspect had been compiled by using bugging, which is not allowed to be used as evidence in court, or where sources needed to be kept secret. Control orders can take many forms, such as restricting an individual's movement, work or communication with others, curfews, electronic tagging, requiring the individual to report at a certain place and time and confiscating a suspect's passport. In 2007 the Law Lords ruled that 18-hour curfews were too long to be imposed as part of control orders, but otherwise that control orders were not unlawful.

The right to privacy

CCTV has been used by Labour as their main way of fighting crime. Since the 1998 Crime Reduction Act, the number of CCTV cameras in the UK has risen astronomically from a few thousand to over a million (exactly how many is unknown). It is unclear whether CCTV has been effective in reducing crime, and the ubiquitous cameras have led critics to talk of the UK's transformation into a 'Big Brother' or a 'nanny' state. Other government measures have added weight to these Orwellian concerns. The 2006 Identity Cards Act provided the legal framework for compulsory ID cards to be issued to everyone over 16 who remains in the UK for longer than 3 months. The proposed card can store 52 pieces of information on the National Identity Register (NIR) about every individual, any of which could be passed on by the Home Office to any other public authority when deemed necessary. The cards have been criticised as being too expensive, both for the government (around £10 billion) and the individual (they could cost up to £60 each), and for being ineffectual in tackling terrorism and stopping illegal immigration, two of their intended aims. The launch of the card has been delayed several times, but is currently tabled for all new passport applicants for 2012.

The NIR is one of several controversial government databases: the National DNA database, which was set up in 1995 to retain the DNA records of criminals, is the largest in the world except for that of the US, and contains the DNA records of over 4.4 million people. Of these, 850,000 are innocent, including 40,000 children, while 40% of convicted criminals in the UK do not appear. In December 2008 the European Court of Human Rights judged that the database was in breach of the European Convention on Human Rights. Other databases labelled illegal by groups such as the Joseph Rowntree Reform Trust include ContactPoint, which contains the personal details of children; Onset, which identifies potential child offenders by examining their behaviour and social background; and the Detailed Care Record, which enables GPs, nurses and social workers to make unmonitored updates of patients' NHS records. David Cameron has pledged to scrap ID cards and ContactPoint if he is elected.

The UK public's fears for their privacy were heightened by a number of high-profile cases in 2007–8 in which confidential records concerning child benefits, the armed forces, justice staff, driving test candidates and criminals were lost in incidents involving stolen laptops, mislaid memory sticks, computer disks and documents left on commuter trains.

A British Bill of Rights?

One of the most high profile and controversial laws passed in the UK in recent years was the Human Rights Act 1998, which applied to UK law the European Convention on Human Rights. While some have welcomed it, others, notably Tory leader David Cameron, have criticised it for making it difficult to deport terror suspects and for providing a 'veneer of respectability' underneath which civil liberties can be eroded. Because of what Cameron calls 'the need to enshrine civil liberties in a way that is relevant to our British traditions and the need to guide the judiciary and the executive towards proportionality and common sense', he believes the Human Rights Act should be replaced with a British Bill of Rights. If the Tories win the next election this will be high on their to-do list.

'He that would make his own liberty secure must guard even his enemy from oppression; for if he violates this duty he establishes a precedent that will reach to himself.'

THOMAS PAINE *(1737–1809), author of* Rights of Man

'We can live in a world with airy-fairy civil liberties and believe the best of everybody – and then they destroy us. This is not the world we live in.'

DAVID BLUNKETT, *UK Home Secretary, 11 November 2001*

Climate Change

Is it really happening?

Yes. In 2007 the Fourth Assessment Report of the IPCC
(Intergovernmental Panel on Climate Change) established that
global warming is a certainty and provided overwhelming
evidence that man is to blame. It concluded that 'warming of
the climate system is unequivocal' and that 'most of the
observed increase in global average temperatures since the mid-

20th century is very likely due to the observed increase in anthropogenic [man-made] greenhouse gas concentrations'. Their findings have largely silenced the minority of politicians, industrialists and lobbyists who had previously denied the reality of climate change despite the mounting evidence.

How do greenhouse gases cause climate change?

Most greenhouse gases (carbon dioxide, methane, nitrous oxide, chlorofluorocarbons (CFCs) and others) are naturally produced by the earth's ecosystem and are essential to maintaining its temperature by absorbing and emitting radiation in the atmosphere. However, an excess of greenhouse gases leads to a phenomenon known as radiative forcing, whereby heat that would normally leave the earth becomes trapped, causing the atmosphere to warm up. By examining ice cores which contain bubbles of the earth's atmosphere dating back thousands of years, IPCC scientists have shown that greenhouse gases have increased 'markedly as a result of human activities since 1750 and now far exceed pre-industrial values'. CO_2 levels are now the highest they have been for over 650,000 years, due to an increase of around 30% in the last 50 years, and there is over twice as much methane in the atmosphere now as there was in pre-industrial times.

Which human activities create greenhouse gases?

Burning fossil fuels and land use change are the two main causes of global increases in carbon dioxide, the principal greenhouse gas. Fossil fuels – such as coal, oil and natural gas – are hydrocarbons, and are burnt in order to generate electricity, provide heating and power transport. The most common example of land use change is the destruction of forests to make way for agriculture. Deforestation accounts for at least a fifth of daily carbon emissions, leaving CO_2 in the atmosphere which would otherwise be removed by trees for use in photosynthesis. Increases in methane, the other most significant greenhouse gas, are principally due to agriculture (especially rice cultivation and flatulence in livestock), leakage during fossil fuel production and the burning of biomass (plant matter).

Positive feedbacks
As the atmosphere warms, its capacity to hold water vapour (in the form of clouds and humidity) increases; water vapour is itself a greenhouse gas, and so the warmer the atmosphere gets, the greater its potential to continue doing so. This is one of several 'positive feedback' processes associated with climate change. Ice and snow reflect sunlight, so in areas where they are melting, solar energy is absorbed instead by the sea or land beneath, causing the earth to heat up further. Permafrost, the deep frozen soil of the arctic and subarctic regions which locks away carbon dioxide and methane in the form of long-dead vegetation, is also melting as the earth warms, releasing more and more of the greenhouse gases into the atmosphere. Rising sea temperatures are threatening to wipe out plankton, microscopic organisms which act as a vital carbon 'sink' by ingesting carbon dioxide. This would leave yet more of the greenhouse gas in the atmosphere. Some scientists also fear that rising sea temperatures could cause a sudden release of methane from clathrate compounds on ocean floors. These are vast deposits of solid water crystals containing methane which, if melted, could create a runaway greenhouse effect. Such an occurrence is believed to have caused the Permian–Triassic event, or the 'mother of all mass extinctions', around 250 million years ago.

How does global warming cause the climate to change?
Increases in average air and ocean temperatures destabilise
climate systems and create extreme and unpredictable weather.
In some regions this means heavier rainfall, which causes
flooding (and often more erosion and subsequent
desertification), whereas other areas experience longer
droughts, heat waves and forest fires. When water gets warmer,
it expands, which, along with the extra meltwater from
disappearing ice caps, snow and glaciers, is causing sea levels to
rise at the rate of several millimetres per year. The incidence of
strong hurricanes (category 4 or 5) has nearly doubled in the
past thirty years. Their relationship with global warming
remains uncertain, although they have been linked to increased
evaporation caused by rising tropical sea temperatures.

What could be the effects of climate change for life on earth?
It is well known that climate change is endangering the polar
bear, but according to the International Union for the
Conservation of Nature (IUCN) there are as many as 10,000
species likely to become extinct as a result of climate change in
the next 50 years alone. The bleaching of coral reefs and death
of plankton caused by rising sea temperatures will seriously
affect marine biodiversity and the ocean food chain (and
dependent bird species). Amongst many other adverse effects on
ecosystems, global warming is causing infestations of tree-
killing beetles and playing havoc with the migratory habits of
animals and birds.

What could be the human costs of climate change?
It depends on how much action we take to stop it. If allowed to
continue unchecked, the potential costs are huge. Rising
temperatures will diminish yields of staple food crops such as

rice and wheat, creating more hunger and malnutrition in developing countries. Mosquitoes will inhabit more of the planet as it warms, enabling malaria to spread further. Flooding caused by heavier rainfalls or meltwater could contaminate water supplies, damage homes and spread water-borne diseases. Heat waves will continue to kill people (35,000 died in the European heat wave of 2003). The world's freshwater supply will decrease as snow and glaciers melt. Island states such as Tuvalu and the Maldives are likely to be submerged or become uninhabitable during this century, while low-lying countries (e.g. Bangladesh, the Netherlands) and coastal cities (e.g. New York, Shanghai) could soon be threatened. Desertification is causing pasture to disappear, creating competition over land – this has already been a cause of war (see **Darfur**). A World Health Organisation study in 2005 established that around 150,000 people die every year from the effects of global warming, a number which could almost double by 2020. In economic terms, it will cost much less to act now to combat climate change than to pay for it later (1% of global GDP compared to 20%, according to the 2006 Stern Review into the Economics of Climate Change).

Are there any positives?
In the UK, we're already enjoying shorter winters and warmer average temperatures as a result of climate change, and tourism and agriculture could benefit from the rising temperatures in the short term. In the Arctic, the melting ice sheet is likely to open up the Northwest Passage (between Canada and the North Pole) within a couple of decades, dramatically shortening shipping times from Asia to Europe. It is also going to enable access to the vast reserves of oil and gas believed to lie under the Arctic seabed; international squabbling over their ownership

has already started, with Russia sending a mini-submarine to plant a flag on the seabed beneath the North Pole in August 2007. Whoever gets their hands on the oil and gas, it will all get burnt, warming up the atmosphere that little bit more.

Colombia

When was the country formed?
The area now known as Colombia was colonised by the Spanish
in the 16th century, along with much of South and Central
America. In the 18th century, Bogotá (capital of present-day
Colombia) became, with Mexico City and Lima, one of the
main administrative centres of the Spanish colonies in America.
Napoleon's conquest of Spain in 1810 caused several of its

South American colonies to break away and declare their independence, which was properly achieved for Colombia by 1819 after an independence struggle spearheaded by Simón Bolívar ('the Liberator') and Francisco de Paula Santander. The resulting state was called Gran Colombia and included Colombia, Panama, Ecuador and Venezuela. The latter two countries broke away in 1830, however, and the country went through various changes of name before the Republic of Colombia was founded in 1886. Panama declared its independence in 1903.

Conservatives vs Liberals
In 1849 Colombia's Conservative and Liberal parties were founded, with contrasting political visions based on those of the country's two founders, Bolívar and Santander. Over the next century, competition between these parties often spilled over into political violence when extremist factions sought to eliminate their rivals by any means possible. Sometimes this violence led to wider civil unrest, most notably the 'Thousand Days War' (1899–1902), which resulted in over 100,000 deaths, and 'La Violencia' (1948–57), which caused more than 250,000. To end 'La Violencia', Conservatives and Liberals agreed to form a National Front from 1958–74; this was a power-sharing arrangement in which each party took turns to rule for four years at a time.

Rebels with a cause
In the 1960s, however, left-wing guerrilla groups started appearing; the two most prominent of these were, and still are, the Revolutionary Armed Forces of Colombia (FARC), and National Revolution Army (ELN), both established in 1964. These two rival groups were founded upon Marxist principles,

are based in the mountains of southern and eastern Colombia and claim to fight for the poor and against the disparity of wealth in the country. Various right-wing paramilitary groups also sprang up to protect local interests and fight the guerrillas, combining forces in 1997 to create the United Self-Defence Forces of Colombia (AUC). All of the above groups are listed as terrorist organisations by the US and EU and fund their operations largely via their links to the cocaine trade. Between them they have been responsible for thousands of kidnappings over the last few decades, as well as assassinations, hijacks, massacres of civilians, rapes and the use of child soldiers. For decades the guerrillas and the paramilitaries have fought against each other and the government in a sporadic and bloody ongoing conflict.

Coca-Colombia
Although Colombia is the world's largest producer of emeralds, it is most famous – or infamous – for its cocaine production. There was relatively little cocaine trafficking from Colombia in the 1960s, but in the following decade a growing demand for the new drug of choice in the US and Europe saw production boom. Soon Colombian drug cartels and kingpins became extremely rich off the back of this illegal trade; the drug baron Pablo Escobar even made it on to the Forbes Rich List before he was killed in 1993. Since 2000, the US has spent $6 billion on 'Plan Colombia', a programme to combat the drugs trade, which includes providing the Colombian army with training and equipment. The initial targets of the plan were not met, and Colombia still supplies the US with 90% of its cocaine. There are signs, however, that anti-narcotic operations may be beginning to work: 2008 saw Colombian coca cultivation fall by 18% and cocaine production fall by 28%.

El Presidente

President Álvaro Uribe has won praise both at home and abroad for his aggressive stance against the rebels. He was elected president in 2002 and won a second term four years later. He has been consistently popular, with approval ratings of at least 65% – a figure that would be the envy of most other politicians worldwide. He is in favour of free trade and privatisation (see **Free Trade**), while his economic policies and efforts to deal with guerrilla groups and paramilitaries have given the economy a boost.

Kidnappings have gone down in number during his presidency; in 2000 there were 3,572 kidnappings, but by 2006 this had been reduced to 521. In July 2007 the dramatic rescue of former Colombian presidential candidate Ingrid Betancourt, along with 14 other hostages, caught the world's attention and dealt a blow to their captors, FARC. With the paramilitaries he has also had some success, including demobilising 31,000 soldiers, although this was on the condition (heavily criticised by some) that they received comparably soft sentences and were exempt from extradition.

Despite these developments, Uribe's reign has not been free from scandal. In 2006 some lawmakers within his government were discovered to have links with the AUC. Although this 'parapolitics' scandal didn't embroil the president himself, his cousin Mario Uribe was arrested. Also, despite the government's efforts, cocaine production and export remains a huge problem, while the guerrilla groups and paramilitaries, if somewhat depleted, remain at large.

Gabriel García Márquez

Márquez is probably the best-known living Colombian. Born in 1928 in Aracataca, a town in the north of the country, he studied as a lawyer but soon switched to journalism. He was sent on a writing assignment to Europe in 1955, and while there one of the Colombian newspapers for which he was writing shut down, prompting him to stay in Paris. He has since lived mostly outside his homeland in a number of different countries, including Mexico, Spain and Venezuela. His novels include *One Hundred Years of Solitude* and *Love in the Time of Cholera*. Márquez was awarded the Nobel Prize for Literature in 1982.

Congo

Where is it?
The Democratic Republic of Congo (as distinct from its western neighbour, the smaller Republic of Congo) is a central African country roughly the size of western Europe that straddles the Equator and includes the vast Congo river basin and the world's second largest rainforest. It is a land rich in natural resources, including diamonds, gold, cobalt and coltan (an essential component of mobile phone chips).

What is going on there?
A decade-long war in the east of the country between national, local and rebel groups motivated by a combination of racial hatred, power and greed. So far it has claimed the lives of an estimated 5 million civilians, mostly through disease and starvation, making it the most deadly conflict since World War II. The humanitarian crisis accompanying this still-rising death toll is one of the most serious in the world at the time of writing: hundreds of thousands have been uprooted from their homes and forced into the jungle or inadequate refugee camps where aid and food are scarce, child soldiers are forced to fight by all sides, and rape and sexual violence, unprecedented in scale and brutality, is commonly used as a tactic of terror. The UN and various charities are doing what they can, but many have criticised the international community for not doing enough to intervene and bring an end to the suffering.

How did the war start?
The war has its roots in the aftermath of the conflict in neighbouring Rwanda in 1994. This was a civil war between two

ethnic groups, the Hutu and the Tutsi, which left an estimated 1 million dead in 100 days (April–July 1994). Most of these were Tutsis, killed in a systematic genocide at the hands of Hutu militias. However, Tutsi forces (the Rwandan Patriotic Front) ended up victorious and overthrew the Hutu regime. Fearing retaliatory genocide, around a million Hutus (many of them *genocidaires* – those who had committed the genocide) fled the country into Congo, which was at the time called Zaire.

What happened then?
The first Congo War, from 1996–7. The Hutu militias (Interahamwe), aided for political reasons by the weakening US-backed dictatorship of President Mobutu, started attacking Congolese Tutsis (Banyamulenge) in the states of North and South Kivu in the east. The Tutsis fought back with the support of Rwanda (which feared an invasion from the Hutus), Uganda and Angola, under the leadership of Laurent-Désiré Kabila, a long-time opponent of Mobutu (but not himself a Tutsi). The war culminated in Kabila marching on the capital Kinshasa, deposing Mobutu, declaring himself president and renaming the country the Democratic Republic of Congo (DR Congo).

Then what?
In 1998, Kabila asked Rwandan and Ugandan military forces to leave the country as it was creating tensions and making him look weak. This left the Congolese Tutsis vulnerable, and they formed a well-armed rebel group, the RCD (Rally for Congolese Democracy), backed by Rwandan and Ugandan forces who, having just left the Congo, now invaded to support them. Uganda also set up another rebel group, the MLC (Movement for the Liberation of the Congo), which operated in the north of the country. The Rwandan government claimed it was

intervening to prevent a genocide against the Tutsis that Kabila was organising; however, it is equally possible that territorial aspirations in eastern Congo were a motivating factor. In response, President Kabila enlisted the help of Hutu extremists to expel the occupying forces, as well as military support from Angola, Zimbabwe and Namibia (and later Chad, Sudan and Libya). The resulting 'Great War of Africa' was fought partly over the Congo's natural and mineral resources, many of which were plundered by neighbouring countries such as Uganda. The war had no outright victor and ended officially when a transitional government was installed in 2003. In 2006 Joseph Kabila (son of Laurent-Désiré, who was assassinated in 2001) was declared president in a democratic election, although his government was ineffective in the lawless east, where the fighting continued and has never really stopped. A UN peacekeeping mission, MONUC, was set up in 2000 and is still firmly embedded in the Congo. It is the most expensive UN mission in history, but its 17,000 personnel are limited in their ability to control and contain the situation.

Which groups are fighting there still?

The current situation is very complicated, due to the many breakaway groups and rival militias that have formed in the last decade. There are three main factions: the ill-disciplined and poorly paid Congolese national army, or FARDC; the Hutu extremist FDLR (Democratic Forces for the Liberation of Rwanda), many of whom carried out the Rwandan genocide in 1994 and who finance themselves by illegal mining; and the Rwandan-sponsored CNDP (National Congress for the Defence of the People). This Tutsi rebel group fought against both the FARDC and the FDLR until January 2009, when President Kabila, realising that they could not be defeated, made a deal with Rwanda in a rare instance of co-operation between the two countries. He allowed the Rwandan army to enter the country to fight the FDLR directly, in exchange for the arrest in Rwanda of the CNDP leader Laurent Nkunda ('the Butcher of Kisangani'). The new CNDP leader Bosco Ntaganda, also known as 'the Terminator', has agreed to integrate his forces into the Congolese army, although at the time of writing they appear to retain a degree of autonomy. Both Nkunda and Ntaganda have been indicted for war crimes by the International Criminal Court. Besides these, there are Hutu splinter groups such as the Rastas, 'a mysterious gang of dreadlocked fugitives who live deep in the forest, wear shiny tracksuits and Los Angeles Lakers jerseys and are notorious for burning babies, kidnapping women and literally chopping up anybody who gets in their way' (*New York Times*), and also the Mai-Mai, locally formed militias who believe they possess magical powers and fight, often naked and smeared in oil, against all of the above groups, especially the CNDP.

According to UN reports, Angolan troops are also present, co-operating with the government forces, while 2008 saw the arrival of Ugandan and South Sudanese armies as well. Their aim was to crush the Lord's Resistance Army (LRA), a cannibalistic cult who have been fighting the Ugandan government for 20 years and are now terrorising north-eastern Congo. Their leader, Joseph Kony, claims to be a spirit medium and a messenger of God. He too has been indicted by the ICC, and if arrested and brought to trial he will face 21 charges of war crimes and 12 charges of crimes against humanity.

Is this the worst suffering the Congo has ever seen?
Possibly not. From 1885–1908 the country was acquired by King Leopold II of Belgium, who looted its resources and enslaved its

people. During this period, half the population (around 10 million people) were wiped out as a direct result of colonial exploitation. The unnamed African country in Joseph Conrad's novella *Heart of Darkness* (serialised 1899; first published 1902) is generally thought to be the Congo of this period.

'It is the only war I have ever known where the worse things get, the more they are ignored.'

MARTIN BELL, *British UNICEF Ambassador*

Credit Crunch

What does it mean?
A 'credit crunch' is a financial crisis in which banks refuse to issue credit, i.e. lend any money, to other banks. Where they will lend, for example on mortgages or credit cards, they raise interest rates; this makes it expensive to borrow money, which slows economic growth. The term is often used to refer to the global economic downturn that started in 2007, though the tightening of credit itself was only part (albeit a crucial part) of the wider economic catastrophe.

What caused it?
The credit crunch actually had its roots in a credit binge, an unprecedented borrowing spree in the US and Western Europe from 2003–7. In 2001, interest rates were set low to let the markets recover from the effects of two disasters: 9/11, and the

bursting of the dotcom bubble (a financial crash caused by overheated speculation in internet and technology companies). Low interest rates made it very cheap to borrow money, and the US and UK in particular borrowed record amounts during this period (it was estimated in 2009 that the total debts of the US and the UK were three times as large as their combined GDP, or annual economic output). The money came from the growing economies of China, Russia and the Middle East, where people were saving instead of spending, and it filtered through the global banking system and ended up in the West as loans. Businesses and private equity firms borrowed money to expand or buy up other companies, and individuals used it to take out mortgages or buy consumer goods. The biggest borrowers were the banks themselves (in particular the investment banks of New York and London), which borrowed – or 'leveraged' themselves – on a massive scale. But the influx of all this money resulted in a bull market; businesses were performing well and their shares collectively rose. This put pressure on companies to continue borrowing, as their shareholders expected them to keep up with or outperform their rivals to maintain their high share prices. Meanwhile, house prices were rising, which created a property bubble; easy access to cheap credit kept driving prices up and encouraging yet more borrowing. Those already repaying mortgages also borrowed money in the knowledge that the value of their house was rising above its mortgage value. Everything was rosy, as long as it all kept going up.

What about sub-prime mortgages?
In the US, banks and building societies began loosening their lending policies, with many offering 0% downpayments on mortgages so that borrowers weren't required to stump up any

initial capital for their new home. This attracted many people in the 'sub-prime' category – those to whom credit would normally be denied because they were considered at risk of defaulting on repayments. With no capital invested, the sub-primers had nothing to lose and everything to gain: if house prices continued to rise, they would make money for nothing; if they fell, they could default on their repayments and declare themselves bankrupt (which carries little stigma in the US). Sub-prime borrowers were also attracted by, and in some cases mis-sold, 'adjustable' or 'floating interest rate' mortgages, many of which offered low rates for the first couple of years. While interest rates were low, floating rates seemed like a better deal than fixed rates to borrowers who were unaware of the risks involved.

Why on earth would the mortgage lenders want to offer mortgages to these people?
For two reasons. First, if the mortgage holders did default, the lenders could take possession of the house and sell it on for a profit in the rising market. Second, lenders didn't usually hang around until the defaults happened; they sold the mortgages on to other financial institutions round the world and reinvested the money they got in return. One method of selling involved slicing up these debts and packaging them together with other pieces of debt in financial products such as Collateralised Debt Obligations (CDOs). These were a recent innovation, and often so complex as to mask the true levels of risk inherent within them, but the market for these grew quickly, with more exotic types being developed and staggering amounts of money changing hands between banks, pension funds and hedge funds during this period (£3 trillion worth of CDOs were sold in 2006 alone). The banks were making huge amounts of money

by operating increasing degrees of leverage to magnify their returns, all the while exposing themselves to greater and greater risk. At the bull market's peak some investment banks were borrowing up to 100 times what they had in capital, which meant that a mere 1% downturn in asset value would be sufficient to wipe that capital out.

... and it all ended in tears

The US housing bubble finally burst when people realised how much the market was overvalued, and house prices started to fall. Interest rates were already on the rise, sparking the first wave of sub-prime defaults in late 2006. By March 2007 Wall Street was panicking, and by August the crisis was beginning to unravel across the world. Banks that had bought mortgage-backed securities (including those in the US, UK, Germany, France and Australia) realised that they, and the credit-rating agencies that they had employed, had massively underestimated their exposure to risk. No one wanted to buy securities any more, and their market value plummeted, along with the share prices of the companies that held them. The financial institutions that had lent the vast sums to the banks now wanted to 'deleverage' themselves and turn their loans back into capital. In other words, they wanted their money back. Some of the banks in question faced insolvency (not being able to pay back their creditors) and many had liquidity problems (not having enough available money to meet their day-to-day needs). Banks no longer trusted one another and refused to lend to each other; the credit crunch had set in. No bank was beyond suspicion of going bust as a result of the 'toxic debt' that potentially lurked within them.

February 2008 saw the first bank run in Britain in 150 years as Northern Rock fell victim to the credit crunch – it ended up having to be nationalised by the British government. The bank wasn't riddled with sub-prime debts, but it had relied for 73% of its funding on loans from international money markets, so when these froze up it had nowhere to turn but the Bank of England. Next to go was US investment bank Bear Stearns in March, which was bought up by JP Morgan after its share price plummeted. The summer break provided a brief respite, but in September heads really began to roll. American mortgage financers Fannie Mae and Freddie Mac were bailed out by the US government in the biggest nationalisation in history; Lehman Brothers was allowed to collapse (which caused even more panic); insurers AIG were bailed out by the Federal Reserve; Bank of America bought out Merrill Lynch; Goldman Sachs and Morgan Stanley surrendered their status as investment banks and Washington Mutual went into receivership. In the UK, Lloyd's took over HBOS and Bradford & Bingley was nationalised, while the Icelandic government was forced to nationalise its three biggest banks and the turmoil spread around Europe. By early October the global banking system was on the verge of total meltdown, needing enormous cash injections from governments worldwide to keep it functioning. Interest rates were cut to encourage borrowing and lending, but the world slid into recession nevertheless: companies went into administration, demand for goods slowed, jobs were cut and house prices sank, causing widespread negative equity and further mortgage defaults.

British banks were £740 billion in debt, prompting Gordon Brown to pledge taxpayers' money to recapitalise them to stop them going broke, and provide them with short-term loans and loan guarantees to encourage them to start issuing credit again. He also set up an Asset Protection Scheme, a sort of insurance policy for the banks in which the UK government absorbed further losses from toxic debt exposures in exchange for a fee. By May 2009, it was estimated that British taxpayers owned 65% of the merged Lloyd's–HBOS and 95% of Royal Bank of Scotland (the largest company in the world by asset size), which had suffered the biggest loss in British corporate history the previous year.

What's going to happen next?

Opinion is divided over what lies in store. Some were already claiming to see the 'green shoots' of recovery as early as spring 2009, while others fear that the problems are much more deep-seated, and that the recession will last many years. Some economic analysts are proclaiming the end of the 'turbo-capitalism' of the last 20 years – seeing a continued role for governments in global finance and tighter control of credit and leveraged risk in the future – while others see the credit crunch as a turning point in the balance of world power, as Western economic hegemony ends and the pendulum swings decisively over to China and South Asia.

'When the music stops, in terms of liquidity, things will be complicated. But as long as the music is playing, you've got to get up and dance. We're still dancing.'

Citigroup Chief Executive CHUCK PRINCE, *July 2007,*
a few weeks before the bank was crippled by sub-prime
mortgage exposure that led to it losing $32 billion

Cuba

Columbus claims Cuba

Christopher Columbus arrived on the north Caribbean island of Cuba in 1492 – the same year he discovered America – and claimed it for Spain. From then until the close of the 19th century, Cuba remained in Spanish hands despite threats from pirates and other countries (including the British, who in 1762 occupied Havana for 11 months). In the late 19th century there were two wars of independence as Cuba sought to free itself from Spain. The first, from 1868–78, ended with the Spanish promising various economic and political reforms to the Cuban people, some of which never materialised. This led to another drive for independence inspired by the revolutionary and poet José Martí, and a second war, from 1895–8, which ended in victory for the Cubans after the US joined in and helped them defeat the Spanish.

When was independence established?

Cuba became an independent republic in 1902, and the following year signed the Platt Amendment with the US, which gave the US the right to intervene when necessary to maintain successful independence. One of the conditions in the agreement was for the new government to sell or lease land to the US that could be used for coaling or naval bases. The right of the US to intervene in Cuba's internal affairs ended with another agreement in 1934, but their rights to maintain the naval base at Guantánamo Bay were kept.

Viva la Revolución!

The year before the 1934 agreement General Fulgencio Batista led a successful coup that propelled him to power. He ruled Cuba from 1933–44 and again from 1952–59. Shortly after regaining power, Batista was confronted by a band of socialist revolutionaries led by Fidel Castro who attempted, but failed, to overthrow the regime. Castro was arrested and jailed, but didn't spend long there as all political prisoners were freed by Batista in 1955. When free, Castro went to Mexico to regroup, and in 1959 led a successful revolution flanked by his brother Raul and Ernesto 'Che' Guevara. Che was an Argentinean doctor, renowned as a key strategist in the revolutionary struggle and for his bravery as a guerrilla commander. As teenagers all over the world will know, Che has come to embody the spirit of the socialist revolution. He was just 39 years old when he was hunted down and killed by CIA-backed Bolivian special forces while leading a group of Marxist-Leninist guerrillas in Bolivia in 1967.

Getting through the Cold War

After the successful revolution, relations soured between the US and Cuba, which officially became a communist state in 1961 and began developing close ties with the USSR (Cuba is now one of only five remaining communist states, along with China, North Korea, Laos and Vietnam). That same year the US backed the unsuccessful 'Bay of Pigs' invasion, so named after the inlet on the island's south coast where a group of Cuban exiles landed in an attempt to topple Castro and his regime. In October 1962 the Cuban Missile Crisis brought the world to the brink of nuclear war: in a bid to protect Cuba from further American threats, Castro had allowed Soviet premier Khrushchev to station nuclear missiles on the island, from where the USSR could potentially hit New York or Washington. When the US spotted the missiles, they imposed a naval blockade on Cuba, and after tense negotiations they were removed in return for American missiles being withdrawn from Turkey. After this narrowly averted crisis, Cuba continued to benefit from aid and trade with the USSR until its collapse in 1991.

From one brother to another

Despite the loss of support from the USSR, Cuba's old revolutionary guard pushed on doggedly. Some measures have been introduced to improve conditions in the country, and tourism has been encouraged to replace the lost revenue. However, there are internal frustrations from citizens locked in what they regard as a weary and run-down Communist state. The international community has also widely condemned the human rights situation, from the tightly controlled media to the arrests of dissidents legally protesting against the one-party regime. Fidel retained power until 2006 when abdominal surgery forced him to hand over the reins to his brother Raul, who officially became president in early 2008. Fidel is thought to have terminal cancer and is not expected to survive for much longer: many feel that a political system and a regime built and dominated for so long by one man will not be able to survive his death, fuelling speculation that Cuba would undergo major economic and political reforms that might lead to the US lifting its trade embargo with the island and attempting to exert its influence over it.

What is Guantánamo Bay?

Guantánamo Bay, on Cuba's south-east coast, is home to a US Naval base. This 45-square-mile area was originally leased by the US government a few years after they defeated the Spanish.

The Mojito and how to make one

This cocktail, now a favourite in bars and clubs everywhere, became popular in 1920s Havana, which at that time was one of the most fashionable cities in the world. The Mojito is said to have been invented by the 16th-century pirate Richard Drake, who named it 'El Draque' (the dragon) after Sir Francis Drake (no relation) – the first Englishman to sail around the globe. To make one, put a few mint leaves in a tall glass, squeeze in the juice of a lime and add a teaspoon of powdered sugar. Smash all this together with a blunt wooden implement, add crushed ice and a decent slug of good white rum, and top it off with some club soda. Stir, light up a Montecristo cigar, sit back and transport yourself to downtown Havana.

The US drew fierce criticism when the detention centre on the base began housing terror suspects shortly after the British and American war in Afghanistan began in October 2001. Campaigners, governments and international organisations strongly condemned the unlawful treatment of prisoners, including controversial methods of interrogation and alleged torture. In January 2009 US President Barack Obama came true on a campaign promise just two days after entering the White House by giving orders for the detention camp to be closed within a year.

You're Havana laugh

According to Fabian Escalante, former head of the Cuban secret service, there have been 638 attempts to kill Fidel since 1959, made by the CIA or Cuban exiles. Methods have ranged from packing high explosives under his podium before a speech in Panama in 2000 (discovered by his security team), to the infamous exploding cigars that were laced with botulinum toxin, which never made it to Castro's lips. Some of the more imaginative methods dreamt up by the CIA to take out the indestructible leader were never implemented. One such idea was to take advantage of his love of scuba diving; the plan was to get hold of some large Caribbean molluscs, cram them with explosives and paint them so as to attract Fidel's attention when he was enjoying a paddle off the coast.

Darfur

Where is it?
Darfur is a semi-arid region of western Sudan roughly the size of France, bordering Chad, Libya and the Central African Republic (CAR) to the west. Since 2003 it has been mired in a war between government forces, local militias and rebel groups that has claimed around 300,000 lives and displaced 2.7 million people.

Some background on Sudan
Sudan (capital Khartoum) is Africa's largest country. It was effectively a British colony from 1899 until independence in 1956, although nominally this was Anglo-Egyptian rule because an Egyptian filled the post of governor-general. For the past century, Sudan's history has been dominated by the religious divide between its north, which is Muslim, and its south, which is a mixture of Christian and Animist (believers in various spirits of nature). From 1924–56 north and south were run by the British as two separate territories, but from 1955–72 and 1983–2005, the two sides were engaged in a bloody civil war which killed and displaced millions. The Naivasha Agreement of 2005 created a shaky power-sharing agreement between the authoritarian Islamic-orientated Sudanese government of Omar al-Bashir and the southern secular SPLM (Sudan People's Liberation Movement). This arrangement is temporary, pending a referendum in 2011 in which the south will determine whether or not it becomes an independent state. President Bashir's National Islamic Front (now National Congress Party) seized power in a military coup in 1989. Sharia law has held sway in the north of Sudan since 1983.

What caused the war in Darfur?

A combination of geographical, ethnic and political disputes. Broadly speaking, Darfur's people fall into two categories; the nomadic Baggara Arab cattle herders in the north – who, although culturally Arab, mostly have Nubian roots – and the Black African farmers further south, who are Muslim. These latter make up the majority of Darfur's population and fall into three ethnic groups: the Zaghawa, Masalit and Fur, after whom the region is named (Darfur: 'realm of the Fur'). Increasing desertification and frequent droughts as a result of climate change forced the northern nomads to encroach further and further into non-Arab farmland, sparking tensions between the groups over food, water and land. The rising population of the region made resources even scarcer.

In 2003, two rebel groups supported by Darfur's non-Arab peoples, the JEM and the SLA, rose up in armed protest against the Sudanese government, whom they accused of neglecting Darfuri interests and favouring the black Arabs in these disputes over resources. The government hit back by waging a proxy war against these groups by deploying Baggara Arab militias known as the Janjawid as a counter-insurgency force. The Janjawid (meaning 'gunmen on horseback', although they also ride camels and drive pick-up trucks) were active throughout the 1990s pursuing agendas of land control in Darfur, but were armed by the government in 1999–2000 in preparation for the growing likelihood of rebel insurgencies. In 2003, following the JEM and SLA uprisings, the Janjawid began enacting what the US government have termed a genocide on the Black African population of Darfur. Aided by Sudanese government airstrikes, they embarked on a campaign of killing, raping, looting and burning which targeted non-Arab villages. This created an ongoing humanitarian crisis with a total of 2.7 million leaving their homes and fleeing to refugee camps either in Darfur itself or over the border in Chad. Fighting has also spilled over into Chad and the Central African Republic, whose governments accuse Sudan of trying to destabilise their countries.

Which are the main rebel groups in Darfur?
JEM – The Justice and Equality Movement, led by Khalil Ibrahim. The movement's ideological roots are Islamist. JEM has bases in neighbouring Chad, whose president, Idriss Déby, belongs to the same Zaghawa ethnic group as Ibrahim. The Sudanese government accuses Chad of funding JEM.

SLA – The Sudan Liberation Army, founded by Abdel Wahid in 1992 as a secular, pro-democratic, multi-ethnic movement in response to the divisive Islamist policies of Bashir. This has broken into three splinter groups, divided mainly along ethnic lines. Abdel Wahid's faction enjoys widespread support amongst displaced Fur but is losing ground due to the leader's refusal to return to Sudan from exile in Paris. Minni Minnawi's mainly Zaghawa faction has lost support since Minnawi, a former English teacher, signed a troubled peace agreement in 2006 (the only rebel leader to do so). SLA-Unity is based in North Darfur and gained support mainly from Zaghawas who were dissatisfied with both Wahid and Minnawi's groups.

URF – The United Resistance Front, formed in April 2008 out of five smaller rebel groups. They have refused to take part in any peace talks.

What has been the international response?
The African Union (see fact box) sent a small peacekeeping presence to monitor the situation in Darfur in 2004, and in

---

What is the African Union?

The African Union (AU) is an intergovernmental organisation made up of all the African states (except Morocco, which disputes the membership of Western Sahara due to its claims over it). Founded in 2002, the AU aims to promote co-operation amongst African nations, solve problems such as the AIDS epidemic, and keep the peace, intervening when necessary in conflict situations. Like the European Union, the AU is comprised of several different legislative bodies including the Assembly, currently chaired by Libyan leader Muammar al-Gaddafi, and the Pan-African Parliament. Gaddafi was instrumental in founding the AU; one of his long-stated aims is to create a United States of Africa, a federation of states modelled on the United States of America.

2007 this was bolstered by the UN to become the hybrid force UNAMID – the first operation of its kind between UN and AU forces. However, UNAMID has been roundly criticised for being too small (only 15,000 troops at the time of writing), lacking in equipment and thus powerless to prevent the fighting or protect the refugees in the camps. The peacekeeping mission is also unpopular with the refugees themselves who see it as pandering to President Bashir. Young men who have lived in the camps for years are now becoming increasingly politicised, forming vigilante groups calling for Bashir's overthrow and opposing any notion of compromise with the government. In March 2009 Bashir became the first sitting head of state to be indicted by the International Criminal Court (ICC); although he was formally accused of war crimes and crimes against humanity by

Prosecutor Luis Moreno-Ocampo, his arrest is unlikely to happen in the near future. In response, Bashir informed the ICC that they could 'eat' the warrant for his arrest. The indictment was celebrated in the West as a victory for human rights, but met with protests in Sudan and concern from the wider international community (including the Arab League, Russia and China) that it would set a damaging precedent and undermine peace prospects. China imports oil from Sudan and has strong business links with it. It has been accused of sponsoring the Sudanese government's military and stalling UN talks over taking more action in Darfur.

'I swear to God I will not surrender even a single cat from Sudan because we can make a shoe out of its skin.'

OMAR AL-BASHIR, *17 December 2008, in reference to two other Sudanese indicted for war crimes in Darfur by the ICC*

Devolution

What does it mean?
Devolution is the transfer of power from central government to regional authorities. This power may be administrative, executive or legislative.

How did the United Kingdom come to be?
The process began in 1536 with the Act of Union between England and Wales, although Wales had been under the English yoke since Edward I's conquest of the country in 1283. The Act of Union stated that Wales would have representatives in England's parliament and that English law would be the only law used in Wales. It also sidelined the Welsh language by

banning those who used it from public office, and forbidding it from being spoken in Welsh courts. In 1707 another Act of Union was signed, this time bringing together the independent kingdoms of England and Scotland, which had shared the same monarchy since 1603. This created Great Britain, made up of England, Scotland and Wales. Although Scottish law and its courts remained unaffected by the 1707 Act, it did bring about the end of the Scottish parliament, whose representatives instead joined the new parliament of Great Britain, based in London.

Almost a century later, in 1801, there was a further Act of Union with Ireland – thereby creating the United Kingdom of Great Britain and Ireland. As with Scotland, the Irish parliament ceased to exist and a certain number of representatives were allocated to the British parliament. When Ireland was partitioned in 1921, the South became independent while the North remained part of the UK. This prompted a final change of name, with legislation in 1927 creating the United Kingdom of Great Britain and Northern Ireland.

Devolution in the UK

Soon after the Labour government came to power in 1997, the UK parliament passed several Acts which saw different degrees of power being devolved to Northern Ireland, Scotland and Wales, each with a different set-up.

Northern Ireland

Devolution began in Northern Ireland as part of the Good Friday Agreement in 1998 (see **Northern Ireland**). It led to the creation of the Northern Ireland Assembly, which has legislative powers on various economic and social issues – often referred to as 'transferred matters' – such as pensions and child support, housing, health and social services, and transport. There are some 'excepted matters' (e.g. nuclear energy, defence, and nationality and immigration) that are still controlled by the UK parliament in Westminster. There are also 'reserved matters' (e.g. firearms and explosives, and financial services and pensions regulation) which are not seen as devolved powers, except in circumstances when Northern Ireland's Secretary of State interjects to say that they should be.

As well as this legislative role, the 108 Members of the Assembly also scrutinise the actions of Northern Ireland's government departments. These departments have executive responsibilities in the same 'transferred matters' on which the Assembly makes laws. The devolved powers of the Northern Ireland Assembly have been suspended by the British government a few times, including in 2002 when there were allegations of spies within the government garnering information for republicans. These responsibilities have been back in play since May 2007, however, when Sinn Féin and the Democratic Unionist Party reached an historic power-sharing agreement. The Northern Ireland First Minister is currently Peter Robinson, of the DUP, while the Deputy First Minister is Martin McGuinness of Sinn Féin.

Wales

Despite calls for devolved power in Wales during the 1970s, a referendum held in 1979 showed that opinion was decisively against it. Nearly twenty years later another referendum yielded different results, with those in favour of devolution narrowly winning with 50.3% of the vote. This led to the Government of Wales Act 1998 and the creation of the National Assembly for Wales. At first this had no power to initiate primary legislation, but a further Government of Wales Act in 2006 allowed it to legislate on certain devolved matters including education and training, food, tourism and flood defence. Before these Welsh laws – known as Assembly Measures – are passed, however, the UK parliament must be approached on a case-by-case basis. The 2006 Act also established the Welsh Assembly Government as the executive, composed of Welsh Ministers and headed by First Minister Rhodri Morgan. This is responsible for implementing policy, proposing assembly measures (Welsh laws) and making subordinate legislation, while the 60 members of the National Assembly monitor the Assembly Government's decisions and sign off on budgets for its programmes.

Scotland

A referendum on devolved responsibilities in Scotland was held in 1979 but failed to muster 40% of the vote, which was required for it to be pursued. However, a second referendum held in September 1997 got much healthier backing and led to the Scotland Act 1998. This established the Scottish Executive and Parliament, which convened for the first time in 1999. Like the Northern Ireland Assembly, the Scottish Parliament, which has 129 Members (MSPs), was given legislative authority to pass laws on matters from health to housing, planning, tourism, education and training, and sports and the arts, but there are some 'reserved matters' which the UK parliament retains power to legislate on (such as UK foreign policy, trade and industry, constitutional matters and employment legislation). Scotland's parliament can also tinker with income tax, raising or lowering the basic rate three pence either way. It scrutinises the actions of the Scottish government (called the Scottish Executive), made up of ministers who look after portfolios on devolved executive powers.

He wants to break free

Alex Salmond of the Scottish Nationalist Party is First Minister in Scotland's parliament, and is keen to hold a referendum on Scottish independence. His plans have suffered setbacks recently, however; in March 2009 an opinion poll found that only 57% supported the holding of such a referendum – a big drop from the 74% two years earlier – and, because of the economic crisis, only 32% of those polled thought a referendum should be held in 2010.

What about England?

In the 1970s, when devolution was being mooted, then Labour MP for West Lothian Tam Dalyell raised what became known as the West Lothian question, highlighting an unjust aspect of the system for English constituencies and their MPs. As a result of devolution, the parliaments of Northern Ireland, Scotland and Wales vote on certain issues specific to their region, such as education. However, whenever there is a vote on a particular issue only relevant to England, it is open to all members of the UK parliament. The Conservative Party has proposed 'English votes for English laws', whereby MPs with constituencies in England would be the only eligible voters on certain issues. Gordon Brown is against this idea, claiming it would 'create two classes of MPs – some entitled to vote on all issues, some invited to vote only on some'. There are also other groups, such as the Campaign for an English Parliament, who are calling for devolution in England.

Divvying up public funds

The way in which public funds are divided between England, Northern Ireland, Scotland and Wales has been met with heavy criticism. The system currently in place was thought up by Lord

Barnett in 1978, when he was Chief Secretary to the Treasury. His system, known as the Barnett Formula, was never intended to last as long as it has, and even its creator has admitted it is in need of reform; for example, recent figures from the Treasury have shown that, for the 2007/8 financial year, the average public expenditure was £1,600 per head more in Scotland than in England. In December 2008 a House of Lords Select Committee was set up to look into the effectiveness of this formula. In May 2009 the House of Commons' Justice Committee weighed in to the debate, calling for reform of the 'unfair' system.

'It's great that after 700 years William Wallace has finally had a proper burial. He did so much for the country. You should be proud of what you have achieved through devolution.'

MEL GIBSON

Energy

What are the world's current energy sources?
According to the US Department of Energy, the world currently
derives 85% of its energy from non-renewable hydrocarbons
such as coal, oil and gas, 9% from renewable sources and 6%
from nuclear power. The carbon dioxide emissions created by
the burning of hydrocarbons are the single biggest contributor

to the greenhouse effect (see **Climate Change**). Aside from environmental concerns, coal, oil and gas are running out, and may only last a matter of decades; the need to develop alternative sources of energy in sufficient quantities is one of the biggest challenges facing humanity in the near future.

What is it used for?
Some 29% of the world's energy is lost in the transmission and distribution of electric power without being used. Of the remaining energy that is delivered, 51% is used in the industrial sector (e.g. agriculture, mining, manufacturing, construction), 26% in transportation, 15% in residential (heating, lighting and appliances for homes) and 8% in commercial (businesses, water and sewer services).

What is energy independence?
Energy independence, or energy security, describes a desired situation in which a country does not need to rely on foreign energy imports but can create enough energy on its own. Much of Europe depends on Russian oil and natural gas for its energy, a supply which has proved unreliable in the past during pricing disputes between Russia and its former Soviet neighbours such as Belarus and the Ukraine (most recently in January 2009, when Russia cut off natural gas supplies via the Ukraine for three weeks). In 1973, OPEC (the Organisation of Petroleum Exporting Countries, a cartel of twelve countries, eight of which are Middle Eastern or North African) cut off oil supplies to Western countries for funding Israel in the Six-Day War, causing a four-fold rise in the price of oil and a six-month-long energy crisis.

What is peak oil?

Peak oil is a theoretical point in time when global oil production, after rising steeply, reaches its peak before entering into terminal and swift decline, causing a global energy crisis. The idea is based on the work of M. King Hubbert, who formulated his 'bell-shaped production curve' theory by observing the production rates of individual oil wells in the US in the 1950s. Optimistic proponents of the theory suggest that the peak will occur around 2020, while the real doom-mongers claim that the peak has already occurred and that the end of industrialised civilisation is nigh. Of the three hydrocarbon types, oil is the most crucial to humanity, powering 90% of the world's vehicles and providing the basis for plastics, solvents, fertilisers, pesticides and pharmaceuticals as well as being burnt, like coal and gas, to produce electricity and heating.

How much energy will the world need in 20 years' time?

Global energy consumption is forecasted to increase by 44% between now and 2030. This sharp rise is largely due to the growing economies and increasing industrialisation of non-OECD countries, whose energy demands will rise by 73% during this time (compared to 15% in OECD countries). To meet these demands, output from all available fuel sources is projected to rise. Meanwhile, global carbon dioxide emissions are set to rise by a third by 2030 – again, mostly due to the rapid industrialisation of the developing world.

What is renewable energy?

Any type of energy created using sources which replenish themselves naturally – this includes wind, solar, hydro-electric, wave, tidal and geothermal power. Renewables are the fastest-growing energy sector and their use is projected to rise by 63% between 2010 and 2030.

Of all the types, hydro-electricity is by far the largest energy producer, but wind power, which is currently in second place, is the fastest growing, expanding by 29% in 2008 alone. Germany is the world leader in wind power, generating the most by unit, while Denmark leads on a per capita basis, providing a fifth of its electricity in this way. The UK has lagged behind most of its European neighbours in switching to renewable energy, but in July 2009 the government unveiled ambitious Low Carbon Transition plans which aim to bring about huge changes in the country's energy usage by 2020. These would see renewables grow from providing 6% of our electricity to 31%, mainly by developing offshore wind power, with additional help from wave, tidal and geothermal sources.

What are biofuels?
Biofuels are a variety of fuels made from living things or from the waste they generate. They include liquid fuels, such as ethanol and biodiesel, wood pellets or chippings and biogas, which is methane collected from animals' excrement or landfill sites. Brazil is the world leader in biofuels, powering 60% of its cars on ethanol derived from the country's large sugar-cane industry. Burning biofuels produces carbon dioxide, but the net output is lower than that of petroleum-based fuels because the plants remove carbon dioxide from the atmosphere while they are growing. However, the total energy used in farming and processing the crops (and especially exporting the fuel) can sometimes make biofuels as polluting as petroleum-based fuels. Although on the increase, biofuels threaten biodiversity by requiring monoculture farming and adversely affect the price and availability of food by using up large areas of land.

What about nuclear power?

Nuclear energy does not generate carbon dioxide, but it is not renewable because it relies on finite stocks of uranium, which has to be mined in large quantities. It remains a controversial energy source due to environmental concerns over the safety of storing radioactive waste and its potential use in nuclear weapons manufacture (see **Nuclear Weapons**). Nevertheless, global nuclear energy production is projected to rise by 39% in the next 20 years, with China and India the fastest growers in this sector. France relies on nuclear power for around 80% of its energy, more than any other country in the world.

What about coal-fired power stations?

Coal-fired power stations are the biggest producers of carbon emissions, but we don't yet have the alternatives in place to stop using them, and more are being built around the world – in China, a new one opens every week. In the UK, the new coal power station being built at Kingsnorth in Kent has been the subject of massive protests by environmental campaigners, and in 2008 a group of 29 environmentalists hijacked and stopped a train carrying coal to the country's largest power station at Drax in North Yorkshire, an act of civil disobedience for which they were prosecuted and sentenced to community service. The polluting effect of coal-fired power stations could be massively reduced with 'carbon capture and storage' (CCS) technology currently being pioneered. This involves various methods of removing carbon from a power station's emissions and storing it deep underground or at the bottom of the sea. CCS would reduce a fossil-fuel power plant's carbon emissions by 80–90%, but would increase its fuel needs by up to 40% and therefore increase the cost of its energy.

What is the Kyoto Protocol?

The Kyoto Protocol, which was adopted in 1997 and came into force in 2005, is an international treaty aimed at reducing greenhouse gases to below their 1990 levels. It imposed legal limitations on the emissions of developed countries, while imposing other, less stringent commitments on developing countries. Notably, the US refused to commit to the treaty due to the damage that it would cause to its economy, while arguing that developing countries should be subject to the same restrictions as the industrialised. The emissions of China and India, which are developing countries, are increasing at an astronomical rate as they industrialise; China alone is projected to account for 29% of the world's emissions by 2030, and will account for three-quarters of the global increase in coal-related emissions from 2006–30. China and India argue that on a per capita basis, their emissions are still small in comparison to the US and other developed countries, which is quite true – electricity production in the US generates four times as much carbon dioxide per person as China and twenty times as much as India.

Despite the US's rejection of the Kyoto Protocol, several of its states, including California (whose emissions would rank 12th highest in the world if it was a country) have voluntarily imposed their own limitations on emissions, putting them roughly in line with the terms of Kyoto. The next big round of climate-change talks is the United Nations Climate Change Conference, which will take place in Copenhagen in December 2009. If they go well, the talks will result in a successor to the Kyoto Protocol to come into force in 2012 and introduce a new international framework for combating climate change which might include a global cap and trade system.

What are flexible mechanisms?

These are three alternative ways for developed countries to meet their Kyoto limitations without actually reducing their emissions:

Cap and Trade – industrialised countries that exceed their emissions quotas can buy carbon credits in emissions trading markets such as the EU Emissions Trading Scheme, the largest of its kind (the UK was the first to pioneer this kind of scheme, between 2002–6). These function like other commodities markets, with emission credits being bought and sold in units each representing one metric tonne of carbon dioxide. Much International Emissions Trading creates a financial incentive to reduce emissions, as countries or companies who have not used their whole allowance can sell on their extra credits.

Joint Implementation – Carbon credits can be earned by funding emission-reducing projects in other developed countries where the costs of emission reduction are cheaper (such as Russia or the Ukraine).

Clean Development Mechanism – by investing in 'clean technology' in developing countries, where costs are much lower but the global benefit is equal.

What is voluntary offsetting?

Since international emissions trading has put a price on carbon, people have become more aware of their own carbon footprint, or the amount of emissions for which they are personally responsible. This has led to the rise of the voluntary offset market, in which individuals compensate for their own emissions by buying offsets which go towards funding renewable energy, reforestation or emissions reduction schemes.

The average Briton was estimated in 2006 to produce 10.92 tonnes of carbon dioxide per year, which would cost around £80 to offset voluntarily through companies that now exist to finance clean schemes. These companies should be treated with caution, however, as there is no single set of standards governing the industry, making it difficult to tell how efficiently the money is being used to combat climate change; some reforestation schemes, for instance, have failed due to mismanagement.

What can I do to help reduce my carbon footprint?
The best thing you could do would be to stop flying. Your share of the carbon emissions on one long-haul return flight is equivalent to driving a car 50 km every day for a year. Driving is also bad news; swap your car for an electric one, or better still, walk or cycle instead. In your home, energy efficiency can greatly reduce emissions as well as the bills. Turn the thermostat down – each degree lower will knock 10% off your heating costs. Make sure your house is well insulated and glazed, install a solar water heater on your roof and swap your boiler for a heat pump – these suck in heat from outside, are powered by electricity and are much more efficient than oil or gas heaters. Don't imagine that turning off your mobile phone charger at the mains is going to make any meaningful difference; the energy saved by doing this for a year would be used up by taking a single hot bath.

EU

What is it?
The EU, or European Union, is a union of states, currently numbering 27, founded to enhance political, economic and social co-operation between its members. It came into existence in 1993 as a result of the Maastricht Treaty, but was based on the pre-existing European Economic Community (EEC).

What was the EEC?
The European Economic Community was a common market in trade and agriculture adopted initially between six countries (France, Germany, Italy, the Netherlands, Belgium and Luxembourg) at the Treaty of Rome in 1957. This built upon the European Coal and Steel Community which the same countries had founded in 1951. The UK, under the leadership of Edward Heath, joined the EEC with Denmark and Ireland in 1973, when new social and environmental policies were also introduced. In 1991 the member states (which by then also included Greece, Spain and Portugal) negotiated the Maastricht Treaty on European Union, which added areas of intergovernmental co-operation to the pre-existing structures of the EEC.

What is the single market?
The single, or common market, is an evolving process of trade liberalisation set in motion by the Treaty of Rome, which abolished customs barriers between EEC members and implemented the Common Agricultural Policy (CAP). The 1987 Single European Act enabled the elimination of many other national restrictions and regulations which hampered the free

movement of people, goods and capital. National laws still
govern some economic sectors (public services, for example),
and individual governments are responsible for taxation and
social welfare.

How does the EU work?
It's pretty complicated. The EU derives its activities from the
treaties that have been signed over the years, most recently the
Treaty of Nice (2001) and Lisbon (2007 – yet to be ratified
unanimously). All other legislation is decided upon by a
triangle of institutions. The first and most important of these
is the Council of the European Union, which represents
national governments. This makes decisions on the basis of
meetings attended by one minister from each EU country
(which minister attends, and the number of votes needed to
secure legislation, depends on the topic being discussed). Each
EU country takes it in turns to hold the Council presidency for
six months at a time (Sweden from July–December 2009,
Spain from January–June 2010). The European Council,
chaired by the president or prime minister of the state holding
Council presidency, meets four times a year to settle difficult
issues arising in the Council of the EU meetings, as well as
initiating new major policies and dealing with pressing
international issues through the Common Foreign and
Security Policy (CFSP).

The second institution in the triangle is the European
Parliament, based in Brussels and Strasbourg and founded in
1979. This represents the people, and in certain respects,
including the adoption of the EU budget, shares responsibility
with the Council. MEPs (Members of the European
Parliament), of whom there are currently 736, are elected every
five years, each state's number of seats being allocated

according to its population (the UK has 72). MEPs are normally affiliated with parties from their own individual nations, which then group together in large blocs with like-minded parties from other nations. There are seven such blocs – Left, Socialists, Greens, Liberals, European People's Party, Union for Europe of the Nations (which promotes national sovereignty) and Independence and Democracy (which encompasses those who advocate withdrawal from the EU altogether) – as well as MEPs who choose not to join any of these groupings. The European Parliament elections of June 2009 were the biggest trans-national elections in history, and saw victory for the centre-right EPP (with 264 seats) and a general swing to the right from the previous parliament. As far as British parties were concerned, it was a disastrous performance by Labour, who were beaten into third place by the Conservatives and the UK Independence Party, while the British National Party won their first two seats in Europe thanks to the collapse of Labour's support. Normally the European Parliament sits in Brussels, but for one week in every month MEPs and staff – 2,500 people in total – must relocate to Strasbourg in a 'travelling circus' which costs 200 million euros a year; this has been widely condemned as a waste of taxpayers' money. Supporters of the policy maintain that having a seat for the parliament at Strasbourg is of important symbolic value due to the city's location on the border between the historic enemies of France and Germany.

The third institution is the European Commission, consisting of one member from each state and based in Brussels and Luxembourg. Although answerable to the European Parliament, it acts independently from the instruction of any national government. As the executive arm of the EU, its job is to uphold the common interest and make sure EU policies are being implemented in all of the member states. Any offending parties can be taken to the Court of Justice, yet another of the EU's many institutions.

What is the Lisbon Treaty?

The Lisbon Treaty is a major piece of legislation intended to reform the EU by streamlining its institutions and making it 'more democratic, more transparent and more efficient', according to its proposers. Negotiations to reform the EU have been under way since 2001, and the first attempt at doing so – the draft European Constitution – was rejected by French and Dutch voters in 2005. The Lisbon Treaty is not as radical as the constitution, amending only the treaties of Rome and Maastricht rather than replacing all previous treaties, but it is nevertheless seen by its opponents as a threat to national sovereignty and a step towards creating a federal European superstate. It was rejected by Irish voters in 2008 and its fate depends on the results of another referendum in Ireland, to be held by November 2009. The EU has pledged not to impose rules on Ireland which might interfere with the country's taxation policy, abortion laws or military neutrality, which were some of the initial Irish concerns. Germany, Poland and the Czech Republic are also yet to ratify the treaty – the UK ratified it in July 2008, clearing it by 346 to 206 votes in the Commons after a proposal from the Conservatives to hold a referendum on the treaty had been defeated.

What about the euro?

The EU's single currency has been around since 1999 (for non-cash transactions) and has circulated as cash since 2002. The UK opted out, along with Denmark and Sweden.

How is the EU funded?
The annual budget of over 120 billion euros is financed partly
by member states, who contribute according to their wealth,
and also by a percentage of VAT and custom duties on products
imported from outside the EU.

Which European countries aren't members of the EU?
Iceland, Norway, Switzerland and Liechtenstein; despite
fulfilling the membership criteria, and committing to some of
the EU regulations, public opinion in these countries is against
joining fully. The microstates of Andorra, San Marino, Monaco
and the Vatican City are not members either, but co-operate
with the EU in many ways, including their use of the euro.
Croatia, Turkey, FYR Macedonia, Bosnia and Herzegovina,
Serbia, Montenegro, Albania, Ukraine, Belarus and Moldova do
not currently fulfil the Copenhagen criteria established by the
Council in 1993. These stipulate that, to join the EU, a country
must be governed democratically, have a functioning market
economy and respect the rule of law and human rights. Turkey,
Croatia and the Former Yugoslav Republic of Macedonia have
been official candidates to join the EU since 2005, although no
dates for accession have yet been announced. The EU has no
rules setting out exactly what constitutes Europe in a
geographical sense, or whether non-European countries should
be allowed to join; however, Morocco's rather hopeful
application to join the (then) European Communities in 1987
was rejected on the grounds that it wasn't a European country
(its poor human rights record may have also counted against it).
    The eastern edges of Europe are generally considered to be
the Ural mountains, the Caucasus mountains and the
Bosphorus straits, putative boundaries which have led some
opponents of Turkey's application to complain that only 3% of

its land mass lies within Europe. In response, Turkey can point to the examples of Cyprus, which is an EU member despite being geographically Asian, as well as various overseas territories of EU nations such as the Canary Islands, Reunion and French Guiana, which are part of the EU despite belonging to different continents altogether (though some other overseas territories, including Greenland, Aruba and the Netherlands Antilles, are not part of the EU).

What is the Council of Europe?

The Council of the European Union and the European Council should not be confused with the Council of Europe which, confusingly, has nothing to do with the EU. The Council of Europe was established in 1949 to promote democracy, human rights and the rule of law across Europe, and one of its most important institutions is the European Court of Human Rights. Its 47 members include Turkey, Russia and the Caucasian states (Georgia, Armenia and Azerbaijan) as well as all the countries of the European continent except for Belarus, which is left out (and isn't in the EU either) because of its human rights record and authoritarian regime.

A bridge too far

Austrian Robert Kalina won a competition in 1996 to create designs for the new euro banknotes on the theme of historic windows and bridges. However, his initial designs were rejected because they depicted real bridges (such as the Rialto in Venice and the Pont de Neuilly in Paris), and this was deemed too partisan for a pan-European currency. The bridges that are depicted on the notes don't actually exist.

Euthanasia

What is it?
Euthanasia is the act of intentionally ending a person's life for their benefit (from the Greek *eu*, 'good' and *thánatos*, 'death'). Euthanasia takes place either after a request from an individual who wishes to die or in situations when a person is not able to ask for assistance because of their physical and/or mental state.

How is it carried out?
Euthanasia is carried out either by giving a person a fatal drug, or by withholding treatment in the knowledge that this inaction will lead to their death.

What is the difference between euthanasia and assisted suicide?
With assisted suicide a person is given the means to kill themselves – such as a lethal drug – but takes their own life, whereas with euthanasia the act itself is carried out by someone else.

Is it legal in the UK?
No. In fact, in England and Wales, aiding, abetting, counselling or procuring a suicide or attempted suicide is an offence under the 1961 Suicide Act and punishable by up to 14 years in jail. This is also the case in Northern Ireland under the Criminal Justice Act (Northern Ireland) 1966. In Scotland, although there is no specific legislation, experts believe assisted suicide could result in a charge of culpable homicide, Scotland's equivalent of manslaughter. There have been several attempts to legalise assisted suicide; the most recent was in 2006, when the House of Lords rejected a bill, which would have allowed the terminally ill

to end their own lives, by 148 to 100. Margo MacDonald, an independent Member of the Scottish Parliament (MSP), who suffers from Parkinson's disease, launched a campaign in December 2008 to legalise assisted suicide in Scotland. All known assisted suicides in the UK, which number at least 115, have chosen to end their life by going to Dignitas, a clinic in Switzerland.

Where is it legal?

Euthanasia or assisted suicide is legal in some form in Belgium, Luxembourg, the Netherlands, the American states of Oregon and Washington, and Switzerland.

Has anyone challenged the UK law?

Yes. In 2001, Diane Pretty, who suffered from motor neurone disease, campaigned to get immunity for her husband if he helped her die in the UK. The mother of two lost her final challenge to end her life at a time and manner of her own choosing at the European Court of Human Rights in April 2002. The following month she had severe difficulty breathing and went to a hospice near her home where she died less than two weeks later. 'Diane had to go through the one thing she had foreseen and was afraid of – and there was nothing I could do to help,' said her husband Brian.

More recently, in October 2008, Debbie Purdy went to the High Court to clarify the law on assisted suicide. Purdy, who suffers from multiple sclerosis, indicated that if her condition worsened there may come a time when she wishes to travel to Dignitas. Her concern lies in the fact that if her husband travels with her, he may face prosecution. She argued that the law may push her to die before she is ready, because she will have to travel to Switzerland without assistance in order to protect her husband. Judges ruled that Mrs Purdy's human rights had not been breached and that the existing guidelines were sufficient. She then took the case to the Court of Appeal and, subsequently, to the House of Lords; in July 2009 the law lords ruled that guidance must be issued by the Director of Public Prosecutions to clarify the circumstances under which a person will be prosecuted for helping someone die abroad. A final policy statement on this issue is expected by spring 2010.

'One should die proudly when it is no longer possible to live proudly. Death freely chosen, death at the right time, brightly and cheerfully accomplished amid children and witnesses: then a real farewell is still possible, as the one who is taking leave is still there; also a real estimate of what one has wished, drawing the sum of one's life – all in opposition to the wretched and revolting comedy that Christianity has made of the hour of death.'

FRIEDRICH NIETZSCHE, The Twilight of the Idols, or How to Philosophise with a Hammer *(1889)*

'Euthanasia is a false solution to the drama of suffering, a solution unworthy of man. Indeed, the true response cannot be to put someone to death, however "kindly", but rather to witness to the love that helps people to face their pain and agony in a human way.'

POPE BENEDICT XVI, *1 February 2009*

Fairtrade

What is it?

Fairtrade is a form of market intervention which aims to give farmers in the developing world a better deal by guaranteeing them a minimum price for their produce. As a concept, it's been around for about 40 years, but it was organised into a formal labelling scheme in the 1980s. Since then, Fairtrade has become big business, with more than 4,500 certified products on sale

around the world – varying from coffee to bananas to cotton clothing. The UK, where sales of Fairtrade products increased tenfold between 2001–8, is the world's second-biggest market after the US.

How does it work?
Companies wishing to achieve Fairtrade status apply to the Fairtrade Labelling Organisations International (FLOI). This is a not-for-profit body which audits company supply chains and checks that production processes are free from child or slave labour before granting Fairtrade certification. The FLOI also dictates the minimum price that the companies must pay to the growers for each product. This minimum is intended to give farmers a safety net to protect against damaging drops in market prices, cover production costs and provide a 'social premium' designed to go towards community development or children's education. Small-scale farmers participating in Fairtrade schemes are usually organised into democratic co-operatives which implement these development projects. The extra costs involved in providing farmers with a baseline income guarantee are picked up by the consumer, which is why Fairtrade products generally cost more. This is not always the case, however – some big brand names are actually more expensive than Fairtrade products.

Why was it invented?
Fairtrade was introduced as a way of protecting some of the poorest and most vulnerable farmers in the developing world from the negative aspects of free trade (see **Free Trade**). When global prices in a certain crop plummet, farmers of that crop are often forced to operate at a loss, which some producers in the developing world simply cannot afford to do. They often have no option but to abandon their land and move to over-crowded

cities in search of work. Farmers in the US and EU were seen as having an unfair advantage because they were subsidised by the government or had access to capital to manage their risks, whereas those in the developing world generally did not. Developing world farmers were also considered to be too dependent on middlemen for market information, and at the mercy of traders who had the power to dictate prices. Fairtrade was introduced to address these market failures and to ensure a decent standard of living for farmers and a reliable income, enabling them to plan for the future and invest in sustainable development. For those living near or beneath the poverty line, Fairtrade provides an opportunity for farmers to escape the poverty trap and become self-sufficient.

What are the criticisms of Fairtrade?

Fairtrade is accused of causing underdevelopment, increasing inefficiency and being merely a token gesture on the part of the developed world. It is often said to create an incentive for people to start growing certain crops for the financial stability that the scheme offers, which leads to overproduction of those crops. This pushes their prices down, adversely affecting farmers who don't participate in Fairtrade. Others claim that by attracting more people in the developing world to the 'peasant lifestyle' of the primary sector (agriculture), Fairtrade slows down economic development. They contest that farmers become dependent on the Western world continuing to pay premium prices for their goods and become 'locked in' to a relatively small Fairtrade market which puts little pressure on farmers to develop modern agricultural methods. Increasing farmers' wages by small amounts is not what will transform impoverished communities; instead, what is needed are radical changes involving modernisation and mechanisation.

Advocates of free market economics argue that it is exposure to open global competition and real integration in global markets, without protection or interference, that will lift the developing world out of poverty. Finally, Fairtrade doesn't reward farmers for the quality of their produce; it guarantees them a minimum price (crucially), but beyond that it is the fluctuating commodities market which dictates how much they are paid for their crop. This means that some Fairtrade products, particularly in the early days of the scheme, were of average quality but sold to the consumer at a premium price, while some were of excellent quality but sold for too little.

... and some rebuttals

Few supporters of Fairtrade would claim that the scheme is a long-term solution to the problems of poverty and development, but they defend it as an interim measure that protects millions of impoverished producers in the developing world who would otherwise face desperate circumstances. They also accept that the Fairtrade scheme can be improved and extended to address problems of oversupply, including helping farmers to diversify by growing other crops. Advocates of Fairtrade point to cases where premiums have helped to build infrastructure and speed economic as well as social development. For example, the Nicaraguan coffee farming co-operative Prodecoop have put their premiums towards the construction of wet milling facilities which will make production more efficient, reduce labour and improve coffee quality. Fairtrade importers agree that quality has to play more of a part in pricing, and that this requires education both of the producer and the consumer – consumers often buy Fairtrade products because they feel it is the 'right thing to do', rather than making an informed choice about the quality of the product they are buying. Changing this would give farmers an incentive to produce higher quality crops for which they can demand higher prices in return.

Some defenders of Fairtrade answer the free market economists by saying that modernising agricultural methods is not what these farmers need; it would make them dependent on expensive machine parts, fuel and fertilisers, put people out of work and, as production increases, reduce the price of crops. Some blame Western farming methods for causing problems for developing world farmers in the first place, and use coffee as an example; all coffee used to be shade grown (grown amongst other larger plants) whereas now it is produced in open fields, necessitating the use of chemical pesticides and modern tilling techniques, which in turn deplete the soil and create the need for chemical fertiliser. Many of the arguments on both sides about Fairtrade are familiar from the debate about development generally (see **Aid**).

A Rush of Mud to the Head

'We don't care about looking like idiots ... we look totally stupid standing behind a plough. But that doesn't matter as long as you get the words "make trade fair dot com" in the newspaper.'

CHRIS MARTIN, *lead singer, Coldplay*

Free Trade

What does it mean?
Free trade refers to international trade that is not restricted or affected by government intervention. Its theoretical roots lie in the writings of political economists Adam Smith (1723–90) and David Ricardo (1772–1823). The 'Ricardian model' is still commonly used today by economists in order to defend free trade as a mutually beneficial practice to all parties concerned.

Central to this argument is the principle of comparative advantage, the idea that countries should specialise in producing what they do best (wine from Portugal, cloth from England, in Ricardo's example). The opposite of free trade is protectionism, where governments try to protect their own manufacturers and producers from foreign competition by limiting imports from abroad while trying to export as much as possible (sometimes known as a 'beggar-thy-neighbour' approach).

What are the advantages of free trade?
According to the Ricardian model, free trade maximises efficiency, increases production and consumption and creates an integrated global economy. Importing goods from abroad creates competition for domestic firms, which prevents them from monopolising the market, forces them to become more efficient, and gives them an incentive to innovate and develop new products. Exporting goods gives domestic firms access to large foreign markets which makes them more profitable due to economies of scale (the tendency for profits to be higher as production increases due to overhead costs remaining relatively static). Free trade gives consumers more choice because a greater variety of goods are available. It also usually encourages peace between trading countries – it's difficult to trade with a country you're at war with.

And the disadvantages?
When free trade causes industries to be undercut by competitors, this can cause unemployment and economic hardship in the country affected. In the 1960s and 70s foreign competition hit the US car manufacturing industry, devastating a large swathe of the mid-West that later became known as the

'Rust Belt'. Developing countries can also be badly affected: opponents of free trade say that their industries need time to become efficient, and that premature exposure to global competition is unfair on them. Others claim that in order to industrialise, countries must first develop a *range* of productive capabilities, rather than specialising in the free trade of comparative advantage goods early on. They point out that major economic powers such as the US, UK and Japan industrialised in this way, achieving 'dynamic efficiency' under a degree of protectionism before competing in free trade, and they argue that developing countries should be allowed to do the same. In addition, specialisation in a narrow range of goods is risky because a) it exposes countries to unpredictable fluctuations in the markets of those goods (for example, the Windward Islands are at the mercy of world banana prices due to their dependence on this crop), and b) countries can become over-dependent on imports from abroad (for example Japan's reliance on grain from overseas). Finally, some governments of developing countries rely on tariffs as a major source of revenue, and abolishing these tariffs in order to participate in free trade would hamper their ability to pay for health, education and other essential services.

Is protectionism a good idea?
Protectionism can benefit a country more than free trade, but only if its exports continue without other countries raising their own tariffs in response. After the Wall Street Crash of 1929, the US Smoot-Hawley Act raised import tariffs on over 20,000 goods in a bid to protect American companies and limit the economic repercussions of the crash. This led, however, to a 'trade war' as other countries raised their import tariffs in retaliation. The next three years saw a worldwide collapse of

financial markets resulting in deflation of 48% and a 68% reduction of world trade (the Great Depression). The rise of the Nazi party in 1933 was facilitated by the dire economic situation in Germany that had come about as a knock-on effect of the Wall Street Crash. This dark period in world history, both economically and politically, set in motion a restructuring of trading principles that saw the world turn away from protectionism and towards free trade. The 1948 General Agreement on Tariffs and Trade (GATT) between 23 countries was a precursor to the 142-member World Trade Organisation (WTO), established in 1995.

What does 'balance of trade' mean?

The balance of trade is the relationship between a country's imports and its exports. If a country is exporting more (by value) than it imports, it is said to have a trade surplus, whereas if it imports more than it exports, it has a trade deficit. Economists are divided as to the precise advantages and disadvantages of each position, although a long-term trade deficit is generally seen as unfavourable and can cause a country's unemployment to rise, GDP to decrease, or wealth-producing jobs to be replaced by lower-paying, wealth-consuming ones. British economist John Maynard Keynes believed that large trade surpluses could have destabilising effects, and that an equilibrium should therefore be maintained in the balance of trade between nations (see **World Bank/IMF**).

What does the WTO do?

The WTO is an international body which aims to liberalise trade between its members. It provides a forum for trade negotiations, sets rules and acts as an arbitrating body in case of trade disputes. Critics of the WTO – environmental campaigners, social justice groups and trades unions – accuse it of serving the interests of big corporations by giving them an official platform from which to flex their muscles over national governments, particularly those of developing countries. In 2001, prior to its most recent round of talks (the 'Doha round'), the WTO set out an agenda which aimed to take into particular account the interests of poorer countries. One of the key issues of these talks was the Special Safeguards Mechanism, a set of measures designed to give developing countries limited protection against foreign imports. However, the talks stalled in 2006 and a final agreement has yet to be reached.

What is globalisation?

Globalisation is almost impossible to define. Although the word has been around since the 1960s, it really came to prominence in the 1990s when people started referring to the 'anti-globalisation movement'. This was (and still is) a loose confederation of activist groups including environmentalists, anarchists, leftists, trades unionists and fair development campaigners. They united in protest against what they perceived to be the negative effects and injustices of increasing global economic integration, and particularly the activities of multinational corporations as the major players in this process. The grievances of the anti-globalisation lobby include the exploitation of 'sweat shop' workers in developing countries, job losses in developed countries, premature exposure of developing countries to free trade, and the growing influence of big business in political as well as economic affairs. Allied to these are objections to the institutions which have helped enable the multinationals to penetrate so far and wide – chiefly the World Bank, IMF, and WTO (see **World Bank/IMF**).

Types of governmental trade restriction

Tariffs: government taxes on imports or exports.

Quotas: restrictions on the quantity of imports allowed.

Subsidies: payments made by governments to companies in order to assist the manufacture or export of particular goods (not a type of restriction, but an anti-competitive intervention).

Countervailing duties: taxes imposed by a government on imports that are subsidised by the exporting country's government, designed to offset (countervail) the effect of the subsidy.

Antidumping duties: tariffs levied on dumped imports (imports provided at a price considered 'unfairly low').

Voluntary export restraints (VERs): restrictions on a country's imports that are achieved by negotiating with the foreign exporting country.

Trade bans: for example, the EU has banned imports of genetically modified (GM) food, believing it unsafe, and the US doesn't export weapons to countries that might threaten it.

Globalisation is also used in a positive sense by proponents of economic integration who believe that free trade and the global reach of multinationals are of long-term benefit to both the developed and the developing world. Globalisation has also taken on other, vaguer connotations, including a general sense of the 'interconnectedness' of today's world, or the ubiquity of certain forms of cultural consumption, such as American film and TV.

Free trade agreements
Free trade agreements (FTAs) may be made bilaterally (between two countries only) or multilaterally (between several countries). Prominent examples of multilateral FTAs include the EU and NAFTA (the North American Free Trade Agreement between Canada, the US and Mexico). In the run-up to the American presidential elections in 2008, Republican running mate Sarah Palin was reported as being ignorant of which countries were in NAFTA, not knowing Africa was a continent, thinking the US was at war with Iran, and referring to 'our neighbouring country of Afghanistan'.

G8/G20

What is the Group of Eight (G8)?
A group of the world's major industrialised democracies, whose leaders get together once a year to chew the fat over current issues of national and global importance. Discussions cover a broad spectrum, including international trade, terrorism, the environment and economic relations between East and West. The resulting agreements, such as cutting carbon emissions by at least 50% by 2050, are then acted on by the respective governments.

How did it come about?
In 1973, the US Treasury Secretary George P. Shultz gathered his counterparts from France, West Germany and the United Kingdom to meet informally and talk about the gloomy economic climate. Japan instigated another meeting later on that year, which led to its involvement. In 1975 Italy was also present at a summit held in France – this time for heads of government – and the year after that Canada joined in, thus forming the Group of 7. G7 became G8 with the involvement of Russia, which, having been on the fringes since 1991, began to participate fully from 1998 onwards. As well as annual meetings for leaders, ministers and officials from G8 countries may also meet when the need arises, to address any urgent areas of concern in their respective portfolios – from foreign affairs to the environment. The only exception is when economic and fiscal affairs are the order of the day; at these meetings finance ministers and governors of central banks from G7 countries meet without Russia. Although Russia has pushed to be fully included, the door remains closed. 'Russia's economy is too

small and isn't free enough to merit membership, and it has drifted on democracy and reform,' observed Stuart Eizenstat, US Under Secretary of State and Deputy Treasury Secretary under President Bill Clinton, in 2005. Others have argued in favour of Russia joining: 'It does not make sense to have the Russian Federation not as a full member at the table,' German Finance Minister Peer Steinbrück said in 2007. But with other impressive emerging economies like China knocking on the door, Russia's chances of being brought into the fold seem slim.

Who else is involved?
The president of the European Commission and the leader of whichever country holds the EU presidency (this rotates every six months) also get seats at the table. Although involved, the EU will neither chair nor host an annual meeting. Other players can participate when deemed useful; for example, the IMF, World Bank and UN were present in 2008. Other leaders might also join in to discuss a specific issue that is relevant to them. Brazil, China, India, Mexico and South Africa were all invited to the 2005 summit at which climate change was addressed.

How are the summits organised?
In the build-up to these annual summits, representatives of the leaders (known as sherpas) do the legwork on agreeing an agenda. Ministers from the countries also meet at different stages throughout the year to check progress on the work agreed at the summit. Even though agreements and goals are made at the summits, because of the informal nature of the group it is not mandatory to fulfil them.

Does anyone care?

Yes. Eight of the world's most powerful leaders are gathered in one place at the same time, and topics under discussion tend to be those at the top of the global agenda. Any tensions that arise between leaders, such as over the Iraq war, also draw a good deal of interest. Protestors flock to these summits as well – they may either be demonstrating on a particular issue under discussion, or protesting more generally against what they regard as an elitist group in favour of globalisation.

What about G20?

G20 was formally established at the 1999 G7 Finance Ministers meeting to ensure emerging economies were more involved in discussions. It is made up of finance ministers as well as central bank governors. Leaders from G20 countries also meet up to discuss pressing issues of global importance. As well as including all G8 countries, G20's other members are Argentina, Australia, Brazil, China, India, Indonesia, Mexico, Saudi Arabia, South Africa, South Korea and Turkey. The twentieth member is the European Union, represented by the president of the European Council and the European Central Bank. Bosses from the IMF and World Bank also participate.

What do they talk about?

G20 was set up to act as a forum for industrialised and developing economies from all over the world to discuss global economic issues, from how terrorists are financed to the credit crunch. In early April 2009, leaders from G20 countries met in London to hammer out a way to address the global economic crisis. After two days of talks they agreed on a US$1.1 trillion package to strengthen the international economy. Gordon Brown said of the talks that 'this is the day that the world came together, to fight back against the global recession'.

Yo, Blair

Back in 2006, at a G8 meeting in Russia, a conversation between former American president George Bush and former British prime minister Tony Blair was picked up by a microphone. 'Yo, Blair,' Bush began. Their private conversation, which was later broadcast all over the world, covered topics as diverse as the jumper Blair had given Bush as a present – he quipped that he had knitted it himself – to the then president offering a solution to tensions in the Middle East at the time: 'You see, the irony is what they need to do is to get Syria to get Hezbollah to stop doing this shit and it's over.'

Georgia

Where is it?

Georgia is separated from Russia by the Great Caucasus mountain range that runs along its northern border. The Black Sea is on its west coast and other neighbouring states to the south and east are Armenia, Azerbaijan and Turkey.

Under Russia's shadow

At the beginning of the 19th century Georgia was swallowed up by the Russian Empire. It was not until after the 1917 Russian Revolution that it gained independence, under the Treaty of Brest-Litovsk. This wasn't to last, however; in 1922 Georgia was absorbed into the newly formed Union of Soviet Socialist Republics (USSR), where it would remain until the collapse of communism in 1991 (see **Russia**). Like many other ethnic minorities in the USSR, Georgians suffered heavy repression at the hands of the communist authorities during the Soviet period, despite the fact that both Joseph Stalin and his infamous chief of secret police, Lavrentiy Beria, both hailed from Georgia themselves.

What happened when the USSR collapsed?

The nationalist Zviad Gamsakhurdia became president of a newly independent Georgia in 1991, but lost control a year later following internal fighting in the capital, Tbilisi. Eduard Shevardnadze then took charge and remained in power for over a decade. At the tail end of his presidency there were tensions with Russia over Chechen rebels using Georgia as a safe haven, but this was resolved when Georgia offered help in fighting these rebels (see **Chechnya**). Shevardnadze was toppled from power in November 2003 in the non-violent 'Rose Revolution' which saw tens of thousands of demonstrators protest against the flawed parliamentary elections that had recently taken place. His electoral rival Mikheil Saakashvili went to the parliament building surrounded by thousands of his supporters, where, holding a rose above his head, he confronted Shevardnadze, shouting simply 'Resign!' Saakashvili went on to become president after he won elections in January 2004. A few years later he survived allegations of corruption and protests, and went on to win a second term in January 2008. During these early years of independence Georgia's economy got off to a rocky start, but a recent increase in foreign investment has led to sustained growth of its GDP: by 10% in 2006, 12% in 2007 and 7% in 2008.

What about the breakaway regions?
South Ossetia, in the north, and Abkhazia, in the north-west, are two regions that want to be free from Georgian control. Both the Abkhaz and the Ossetians are distinct ethnic groups. While Abkhazia wants complete independence, South Ossetia is looking to join North Ossetia, an autonomous republic in Russia. Both became part of Georgia shortly after the formation of the USSR, but ever since the Soviet Union's collapse these regions have strived for independence.

So what have they done about it?
Both Abkhazia and South Ossetia have established referendums calling for independence, held their own elections, drafted their own constitutions and even declared their own independence. They have also appealed to the international community asking for acknowledgement of their independence. In the last two decades there has been sporadic fighting between Georgia and

the separatists from these regions – several thousand were killed during a conflict between Georgia and South Ossetia from 1990 to 1992, and in Abkhazia fighting during the early 1990s caused an estimated ten thousand deaths and hundreds of thousands of displacements.

Cosying up with the West
Georgia is keen to join NATO and the European Union and has developed a close relationship with the US, none of which Russia is too keen on. The tie with America was highlighted when Georgia allowed oil and gas pipelines for their Western ally to run through their country, bypassing Russia. The US has also lent its assistance by providing Georgian troops with counter-terrorism training.

What happened in August 2008?
Georgian troops began fighting separatists in South Ossetia. Russian forces were consequently dispatched, with Russian president Dmitry Medvedev saying that he must 'protect the life and dignity of Russian citizens wherever they are'. Russia then pushed further into Georgia, but a ceasefire agreement brought an end to the conflict. Shortly afterwards, Russia recognised the independence of South Ossetia and Abkhazia in an act widely condemned by the international community, but symptomatic of the unstable relationship between Russia and Georgia since independence. 'We are not afraid of anything, including the prospect of a Cold War,' Medvedev said at the time. Following this bout of fighting tensions are once again contained, but it is uncertain how long this current period of relative calm will last.

We don't wanna put in

Georgia's entry for the 2009 Eurovision song contest, which took place in Moscow, caused a stir with lyrics which seemed to adopt a political tone – something that is expressly banned by the rules of the competition. The 70s-style disco track, performed by songwriter Stephane Mgebrishvili and a trio of women called 3G, takes a thinly disguised pop at Russian Prime Minister Vladimir Putin with the chorus: 'We don't wanna put in/ Cuz negative move/ It's killin' the groove/ I'm gonna try to shoot in/ Some disco tonight/ Boogie with you.' Organisers laid down an ultimatum that Georgia should either pick another song or rewrite the lyrics. Georgia decided to withdraw from the contest but denied that the song contained any political statement. Anglo-Georgian singer Katie Melua was more even-handed in her analysis of the political situation in August last year, saying, 'Who ever settled anything with war? At the moment it seems to be a lot of posturing and the two sides showing each other how big their guns are.'

GM Food

What is it?

Genetically modified (GM) food contains organisms whose genetic characteristics have been altered using the latest techniques in biotechnology. GM foods currently on sale contain genetically modified crops such as soybeans, corn, canola, tomatoes, potatoes, rice and sugar cane; GM animals have been developed, but not yet sold as food products. Since the first commercial release of GM food in 1994 (the slow-ripening Flavr Savr tomato, by the Californian company Calgene), production has increased rapidly around the world;

according to the ISAAA (the International Service for the Acquisition of Agri-Biotech Applications, a nonprofit group that promotes GM use in developing countries), over 12 million farmers in 23 countries are now growing GM crops. Of these, the US is leading the way by far, producing over half of the world's total, with Argentina, Brazil, Canada, India and China the next biggest growers. In the US, 91% of all corn and 73% of soybeans grown are genetically modified, and an estimated 75% of its processed food contains some kind of GM ingredient. The EU is very different; Europeans have been wary of food safety since the 'mad cow' and dioxin food scares (both non-GM-related) in the 1990s and remain suspicious of GM, which is reflected in strict EU regulations governing its sale and production. Feted by biotechnology companies as the saviour of mankind, and demonised by environmentalists as the monstrous scourge of ecosytems, GM food is one of the most controversial and polarised issues of our times.

What are genes?
Every cell of every living organism contains the famous 'double helix' molecule DNA (Deoxyribonucleic acid) in its nucleus. This carries the coded instructions for every characteristic and function of the organism. Genes are subsections of DNA, each of which correspond to a particular characteristic. Humans have around 25,000 genes, packaged into 23 pairs of bundles called chromosomes, whereas most plants have even more – rice might have up to 55,000. Altering the genes of an organism is like changing the ingredients of a recipe; it changes its fundamental make-up.

Is genetic modification anything new?
No. The genetic modification of crops is as old as agriculture itself; for around ten thousand years farmers have been cross-breeding crops in order to combine and develop their most favourable characteristics into new strains. The 'classical' methods of cross-breeding, or hybridisation, involve the cross-pollination or manual splicing together of different species, resulting in transgenic strains (plants whose genetic information is a combination of genes from different species). What we recognise today as corn was developed by farmers over centuries from a crop that was originally more akin to a rice stalk. Seedless grapes and high-yielding tomatoes are other examples of achievements in GM that predated laboratory techniques. The modern version of GM dates from the 1970s, when it first became possible to isolate individual genes and copy them in other cells.

How does it work?
On the same principle as the classical methods – combining genetic information from different organisms to create new strains of crop – but more precisely, either by directly transferring DNA into other cells, or by 'silencing' a particular gene by copying it and attaching it in the reverse direction. There is a wide array of techniques used to transfer DNA, including biolistics (attaching the DNA to tiny gold particles and forcing them into the cells using intense bursts of gas), calcium phosphate precipitation (which granulates the DNA, enabling it to be ingested by the target cells), electroporation (using electric shocks to temporarily rupture the cell wall and enable the penetration of the DNA) or the use of bacteria or benign viruses as DNA carriers. These modern techniques mean that genes from totally different organisms can be combined if

necessary; indeed, mouse genes have been introduced to potatoes, cow genes to soy beans, and even human genes to corn and rice. It was the potential for radical combinations such as these that led critics to label GM products 'Frankenfood' in the 1990s.

What are the characteristics of GM crops?

Herbicide resistance and resistance to insects and other pests are the two characteristics most commonly found in GM crops. Herbicide-resistant crops enable a whole field to be sprayed with herbicide, killing the weeds but not the crops, and saving time and energy for the farmer (who would otherwise have to apply herbicide very selectively or use labour-intensive weeding methods). Insect-repellent crops have a gene introduced to them from the naturally-occurring bacterium *bacillus thuringiensis*, or *bt*, which has been used for centuries as an organic insecticide. This makes the plant 'sweat' *bt*, which means farmers don't need to buy it and then spray their crops with it.

Other favourable characteristics currently in research and development include drought-resistance, high nitrogen absorption, water-logging resistance, disease resistance, salt tolerance, high nutritional value, high vitamin content (for example 'golden rice', which has been developed to contain high levels of Vitamin A) and vaccine content (for example rice containing a cholera vaccine, which has proved successful in trials on mice). If these traits can be successfully developed and released commercially, GM crops could start to fulfil the promises made by the biotech companies by providing a way both of feeding the world's rising population and of combating the negative effects of climate change on food production by creating resilient crops that can grow in inhospitable conditions.

Do GM crops give higher yields?

Not at the moment. One of the main arguments that the biotech companies put forward for GM crops is their potential to help feed the world's growing population by producing more crop per hectare. In theory, crops that can grow without competition from weeds and the threat of pests should have higher yields, but studies have so far proved inconclusive; one study in India found that GM pest-resistant cotton gave much higher yields than non-GM cotton, but other reports from the USDA (United States Department of Agriculture) and UNFAO (United Nations Food and Agriculture Organisation) have suggested that GM does not in fact improve yields, and in some cases even decreases them.

So what's all the fuss about?

The main objection to GM is that its effect on both humans and the environment is not yet fully understood. GM crops have been growing for 15 years without causing any major disasters, but it may simply be too early to tell what their long-term effects will be. Amongst other health risks yet to be conclusively proved, there are concerns that allergenic properties (from fish or nuts, for example) could be transferred into GM crops. As for the environment, GM could have a negative effect on biodiversity and ecosystems: genetic information from GM crops could infiltrate other plants (including organic or non-GM crops) via cross-pollination, or the animal kingdom via the food chain – an idea known as 'genetic drift' or 'gene pollution'. GM crops could cause long-term soil depletion, either through steady *bt* release over a long period, or due to low biodiversity caused by herbicide usage. On top of this, there is evidence that some insects are developing *bt* resistance, which would render this particular genetic modification pointless. More generally,

Live organisms have been patentable since a landmark legal ruling in 1980 awarded scientist Ananda Chakrabarty the patent for an oil-metabolising bacterium that he had genetically engineered.

releasing new organisms 'into the wild' before they are fully understood is a cause of concern because once they are out they cannot be removed or contained. Due to their time- and labour-saving advantages, GM crops go hand-in-hand with monoculture farming (the mass production of a single crop favoured by big agribusiness), which critics say is unsustainable, especially in the developing world. Anti-GM campaigners also object to the overbearing power of the few vast biotech corporations that dominate the development and sale of GM products, in particular the American-based Monsanto, the largest producer of GM seeds and herbicide in the world. These corporations own the intellectual property rights to the plants they create and generate huge annual profits, for example by creating seeds designed only to work with their own brand of herbicide. Many worry about the influence these companies may have in governmental food regulation, and question the ethical implications of their involvement in the developing world.

'Monsanto should not have to vouchsafe the safety of biotech food. Our interest is in selling as much of it as possible. Assuring its safety is the FDA's [Food and Drug Administration's] job.'
PHIL ANGELL, *Director of Corporate Communications, Monsanto, 1998*

Hedge Funds

What are hedge funds?

Hedge funds are private investment funds, often worth billions of pounds, that are handled by specialist managers on behalf of professional investors such as pension schemes and insurance companies, or super-rich individuals. The minimum requirement to enter a fund is anything from £50,000 to £1 million, and sometimes even more. Although hedge funds are often registered in offshore tax havens such as the Cayman

Islands, the majority of them are managed from London and New York, typically from premium office space in Mayfair, Midtown, or the affluent suburbs of Connecticut or Long Island. It has been estimated that hedge funds carry out up to half of all trades on the New York and London stock exchanges. Despite this they are usually run by only a handful of people (usually between five and twenty), amongst them seasoned investors with a proven track record in mainstream investment banking. Hedge-fund managers charge an annual management fee (typically 2% of their fund's value) as well as a performance fee, usually 20% of profits. They also invest their own money in their fund, traditionally half of their net worth, which stops them taking irresponsible risks and gives them an extra incentive to perform well. Successful hedge-fund managers stand to make enormous profits that far exceed the earnings of conventional bankers – in 2007 alone, John Paulson of Paulson & Co. made $3.7 billion by short-selling sub-prime mortgage-backed securities.

How do they differ from other investment companies?
Hedge funds grew up as a by-product of financial legislation that was passed in the wake of the Great Depression in the 1930s and 40s. This aimed to regulate and limit the practices of investment companies in order to prevent them from taking risks with public money and causing another Wall Street Crash. Hedge funds got round this legislation by going private, only accepting money from accredited investors (rich people, basically) and not advertising to the general public – which they're still not allowed to do. Although much of this legislation has since been lifted for normal investment companies, hedge funds are still governed by fewer regulations; they also trade more frequently, and 'lock in' their money for longer, which

means their positions don't need to be as liquid (readily convertible into money) as other companies' investments. The fact that hedge-fund managers risk their own money sets them apart from bankers somewhat; in the aftermath of the credit crunch, bankers were vilified for running what were perceived to be irresponsible risks with other people's money in the hope of greater and greater returns, and at no personal risk to their own bank balance if it all went wrong (indeed, they received enormous bonuses even when it did).

What do they actually do?
Hedge funds try to deliver 'absolute returns' to their investors, which means aiming to give back more money than they put in. This sounds like an obvious objective, but in fact it differs from other investment houses such as banks, which measure their success in relative terms against the performance of an index or each other.

'Hedge fund' is in fact a blanket term for a huge variety of investment pools employing different sorts of strategies at varying levels of risk, but all with the ultimate purpose of creating profit for their investors, whatever the state of the markets. They were originally set up to be investment vehicles which minimised, or 'hedged' against risk. Australian Alfred Winslow Jones, who set up the first hedge fund in 1949, pioneered the 'equity long/short' strategy, which is still commonly employed by hedge funds today; buying shares in certain stocks he thought would do well ('going long') whilst simultaneously 'shorting' stocks that he thought might fall. 'Shorting' or 'short selling', means borrowing a share from someone else for a fee, and then selling it – enabling you to buy it back for less (if the price goes down) and return it to its owner whilst pocketing the difference. If Winslow's predictions were both correct, he would make money twice over, but if (for example) the overall market fell, and both stocks devalued, he would still make money from the short position, thus minimising his losses. Short selling enables hedge-fund managers to make money even when markets are falling, and can also be used by itself as a potentially risky investment strategy. Nowadays hedge-fund managers don't necessarily 'hedge' to reduce risk, but employ a whole host of fiendish investment strategies, many of which can be described as complex forms of gambling. Here are some of the simpler ones:

Derivatives trading: like stocks or bonds, derivatives are securities, tradeable financial instruments whose value is based on the price of an underlying asset. The most common forms of derivative are options and futures.

Options are contracts giving you the right either to buy or sell a share at a particular price on a particular date in the future. For example, you might spend £400 on the option to buy a speedboat for £40,000 in a year's time. If in a year's time the speedboat is worth £50,000, you exercise your option, buy the speedboat for £40,000 and sell it for £50,000, leaving you with a profit of £9,600. If the speedboat decreases in price, however, you've only lost £400. Options can also be used to protect against risk – if you buy £200,000 worth of shares believing that they'll rise sharply in value, you may also choose to spend a further £20,000 on the option to sell them for the same price in a year – that way, if things go horribly wrong, the most you could lose is the £20,000 you spent on the option.

Futures, or forwards, are like options, except they oblige you either to buy or sell on the agreed date at the agreed price. This makes them much riskier and therefore cheaper. Some of the most damaging investment mistakes can be made by buying futures, as they tie you into paying a much larger amount than you spent on the security itself on something in the future – often shares. This usually means you have to leverage yourself by borrowing that much larger amount from someone else. If those shares go up, you can make a huge profit by selling them at their new price, returning what you borrowed and pocketing the difference, but if they go down you will have made a huge loss, and it's not even your money you've lost, so you've then got to find some way of repaying the difference to your creditor. Not for the faint-hearted.

Derivatives these days are rarely one single product, and more usually consist of complex financial packages involving 'a mix of options and futures and currencies and debt, structured and priced in ways that are the closest real-life thing to rocket science' (John Lanchester, *London Review of Books*).

Fixed-income arbitrage (or convergence trading): this works by exploiting tiny discrepancies in bond market prices (see **Stocks and Bonds**), taking two similar bonds, buying the cheaper one and short selling the more expensive, thus making money when the discrepancy corrects itself, which it nearly always will. To make this worth doing, you need to be highly leveraged to make a decent profit, as the price differences involved are so small. When it goes wrong it can be disastrous due to the amount of leverage exposed: in 1998, unpredictable bond market movements brought about by the Russian debt crisis brought high-flying US fund Long-Term Capital Management to its knees, losing it $4.6 billion in less than four months. A wider meltdown in financial markets was only prevented by a $3.625 billion bailout by 14 major banks organised by the New York Federal Reserve.

Carry trading: taking currency from a country where interest rates are low and investing it in a country where they're high. Easy – until exchange rates start to move against you, in which case you'll need to pull out quick.

Global macro: trying to foresee and profit from large-scale movements in the world's economy, for example by betting on the change in value of a currency. George Soros made a huge profit in 1992 by betting that the value of the pound would fall; in doing so, his £10 billion short position actually worsened the currency's woes, earning him the nickname 'the man who broke the Bank of England'. Over the years, Soros and his Quantum Fund have made vast amounts of money making one-way bets based on macroeconomic analysis, but also lost a fair bit along the way: he was down $2 billion from the Russian debt crisis of 1998 and a further $3 billion from the dotcom crash of 2000–2.

Activist: Buying a lot of shares in a company and then trying to influence the way the company is run in order to boost its share price. Pretty controversial.

The credit crunch and its aftermath

In 2006 Janet Bush, writing in the *New Statesman*, dubbed hedge funds 'lords of havoc', warning that 'if the hedge-fund industry's positions in the market are 20 times the cash they actually hold, their potential impact on the world financial system is about equal to US GDP'. She was referring to the hedge funds' use of leverage, the practice of borrowing vast sums of money to maximise exposure to the securities markets, which multiplies the adverse effect many times over if bets go wrong. Hedge funds, however, did not cause the credit crunch; although they added to the volatility of the markets and exacerbated the problems of some companies during this period, their use of leverage was conservative in comparison with that of the investment banks. In general, hedge funds have suffered as a result of the credit crunch; many had to close down in 2008–9 as investors pulled their money out and managers were forced to liquidate their positions. Some, however, profited from the carnage; Andrew Lahde, a 37-year-old American hedge-fund manager, bowed out of the industry in October 2008 with a huge (undisclosed) fortune, and issued a farewell letter in which he lambasted the Bush administration for its irresponsible lack of financial regulation, extolled the virtues of marijuana as a panacea for society's ills, and encouraged his colleagues in financial services to 'throw away the BlackBerry and enjoy life'.

Hezbollah

What is it?
Hezbollah (also Hizbollah or Hizbu'llah), meaning 'Party of God', is a Lebanese Islamist organisation which functions as a political party, a paramilitary force and a provider of social welfare and development. It also runs its own satellite TV and radio station, al-Manar. Hezbollah is branded a terrorist organisation by the US, Canada and Israel, while the UK and Australia describe only its military wing as terrorist. It is seen as a legitimate resistance movement throughout much of the Arab and Muslim world. Hezbollah's leader since 1992 has been Hassan Nasrallah.

What are its origins?
Hezbollah was founded by Shi'ite clerics in 1982, initially as a militia in order to resist the Israeli occupation of Lebanon. Its founders were inspired by the Ayatollah Khomeini's Islamic revolution in Iran in 1979, and its members trained by a group of Iranian Revolutionary Guards stationed in Lebanon.

What are its aims?
Hezbollah's 1985 manifesto demanded the expulsion of Israeli, American and French forces from Lebanon and proposed the establishment of Islamic rule to replace Lebanon's secular state. This latter aim has since been abandoned and the party has made alliances across religious divides. Hezbollah remains vehemently anti-Israeli and anti-Western, its leaders having issued numerous statements calling for the destruction of the state of Israel, which it considers an illegitimate occupant of Palestinian territory. Although Israel withdrew from Lebanon in

2000, Hezbollah still claims as Lebanese territory the disputed Shebaa farms area in the north of the Golan Heights, which Israel seized from Syria in the Six-Day War of 1967.

Where is it based?
In Shi'ite-dominated areas of Lebanon, which include the south, the Bekaa valley in the north-east, and in parts of the capital Beirut. US Intelligence claims that Hezbollah also operates cells in North and South America, Africa and Europe.

Who are its allies?
Hezbollah provides support to Hamas, the Palestinian Sunni group, and enjoys strong ties with Iran and Syria, from whom it receives financial, organisational and military aid.

What major attacks has it carried out?
Hezbollah was linked to several attacks and kidnappings in the 1980s, including the suicide bombing of a US barracks in Beirut in 1983 and the hijacking of Flight TWA 847 in 1985. It was also blamed for the bombings of two Jewish targets in Argentina in 1992 and 1994, although it has denied any involvement. From 1982 onwards Hezbollah waged a guerrilla campaign against occupying Israeli forces in southern Lebanon until these forces withdrew in May 2000 following a UN resolution. In July 2006 Hezbollah kidnapped two Israeli soldiers and killed several others in a cross-border attack, sparking a month-long war which claimed over 1,300 (mostly civilian) lives and ended in a ceasefire. Hezbollah has also claimed responsibility for operations in Iraq, including attacks against US-led coalition forces.

What is its military capability?

It is estimated that Hezbollah has around 1,000 full-time soldiers and 6–10,000 volunteers. Its weaponry includes the Katyusha rocket and various types of anti-tank, anti-aircraft and anti-ship missiles. It also possesses around 100 long-range missiles which make strikes on the Israeli cities of Haifa and Tel Aviv possible. Despite two UN resolutions demanding the disarmament of Lebanese militias, Hezbollah's military wing not only remains intact but is growing in strength, according to both Israel and Hezbollah itself.

How powerful is Hezbollah in Lebanese politics?

Hezbollah won its first seats in Lebanon's parliament in the 2005 elections and then led the March 8 Alliance, a pro-Syrian bloc consisting of several other parties, in opposition to the US-backed government of Fouad Siniora also elected in that year. In May 2008, Hezbollah invaded West Beirut in response to a government-ordered shutdown of their military communications network. The ensuing violence drove the country to the brink of civil war until the situation was resolved by an Arab-brokered peace deal in which Hezbollah was granted the power of veto and 11 out of 30 seats in the cabinet of a new unity government. This made Hezbollah's political position stronger than ever, and they remain a significant political force despite losing the June 2009 elections to the pro-Western faction of Saad Hariri. Saad is the business tycoon son of former prime minister Rafik Hariri, whose assassination in February 2005 was widely blamed on Syria.

Do they ever get a bit carried away?
In 1996, Hezbollah called on Muslims to boycott the movie
Independence Day, calling it 'propaganda for the so-called genius
of the Jews and their alleged concern for humanity'. In the
movie, a Jewish scientist played by Jeff Goldblum helps save the
world from an alien invasion.

Human Rights

What does it mean?
The term 'human rights' refers to the universal rights of all human beings – civil, political, social, economic and cultural – as set out by the Universal Declaration of Human Rights (UDHR) adopted at the United Nations General Assembly in Paris, 1948. This was a more specific definition of the rights listed in the United Nations Charter (the founding treaty of the UN) drawn up in San Francisco in 1945 in the aftermath of World War II (see UN).

What are they?
The rights specified by the UDHR can be roughly divided into three categories. First, there are the rights necessary for survival and dignified living, which include the right to adequate living standards (food, water and housing), the right to social protection in times of need, the right to the highest attainable standard of health, the right to work (and in humane conditions) and the right to privacy and family life. Second, there are rights necessary for human dignity, creativity and intellectual and spiritual development, which include the right to education and information, freedom of religion, opinion and speech, freedom of association (the right to band together with other individuals to express or defend common interests, such as with workers' unions), the right to take part in the political process and the right to take part in cultural life. Finally, there are the rights necessary for liberty and physical security, which include freedom from slavery, freedom from torture or degrading treatment, freedom from arbitrary arrest or imprisonment and the right to a fair trial.

How are human rights enforced?

The Universal Declaration of Human Rights (UDHR) was not legally binding, but was important in establishing a set of norms and standards to which the global community was expected to adhere – a moral conscience for the world. Over the ensuing decades, the UDHR was embedded into international law by six core human rights treaties, on the themes of racial discrimination (which came into force in 1969), civil and political rights (1976), economic, social and cultural rights (1976), discrimination against women (1981), torture (1987) and the rights of the child (1990). States which have signed these treaties are required to alter their own national law in order to accommodate them. Each of the core treaties has its own committee that monitors the extent to which signatory states are complying with them, and four out of the six have complaints procedures which enable individuals to raise allegations if they believe their rights have been violated. Through the United Nations Human Rights Council, created in 2005, all UN member states have agreed to a public debate on their human rights performance. Non-governmental Organisations (NGOs), such as Amnesty International and Human Rights Watch, also play a role in holding governments accountable for violating human rights.

Have all countries signed up to the six core treaties?

No – in fact, none of them are fully signed and ratified (confirmed) by all the countries in the world. The most complete is the Convention on the Rights of the Child which only lacks Somalia (not signed) and the USA (signed but not yet ratified) from its list of member states. The Convention on the Elimination of All Forms of Discrimination Against Women has not been signed by the Islamic states of Sudan, Iran, Qatar and

Somalia, as well as a handful of Pacific island states. The Convention Against Torture and Other Cruel, Inhuman or Degrading Treatment or Punishment is far from complete, awaiting signature or ratification from around 50 states worldwide.

Do the signatory countries always comply with the treaties?
No – Amnesty International's World Human Rights Report 2008 announced that the Universal Declaration of Human Rights was being observed in only a handful of countries worldwide. It drew attention to thousands of human rights violations that occurred in 2007 alone, including the USA's use of torture and imprisonment of detainees without charge or trial in Iraq, Bagram (Afghanistan), Guantánamo Bay and secret detention centres, and the collusion of many EU countries (including the UK) in CIA activities such as extraordinary rendition (the secret and illegal transfer of prisoners to other countries where they may suffer torture or ill-treatment). The report also pointed to Russia's draconian treatment of political dissenters and its failure to punish human rights abuses in Chechnya, and China's widespread and systematic abuses ranging from repression of religious groups, Tibetans and Uighurs, to torture of political dissenters and human rights activists, to the use of the death penalty, and state restriction of information and freedom of expression. As well as listing notorious flashpoints such as Burma (Myanmar), Gaza, Darfur, Zimbabwe and the Democratic Republic of Congo, other notable violations included particularly high levels of violence against women (including rape) in Egypt; Israel's restriction of the movement of Palestinians in the West Bank and Gaza through its use of checkpoints and 'security fence'; the killing of trade

union members in Colombia; the lack of free anti-retroviral drugs for 97% of HIV/AIDS victims in Malawi; and the trafficking of women for enforced sex work in many countries, notably in Europe.

Is there an international court of human rights?

No. For the 47 members of the Council of Europe, however, there is the European Court of Human Rights in Strasbourg, established under the European Convention on Human Rights of 1950. This binds member states to a code of human rights that, although strict, is more lenient than the UDHR.

Where are the rules of war written down?

The Geneva Conventions of 1949 were a set of four treaties in international law which set the standards for the treatment of victims of war, non-combatants in war and prisoners of war. They outlawed (amongst other things) the taking of hostages, forcing prisoners of war to fight for a hostile power and depriving prisoners of war a fair trial. The use of weapons in war was regulated by the Hague Conventions of 1899 and 1907 and the Geneva Protocol (on the use of gas and biological weapons) of 1925. This was supplemented by the Chemical Weapons Convention, drafted in 1992 and now signed and ratified by nearly all the world's nations. This outlaws the production, stockpiling and use of chemical weapons. White phosphorus, a controversial incendiary substance known to have been used in combat by the US, Israel and Russia in recent years, is not designated a chemical weapon in this convention, although various groups feel that it should be.

What is the ICC?

The International Criminal Court in the Hague was established under the Rome Statute on 1 July 2002, as a permanent tribunal for bringing to justice those responsible for war crimes, genocide and crimes against humanity. The court built on the precedent of two pre-existing international war crimes tribunals for Yugoslavia and Rwanda. The ICC's definitions of war crimes include: any breaches of the Geneva Conventions; attacks on civilians, humanitarian workers or UN peacekeepers; settlement of occupied territory; use of poison weapons; use of civilians as shields; use of child soldiers; summary execution (killing someone on the spot without trial); rape and pillage.

Thomas Lubanga, a Congolese rebel leader, became the first person to be tried at the ICC in January 2009 for conscripting child soldiers in the Ituri district of north-eastern DR Congo in 2002–3 (see **Congo**). So far 14 people, from Uganda, Central African Republic, DR Congo and Sudan have been indicted, seven of whom remain at large (including Sudanese head of state Omar al-Bashir) and two of whom have died. As of mid-2009, 108 states are members of the ICC; notable countries that have not joined include the US, China, Russia, India and Israel, although their citizens can be indicted if accused of war crimes in a participating state. Some non-members fear that the ICC could interfere with their sovereignty or that their citizens could be targeted by politically motivated indictments. Israel doesn't like the fact that settlement of occupied territory is classed as a war crime by the ICC.

Miami Vice

In 2003, the New York Human Rights Commission demanded that the manufacturers of the hugely popular video game *Grand Theft Auto 3: Vice City* remove the phrase 'kill the Haitian dickheads' from their recent release. The two companies that produced the game were investigated for human rights violations and for inciting hatred or violence against the Haitian people.

Immigration

What are immigrants?
People who live in a country that is not their land of origin.

What are asylum-seekers and refugees?
Asylum-seekers are people who have fled their home country because their safety has been threatened on political, religious or ethnic grounds or because of war, and are seeking protection as refugees under the terms of the 1951 UN Refugee Convention. An asylum-seeker is someone who has applied for asylum in a country but is still awaiting the results, while a refugee is someone whose application to stay has been successful.

What are internally displaced people?

People who have fled their homes because of threatening
situations such as armed conflicts and natural disasters, but who
have not left their country. In the aftermath of the conflict in Sri
Lanka in May 2009, the UN Refugee Agency reported that there
were 300,000 internally displaced persons spread across 40
emergency shelter sites.

When did immigration to the UK start?

It's been going on for thousands of years. In Britain's early
history, immigration usually occurred forcibly, as the result of
invasions from Celts, Romans, Anglo-Saxons, Vikings or
Normans. One of the first major influxes of refugees arrived
from 1670–1710, as 50,000 Protestant Huguenots fled to
England to avoid persecution in Catholic France. As the
British Empire grew, London became a hub of trade, attracting
immigrants from around the world, and by the late Victorian
period the capital was home to sizeable communities of
Irish, Chinese, Jews and Italians, while other immigrant
groups established themselves in other port cities or towns. In
the 20th century two World Wars left Britain weak, prompting
the country to look abroad for labourers to help reinvigorate
the economy, and in the few years after World War II over
340,000 Europeans from countries such as Poland, Italy and
Austria arrived on work-permit schemes. When more
economic migrants were needed in the 1950s and 60s, the
government turned further afield to new Commonwealth
countries such as India, Pakistan, the Caribbean and former
African colonies.

A rise in racial tensions

Between 1951 and 1971 the number of non-white residents in Britain rose from around 30,000 to 1.4 million. With this rise grew ethnic tensions and violence, notably the riots in Liverpool in 1948 – home to around 8,000 black residents – and a decade later riots in Notting Hill, London, which saw clashes between young whites and the area's growing Caribbean community.

European neighbours

The fall of the Berlin Wall in 1989 led to a large number of immigrants entering the UK from Eastern Europe. In 2004, when eight new countries joined the European Union, a new wave of migrants arrived, largely from Poland. Although a million crossed the Channel, research from the think-tank IPPR (the Institute for Public Policy Research) in May 2008 indicated that half of these had already left. The increase in Poles living in the UK prompted the *Sun* newspaper to print a Polish language edition during the Euro 2008 football tournament.

What are the latest UK immigration figures?

The latest figures from the Office of National Statistics are for 2007, when net immigration to the UK was 237,000, an increase of 46,000 from the previous year. The number of people arriving to live in the UK actually dropped from 2006–7 (591,000 to 577,000) but this was offset by a bigger drop in emigration (400,000 to 340,000). Since the Labour government came to power in 1997, the UK population has swelled by 1.8 million as a result of immigration. This has been caused by Labour's policy of attracting economic migrants – the number of work permits issued per year trebled between 1997 and 2007 – and of abolishing the 'Primary Purpose Rule' in 1997, making it possible to marry someone purely for the purposes of immigration. Since 1997 the number of people arriving in the UK as new spouses has doubled to 42,000 per year.

Between 1997 and 2002 there was also a sharp rise in the number of asylum-seekers trying to escape conflicts in countries such as Iraq, Zimbabwe, Somalia and Afghanistan: these reached a peak of 84,000 in 2002, before reducing steadily to the current figure of around 26,000 per year. In 2007, 17% of these were granted asylum, 10% were granted humanitarian protection or discretionary leave to stay, and 23% of appeals processed that year against previously refused asylum were allowed. There are also thought to be a large number of illegal immigrants in Britain – 725,000 (518,000 of which are in London), according to estimates by the London School of Economics in March 2009. These have either sneaked in illegally on the back of a truck, are students or visitors who have overstayed their visas, or are rejected asylum-seekers who the authorities have failed to eject. The UK population is projected to rise from 61 million today to 70 million by 2028, 70% of which will be due to immigration.

Is immigration of economic benefit to the UK?
Figures released by the Home Office in October 2007 stated that immigrants contributed around £6 billion to the UK economy in 2006 alone, leading then Home Secretary Jacqui Smith to refer to the 'purity of the macroeconomic case for immigration'. However, a House of Lords committee report in April 2008 found the government's argument 'unconvincing'. Lord Wakeham, who chaired the committee, called the figure of £6 billion 'meaningless' because, while immigrants contribute to the country's GDP (Gross Domestic Product), they also swell its population, which means overall standards of living (GDP per head) stay the same. Lord Wakeham's report

recognised the value of the immigrant workforce in a number of private and public sectors such as the NHS, which currently recruits around 15,000 immigrant nurses per year, but in all other respects it opposed the view that immigration was good for the UK economy. It rubbished claims that immigrants are needed to do jobs that British people 'won't or can't' do (proposing that mechanisation and higher wages could solve this problem instead), and rejected the notion that immigrants would be necessary to stem the looming pension crisis. This crisis is forecasted to result from the combination of an ageing population and a falling birth rate and, according to a 2006 study from the Cass Business School in London, could be solved by the arrival of ten million migrant workers before 2025. Lord Wakeham's report stated that these sorts of arguments 'are based on the unreasonable assumption of a static retirement age as people live longer, and ignore the fact that, in time, immigrants too will grow old and draw pensions'. Lastly, the report voiced concern about immigration's effect on the wages of the lowest-paid; high net immigration of low-skilled workers creates more competition for jobs among the lowest paid, which has a negative effect on their wages while raising slightly the wages of the highest paid. An opinion poll in February 2009 found that immigration was the most pressing issue for Labour and Conservative voters, indicating that this will be a hotly debated topic in the run-up to the next general election.

Sleepwalking to segregation?
In the 1970s and 80s, and particularly from 1997 onwards, British governments adopted multicultural policies as a way of assimilating immigrant communities into their new environment. Broadly speaking, this meant recognising and

celebrating their cultural differences, treating each minority group equitably and not imposing majority British culture on them – policies included supporting the festivals, art and music of minority cultures, accepting religious dress in schools and supporting media in minority languages. However, such policies have been criticised as divisive rather than cohesive in the last few years, emphasising difference rather than similarity, and were blamed for fuelling the Islamic extremism which led to the London bombings of 2005. Not long after 7/7, Trevor Philips, the Chairman of the Commission for Racial Equality, famously warned: 'We are sleepwalking our way to segregation. We are becoming strangers to each other and we are leaving communities to be marooned outside the mainstream.' Since 2005, the Labour government has started to move away from multiculturalism by promoting 'essential' or 'British' values, and introducing measures which advance a common thread of national identity. One example is the Life in the United Kingdom test, a computer-based multiple choice test on aspects of British history, citizenship and everyday affairs for individuals seeking Indefinite Leave to Remain in the UK, or naturalisation as a British citizen.

A matter of shame

The extreme right-wing whites-only British National Party (BNP), led by Nick Griffin, who was convicted for citing racial hatred against Jews, is among the minority fuelling resentment against immigrants in the UK. Griffin and his BNP accomplice Andrew Brons were elected to the European parliament as MEPs on the back of disastrous European election results for Labour in June 2009. Following the results, Griffin said: 'The Labour Party, the Lib Dems and the Tories, by leaving the door to Britain open, have forced people to turn to a party which speaks openly about the problem of immigration and says that while there might be a few good things about it there's also a lot of bad things.' Tony Lloyd, MP for Manchester Central, said: 'I am not just disappointed, it is a matter of shame. This country has a deserved reputation as a tolerant society and it now has representatives who are avowed racists.'

Brits abroad
Emigration has also proved a hot topic in recent years. In 2006, a record 400,000 people left Britain for a minimum of a year, 207,000 of whom were British. This figure dropped in 2007 to 340,000, of whom half were British. Despite this drop emigration remains high, with many Brits emigrating abroad in search of a better life – many cite the cost of living as the main reason for their move. Popular destinations include Australia, which actively seeks workers, and which has an immigration target of over 100,000 for the 2009/10 financial year.

Famous literary immigrants
Joseph Conrad, one of English literature's great writers, was born Józef Korzeniowski in the Ukraine in 1857. English was his third language after Polish and French – he didn't learn it until his twenties, and became a British citizen in 1886 before going on to write such masterpieces as *Heart of Darkness*, *Lord Jim* and *The Secret Agent*. Tom Stoppard, writer of *Arcadia* and *The Real Thing* and one of the most celebrated English playwrights today, was born Tomáš Straussler in Czechoslovakia in 1939, before moving to England at the age of seven and adopting his English stepfather's surname. V.S. Naipaul, perhaps best known for his novel *A House for Mr Biswas*, is of Indian ancestry but was born in Trinidad in 1932 before settling in England in 1950. *Wild Swans* author Jung Chang was born in China in 1952 but has

lived in Britain since 1978, when she arrived on a government scholarship to study for a PhD in linguistics, which she completed before becoming a writer.

Iran

Some basics

Iran was once the seat of the Persian empire, one of the largest and greatest of the ancient world. This vast and varied country was known in the West as Persia until 1935, when its Persian-language name, Iran ('Land of the Aryans'), was introduced internationally. The terrain is mountainous, with areas of desert as well as sub-tropical forests; its capital, Tehran, is the largest city in the Middle East. Islam arrived in Iran in 636 AD, and gradually took over from Zoroastrianism as the major religion, while the country's rich traditions of poetry, art, architecture, science and mathematics blended with Islamic cultural influences. Iran remained non-Arab both in language and ethnicity, however: it retained its distinct language, Farsi, and although its population today of around 70 million comprises many ethnic groups (including Persian (51%), Azeri (24%), Mazandarani (8%) and Gilaki (8%)), only 3% are Arab. Iran is also set apart from most other Muslim countries in the Middle East by its majority (89%) following of Shi'a Islam, which has been the state religion since 1501, as opposed to the Sunni sect which dominates most other Muslim countries (see **Islam**). Iran became the world's first Islamic Republic in 1979 after a revolution led by the Shi'a cleric Ayatollah Ruhollah Khomeini overthrew the pro-Western monarchy of Shah Reza Pahlavi.

Why did the revolution happen and what were its effects?

Mass demonstrations against the monarchy began in 1978. Popular opinion turned against the Shah's programme of modernisation and secularisation, friendly relations with the US and the social injustice, corruption and brutality of his regime.

The Ayatollah Khomeini, a long-standing critic of the Shah, returned from exile in 1979 to lead the revolution, which very quickly restored Islam as the guiding force of social and political life in Iran (ayatollah, meaning 'sign of God', is the name for the highest-ranking clerics from the Usuli Twelver sect, the largest branch of Shi'a Islam; there are over twenty ayatollahs worldwide). The Islamic Revolution expanded health and education services across the country (the literacy rate is now 82%), but it also introduced widespread censorship of the media, suppressed political opposition and denied equal rights for women (despite this, women still occupy some prominent roles in Iranian society and constitute over half of the country's university students). The Shah's hated secret police were disbanded, only to be replaced by the Revolutionary Guard, an elite military force dedicated to upholding the ideology of the revolution, and a morality police (the Basij) designed to enforce *hijab* (the Islamic ruling that women should be appropriately covered up by clothing) and prevent other moral transgressions such as drinking, sex outside marriage and the mixing of the sexes in public.

What happened after the revolution?

A hostage crisis and a war. Relations with the US broke down in October 1979 when Iranian students captured 66 American diplomats at the US Embassy in Tehran and held them hostage for over a year. Initially the students were calling for the Shah to be extradited from America (where he had gone to receive cancer treatment) back to Iran to face trial and execution; the Shah died in Egypt in July 1980, but most of the hostages continued to be held until January 1981 in a symbolic act of defiance to the 'Great Satan', the US. 'America can't do a thing,' said Khomeini at the time. Iran then alienated itself further

from the US during the 1980s by sponsoring Hezbollah (see
Hezbollah), the PLO and, later, Hamas (see **Israel/Palestine**). In
September 1980, Iran was invaded by neighbouring Iraq under
Saddam Hussein (see **Iraq**). Having suffered early setbacks,
Khomeini's Iran hit back hard, seeing the war as a good
opportunity to weaken Saddam's secular Ba'athist regime and
export the Islamic Revolution to Iraq, with its 60% Shi'a
majority. The Iran–Iraq war dragged on until 1988, when it was
finally ended by a UN-brokered peace deal. Neither side gained
any ground, but both suffered heavy losses and damage to their
oil industries. Since the end of the war Iran's centrally planned
economy has grown (it is now classed as 'semi-developed' by the
UN), but it is still inefficient and over-reliant on its oil and
natural gas reserves, which are amongst the largest in the world.

Who holds the power in Iran?
Iran's political system, established under the 1979 constitution,
is a complex combination of Islamic theocracy and subordinate
democratic institutions. On the one hand there are the
unelected ultra-conservative bodies made up of Shi'a clerics, at
the top of which sits the Supreme Leader, currently Ayatollah
Ali Khamenei. The Supreme Leader appoints the heads of the
Judiciary, armed forces, radio and TV as well as a personal
advisory body, the Expediency Council. Then there are the
directly elected institutions: the Majlis (or parliament, made up
of reformist and conservative factions), the President and the
Assembly of Experts (an 86-strong body whose job it is to
appoint and monitor the performance of the Supreme Leader).
Meanwhile the Guardian Council, consisting of six clerics, is co-
appointed by the Supreme Leader, Head of Judiciary and
Parliament. This is a particularly powerful body as it has the
power to veto laws passed by parliament and block people from

standing in elections to any of the directly elected institutions. In 2004 the Guardian Council disqualified 2,300 mostly reformist candidates from parliamentary elections and barred all but 6 of over 1,000 presidential candidates from standing the following year. These interventions ushered in a new era of conservative rule in Iran, ending a period of moderate reformist government under Mohammed Khatami, who had been president since 1997.

Who is the president now?
Mahmoud Ahmadinejad, a hardline conservative, former mayor of Tehran and the first non-cleric to hold the office since 1981. First elected in 2005, he is a famously outspoken critic of the US who has also called for the dissolution of Israel and described the holocaust as a 'myth'. Ahmadinejad began a second term in office in June 2009 after winning elections that were widely believed to have been rigged: not only was his share of the vote, at 63%, unexpectedly high, but the results suggested that he had fared equally well in rural and urban areas and that the other candidates had done badly in their home provinces, all of which aroused suspicion. The results sparked several weeks of mass protests by supporters of the defeated reformist candidates Mir-Hossein Mousavi and Mehdi Karroubi, which were eventually contained by a government crackdown in which foreign media was restricted and at least 17 people were killed. The protests failed to change the election result, but many Iranians lost faith in their political system and a deep rift opened between conservatives and reformists. At the time of writing, Mousavi, Karroubi and former president Khatami, supported by some senior clerics, continue defiantly to reject the legitimacy of Ahmadinejad and call for fresh elections.

Does Iran have nuclear weapons?

No, but it may have before long. For years, Iran has been enriching uranium for what it insists are peaceful purposes, i.e. the creation of nuclear energy. In 2003 Iran passed inspections by the UN's nuclear watchdog, the IAEA – which concluded that there was no evidence of a nuclear weapons programme – before agreeing to suspend most of its uranium enrichment in a deal with the EU the following year. However, after the election of Ahmadinejad in 2005, certain enrichment programmes were resumed which contravened IAEA regulations. Iran refused to stop these programmes, prompting the UN Security Council to impose sanctions in 2007 which included a ban on arms sales and freezing some of the state's assets. Despite these measures, uranium enrichment, centrifuge manufacture and missile testing have all since continued, to the dismay of Israel, the EU and the US. Barack Obama is trying to revive diplomatic relations with Iran and engage in an open dialogue about its nuclear weapons, releasing a special video message to the Iranian people on the occasion of Nowruz (New Year) in March 2009. It remains to be seen how successful these friendly overtures will be; in the same month Supreme Leader Ali Khamenei declared that Obama was following the 'same misguided track' as President Bush, referring to continued American support for Israel and vowing to back the Palestinian cause in return, considering this a 'mandatory duty' for all Muslims.

The next revolution

Of the current population, 70% are under 30 and weren't alive for the revolution that their parents demanded so fervently. Many young Iranians, especially those in the cities, embrace Western culture, music and fashion; the latest trend for 2009 is plastic surgery, which is very popular in Tehran. Despite the authorities' efforts to censor the internet, young Iranians often use it to register their disdain for a political system that they see as backward and out of touch with their views (many used Twitter to keep the world informed about the street protests in June 2009 – see **Social Networking**). Despite the threat of public flogging for moral indecency, some Iranian youths have reacted defiantly to the increase of morality police patrols under Ahmadinejad by proclaiming a 'sexual revolution' and throwing wild parties fuelled by drugs and alcohol.

Rock the Casbah
British punk band The Clash wrote this song (which features on their 1982 album *Combat Rock*) as a protest against oppressive Islamic regimes including Khomeini's, which had introduced a ban on rock music as part of the Islamic Revolution.

Iraq

Between the rivers
Ancient Iraq is sometimes known as the 'cradle of civilisation' due to the early urban societies which grew up in the fertile land between the Tigris and Euphrates rivers (Mesopotamia, an ancient Greek name for the region, literally means 'between the rivers'). By 3000 BC, the Sumerians had developed the first writing, cuneiform, and begun building cities such as Uruk and Ur; they were followed by other local rulers such as the Akkadians, Assyrians and Babylonians, who were responsible for pioneering achievements in agriculture, engineering, science and art. Iraq was then ruled as a province of several different Persian empires for a total of 900 years between the 5th century BC and the 7th century AD, which also saw conquests by Alexander the Great and (briefly) the Romans.

When did Islam arrive in Iraq?
Islam arrived with the Rashidun Caliphate in the 7th century AD and put an end to Persian rule; Baghdad was founded in 762 as the capital of the Abbasid Caliphate, and in the centuries that followed it grew to become the greatest city of the Muslim world, and a key centre of learning during the Islamic Golden Age, until it was sacked by the Mongols in 1257. The Ottoman Empire ruled over Iraq from 1533–1918, when the British invaded and took control over the region. The Kingdom of Iraq came into existence in 1921, but it remained under British administration as a League of Nations Mandate until 1932, when it became fully independent. In 1958 there was a coup in which the royal family was toppled and a republic declared, and in 1968, after a decade of power struggles, General al-Bakr of

the nationalist and socialist Ba'ath Party took power on the back of a bloodless coup. Al-Bakr's nephew, Saddam Hussein, succeeded as president in 1979, a position he held until 2003.

What did Saddam do when he came to power?
In September 1980 Saddam invaded Iran, starting a long and bloody war that lasted until a ceasefire was finally called in August 1988. He claimed that the war was triggered by a territorial dispute over the Shatt al-Arab, a waterway running between the two countries, but he also had territorial designs on the oil-rich Khuzestan region of Iran and wished to improve Iraq's standing as a regional power. By the end of the war – which claimed up to a million and a half lives – the border hadn't changed at all. During the war, Iraq was simultaneously embroiled in a civil war between Saddam's forces and Iraqi Kurds (around 17% of its total population), who had been campaigning for decades for increased autonomy over the northern areas of the country. When Saddam sought to 'Arabise' the region rather than grant this autonomy, the Kurds joined ranks with Iran and attacked military and industrial sites. Iraq responded with the Anfal campaign from 1986–9, during which chemical weapons and concentration camps were used to kill around 180,000 Kurds. Saddam's cousin Ali Hassan al-Majid, known as 'Chemical Ali', was sentenced to death in 2007 for masterminding the genocide.

What is the Sunni/Shi'a split in Iraq?
Iraq's population is 97% Muslim; of these, approximately 60% are Shi'a and 40% Sunni. Iraq has been home to both major Muslim sects ever since they split from one another in the late 7th century AD (see **Islam**). Central Iraq is home to two of the holiest cities in Shi'a Islam, namely Najaf (the centre of Shi'a

learning and site of Ali, the first Shi'a Imam's tomb), and nearby Karbala (the site of the tomb of Hussein, Ali's son, who was martyred at the Battle of Karbala in AD 680). In the 1970s the secular Ba'athist regime began to crack down on Shi'a political activism and Islamism with torture and executions, sparking a resistance movement led by al-Dawa ('the Call'), a political party headed by Mohammad Baqir al-Sadr dedicated to establishing an Islamic state in Iraq. Al-Dawa had close connections with the Iranian Ayatollah Ruhollah Khomeini during his exile in Najaf from 1965–78, and supported his Islamic Revolution in Iran in 1979 (see **Iran**). During the Iran–Iraq War, both Saddam and Khomeini attempted to court Iraq's Shi'a population, with Saddam's propaganda stressing their Arab ethnicity, and Khomeini emphasising their religious affiliation in a bid to export the Islamic Revolution to Iraq.

Why did Iraq invade Kuwait?
Having hardly drawn breath from the previous war, Iraq invaded neighbouring Kuwait with over 100,000 troops on 2 August 1990. Saddam accused Kuwait of taking more than its fair share from a disputed oil field, and of flooding oil into the world's markets at too low a price. There was also a disagreement over Iraq's repayment of debts to Kuwait, incurred during its previous conflict with Iran. Having invaded, Iraq swiftly set up a provisional 'free' government in Kuwait, and on 8 August formally announced that they had taken over the country, much to the condemnation of the international community. The United Nations levied economic sanctions and issued a deadline for Iraqi forces to leave; Iraq's refusal to comply provoked a combined invasion by UK, US and other allied forces known as Operation Desert Storm. This began on 17 January 1991 with an aerial assault, in which 85,000 tons of

bombs peppered hundreds of targets over a period of six weeks, followed by a ground assault that forced Iraq to give up Kuwait, and by 3 March Iraq had agreed to the conditions of a ceasefire. The First Gulf War claimed the lives of around 300 allied soldiers, while estimates for the number of Iraqi casualties range from 60,000 to 200,000.

Coping in the aftermath

Immediately after the war Iraq descended into chaos as a series of violent Shi'a uprisings tried to topple Saddam's regime while the Kurds rebelled simultaneously in the north. Both insurgencies were brutally suppressed by government forces, resulting in tens of thousands of deaths and around two million refugees. Rival Kurdish factions then turned on each other in northern Iraq and fought a civil war from 1994–7. In December 1996 the 'Oil for Food' programme was implemented, which would continue until November 2003. Under this programme regulated oil sales were used to inject badly needed humanitarian supplies into the country (see **United Nations** for details of the corruption of this programme).

What about those Weapons of Mass Destruction?

In 1998 Iraq stopped co-operating with the UN commission charged with overseeing that its Weapons of Mass Destruction (WMD) were destroyed, part of the conditions following the end of the First Gulf War. This led to Operation Desert Fox, when the UK and US dropped bombs on suspected biological, chemical and nuclear weapons bases. More bombings followed over the next few years to cripple Iraq's air-defence network. In 2002, President George W. Bush and Prime Minister Tony Blair built up a case to invade and bring an end to Saddam's regime, which they accused of failing to co-operate with an inspection for WMD. The most infamous justification for the war was Blair's claim in the House of Commons in September 2002 that Saddam had 'existing and active military plans for the use of chemical and biological weapons, which could be activated within 45 minutes'. Two years later, at a Labour conference, Blair admitted that 'evidence about Saddam having actual biological and chemical weapons, as opposed to the capability to develop them, had turned out to be wrong'. The US and the UK met with strong opposition both at home and abroad, including from China, France, Germany and Russia, all of whom wanted more time to be allowed for inspections. Regardless, on 20 March 2003 the invasion began, and a few weeks later, on 9 April 2003, Saddam Hussein was removed from power. In December 2006 he was hanged for crimes against humanity, having been charged with the killing of nearly 150 Shi'a in 1982.

Life after Saddam

After Saddam's deposition, the country descended into an approximation of civil war. There has been significant sectarian violence between Sunnis and Shi'as, as well as attacks against coalition troops ranging from suicide and car bombs to gun battles. Since the US/UK invasion, estimates for the number of Iraqi civilians and combatants who have died as a result of the ongoing conflict range from 151,000 to 1.03 million. Around 5 million citizens have been displaced, half of whom have left the country, mainly to Jordan and Syria. Although allied troops have encountered fierce resistance, they oversaw the establishment of an interim government in June 2004, followed by a new constitution and multi-party parliamentary elections in December 2005. In 2007, Bush embarked on a 'New Way Forward' for Iraq, pouring 20,000 more troops into the country in what became known as 'the surge'; this succeeded in bringing a fragile stability to the region. From the end of May 2009 there was a rapid withdrawal of UK troops from over 4,000 to fewer than 400; the focus of those that remain is on naval training. In February 2009 President Barack Obama also announced a withdrawal plan for American troops: from 142,000 to between 35,000 and 50,000 by 31 August 2010. Their work will include training and advising Iraqi security forces. All remaining US troops will have withdrawn by 31 December 2011.

By the Rivers of Babylon

One of the Seven Wonders of the World, the Hanging Gardens of Babylon were built on the orders of King Nebuchadnezzar II around 600 BC to cheer up his gloomy wife, who was from Media (now Iran) and suffering homesickness. Ancient Greek and Roman historians wrote about the magnificence of stunning gardens on terraces high up in the air, supported by stone columns, in the ancient city of Babylon, which was located a little over 50 miles south of Baghdad. There is, however, doubt over the actual existence of these gardens, of which no physical evidence has been found, and no mention in any recovered Babylonian inscriptions.

Islam

What is Islam?

Islam is the world's second largest religion after Christianity, with around 1.5 billion followers. The Muslim world stretches from West Africa across North Africa to the Middle East and central Asia, and also includes Bangladesh and Indonesia, home to the world's largest Muslim population (228 million). Significant Muslim communities can also be found in the Balkans, the Caribbean, the US, Russia (e.g. Chechnya), western China, western Europe and East Africa. Muslims worship one god (Allah), and believe that their religion was revealed gradually to the world via a succession of prophets culminating in its full revelation to the prophet Muhammad in 610 AD. Muhammad is the final and most important prophet in Islam, the last of a long line that begins with Adam and includes many that are shared by Judaism and Christianity, such as Ibrahim (Abraham), Nuh (Noah), Ayoub (Job) and Musa (Moses). Another Muslim prophet, Isa, is better known by Christians as Jesus.

What are the five pillars of Islam?

These are the five most important practices that Muslims must observe. They are:

The *Shahada* – the basic statement of the Islamic faith: 'There is no God but Allah, and Muhammad is his messenger.' Reciting this out loud three times in front of witnesses is all that is required to convert to Islam.

Salat prayer – good Muslims should do this five times a day: before dawn, at midday, late afternoon, just after sunset, and between sunset and midnight. Prayer involves a set of movements which are intended to unite body with mind and soul.

Zakat charity – Muslims are expected to donate 2.5% of their annual income to benefit the poor.

Sawm fasting – this is done in the month of Ramadan, during which adult Muslims must refrain from eating, smoking or any kind of sexual activity during daylight hours.

Hajj pilgrimage to Mecca – to be undertaken at least once in a Muslim's lifetime. Each year 2–3 million Muslims of all ethnic groups, cultures and social status complete the Hajj. It takes place in the 12th month of the Islamic calendar and consists of a prescribed sequence of rituals at various sites in and around Mecca.

Which are the holy cities of Islam?
Mecca, near Saudi Arabia's Red Sea coastline, is Islam's holiest place. This is where Muhammad was born, in 570, and where he started receiving the divine revelations of the *Qu'ran* (holy scripture) from the angel Jibreel (Gabriel) in 610. Mecca's Great Mosque can accommodate 900,000 people and forms the focus of the Hajj. The second holiest city is Medina, 210 miles to the north, where Muhammad migrated with his followers in 622 and died in 632. Medina's Mosque of the Prophet houses Muhammad's tomb and is also a popular destination for pilgrims. Finally, the Al-Aqsa mosque in Jerusalem, where Muhammad is believed to have been transported during his Night Journey from Mecca around the year 620, is the third holiest site in Islam. This is situated near

the famous Dome of the Rock shrine on the Temple Mount in the east of the city, which has been under Israeli occupation since 1967 (see **Israel/Palestine**).

What are the most important festivals in the Islamic calendar?
Eid ul-Fitr and *Eid ul-Adha* are the two most important festivals of the year. *Eid ul-Fitr* marks the end of Ramadan (the month of fasting) and is a time of celebration and forgiveness on which new clothes are worn. *Eid ul-Adha*, which follows a week later, commemorates the prophet Ibrahim's willingness to kill his son Isma'il when ordered to by God. Muslims remember their own submission to God on this occasion (the word Islam itself means submission), and mark it by sacrificing animals. There are various other special days throughout the year, such as *Al-Hijra*, Muslim New Year. Muslims follow a calendar of 12 lunar months that, at 354 days, is 11 days shorter than the solar year of 365. For this reason Muslim holy days usually shift 11 days earlier in the solar calendar each year.

What is the difference between Sunni and Shi'a Islam?
Sunnis are by far the larger sect, constituting around 85% of all Muslims. The division between the Sunni and Shi'a is almost as old as Islam itself. When Muhammad died in 632, Abu-Bakr succeeded him as Caliph, or politico-social leader, of the fledgling Muslim *ummah*, or community (this would expand rapidly over the course of the 7th and 8th centuries across the Middle East, North Africa and Spain into an empire known as the Caliphate). Sunnis accept Abu-Bakr as First Caliph, but Shi'as believe that Ali, a cousin and son-in-law of Muhammad, should have taken over instead as both a political and spiritual leader (Shi'a is a contraction of Shi'at Ali, meaning 'partisans of Ali'). Ali did in fact rule as Fourth Caliph from 656–61, but by

this time the two branches of Islam were already emerging into distinct groups. When Ali was assassinated by a group called the Khajirites, the Caliphate passed back to the Sunni line, and from this point on, Sunni Islam grew to dominate the Muslim world, eventually spreading to West Africa, Europe, India and South-East Asia. However, the Shi'as continued to follow Ali's descendants, the Twelve Imams (also known as the Prophet's family) as the divinely appointed, rightful rulers of the Islamic world. Today, most Shi'as follow the ayatollahs, religious scholars who act as the representatives of the 12th Imam, Muhammad al-Muntazar al-Mahdi, whom they believe has been hidden by God and will one day return with Jesus to bring peace and justice to the world. With a 90% Shi'a population, Iran is the world centre of Shi'a Islam today, while Iraq, Azerbaijan and Bahrain also have majority Shi'a followings.

What is Sharia?

Sharia (meaning 'path to the watering hole') is a set of moral codes governing all aspects of Islamic life, derived from the Qu'ran, the *sunnah* (example of Muhammad), *ahadith* (oral traditions relating to Muhammad's words and actions) and *fiqh* (the rulings of *ulema* – Islamic jurists and theologians). Most Muslims observe aspects of Sharia in their personal lives as a matter of conscience, and Muslim states incorporate parts of it into their legal systems, especially where banking and family law are concerned. Sharia has a bad name in the West due to the draconian punishments included in its penal system. There are certain violations known as the *hadd* offences, which include sex outside marriage, drinking alcohol, theft and murder, which can be punishable by death or the amputation of a hand. However, these penalties are enforced only in the few areas of the world where full Sharia law has been adopted, and with varying levels of consistency. These areas include the Swat region of Pakistan, northern Nigeria and parts of Sudan and Iran. Otherwise, Sharia courts composed of ulema exist in Muslim communities to give non-binding *fatawa* (religious advice) on issues ranging from divorce, marriage, business and personal dilemmas. In Shi'a Islam, a fatwa can be binding if the scholar issuing it is of a high enough status – for example, the Ayatollah Khomeini's 1989 death sentence on Salman Rushdie, author of *The Satanic Verses*. Some aspects of Sharia law were incorporated into the British legal system in 2008, when Sharia courts were given power to rule on Muslim civil cases; around 90% of these cases are divorce proceedings, brought mainly by women. This legal incorporation followed the example of the Jewish Beth Din courts, which for centuries have had similar powers in the UK.

What is jihad?
Jihad means 'to strive or struggle' in the way of God, and can refer to an offensive or defensive military campaign against the enemies of Islam, an individual struggle against the devil or a personal striving for spiritual perfection. Jihad is the only form of warfare allowed under Islamic law; the early expansion of the Caliphate under the Rashidun (632–61) and Umayyad (661–750) dynasties was carried out in the name of offensive jihad, with the purpose of defeating or converting non-Muslims and spreading Islam as a universal religion. Today, most Muslims interpret the military aspect of jihad only as a defensive measure, although a minority of radical Islamist groups advocate offensive jihad and hope one day to re-establish the Caliphate across the Muslim world and beyond (see **Al-Qaeda**).

Muslims in the UK

Muslims first came to settle in the UK as a result of the British Empire and its trading links with Muslim countries and colonies. There is documentary evidence of 'a sect of Mahometans' living in London as far back as 1641. During the 18th century, Indian Muslims recruited as sailors by the East India Company began settling in English ports, and in the 19th they were followed by Sylhetis (from what is now Bangladesh) and Yemenis, particularly after the opening of the Suez Canal in 1869 strengthened trading links. The first ever mosque in the UK was built in Cardiff in 1860. Most of Britain's Muslim population today (1.5–2 million) are the descendants of immigrants who arrived from Pakistan, India, Bangladesh, Kenya and Uganda in the 1950s, 60s and 70s.

Israel/Palestine

When was Israel founded?
On 14 May 1948. The declaration of the state of Israel was the culmination of roughly a century of Zionism, a movement which called for a Jewish homeland state after centuries of diaspora (exile). From 1920 to 1948, what is now Israel was the mandate of Palestine, which the League of Nations had handed to the British to govern following the collapse of the Ottoman

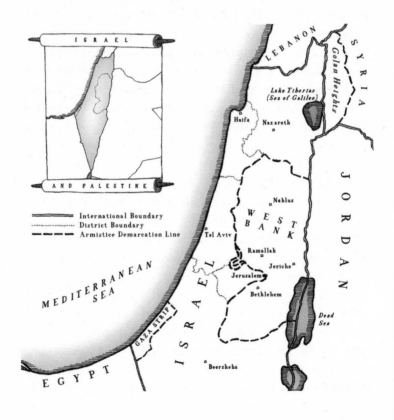

International Boundary
District Boundary
Armistice Demarcation Line

Empire in the First World War. In 1917 Britain had backed the Zionist cause by issuing the Balfour Declaration, which called for the 'establishment in Palestine of a national home for the Jewish people … it being clearly understood that nothing shall be done which may prejudice the civil and religious rights of existing non-Jewish communities in Palestine'. From 1917 the British helped hundreds of thousands of Jews immigrate to Palestine, but from 1936 they started to limit the numbers coming in because of mounting discontent from the Palestinian Arab population. This limit meant that many Jews had to stay in Europe and face persecution and the Holocaust, which angered the Zionist leadership and turned them against their colonial rulers. In 1947, after a series of terrorist attacks from both Jews and Arabs, the British pulled out of Palestine, declaring it ungovernable and handing it to the UN. The UN proposed a plan to partition Palestine into two roughly equal parts (one Jewish, one Arab, with Jerusalem an international area) but this was rejected by the Arabs. When the British finally left in 1948, the Jews declared the foundation of the state of Israel at Tel Aviv.

What happened then?

The surrounding members of the newly formed Arab League (Lebanon, Syria, Jordan, Iraq and Egypt) invaded Israel immediately, starting a war that lasted until January 1949 when Israel emerged victorious. The new state not only survived the onslaught, but increased its territory by roughly 50%. Meanwhile, Jordan annexed the Palestinian Arab area adjoining its border (the West Bank, including eastern Jerusalem) while Egypt occupied the Gaza strip. During this war, 726,000 Palestinian Arab refugees fled from Israel to camps in surrounding Arab countries in an exodus known as *al-nakba*, or 'the disaster', in the Arab world; many of these camps still exist in the West Bank and Gaza. Around 600,000 Jews fled the other way into Israel.

What was the Six-Day War?
This was the Arab League's second invasion of Israel, and second defeat. In May 1967, Egypt, Syria, Jordan, Iraq and Saudi Arabia all moved their troops to the Israeli border. President Gamal Abdel Nasser of Egypt was unsubtle about their objective: 'Our basic goal is the destruction of Israel.' On 5 June, Israel launched a pre-emptive strike on Egypt and Syria; Jordan subsequently attacked Israel. As in 1948–9, Israel was the victor, and made significant territorial gains, but this time much more quickly. In only six days, it won the Gaza Strip and the Sinai peninsula from Egypt, the Golan Heights from Syria, and the West Bank and East Jerusalem from Jordan.

Following this war, Israelis began moving in to these newly captured Arab territories and building settlements there. Israeli politicians were split over these settlements: some justified them on religious grounds as the claiming of the Jewish *Eretz HaMuvtachat* ('promised land') of Judea and Samaria (the West Bank) or as a strategic response to the Arab nations' refusal to negotiate with or recognise Israel after the war. Others opposed the settlements due to the demographic problems they would create, and the fear that they would make Israel look like a colonialist enterprise. In 1977, however, when the right-wing Likud party came to power under Menachem Begin, the settlements became official Israeli policy. There are now around half a million Israeli settlers in the West Bank, East Jerusalem and the Golan Heights, and Israel has ignored repeated UN resolutions to withdraw them or to stop building new settlements. The UN has also condemned Israel's construction of a 703 km-long barrier around the West Bank which it began in 2002 as a way of preventing terrorist attacks. Instead of following the accepted 'Green Line' border between Israel and the West Bank, the 'security fence', which is in fact a network of fences, trenches and walls, encroaches deep into Palestinian territory in some places, keeping Jewish settlements on the Israeli side.

And the Yom Kippur War?

On 6 October 1973, Egypt and Syria combined in an attack on Sinai and the Golan Heights on the most important Jewish holiday of the year (Yom Kippur). The exact day of the attack caught the Israelis off guard, and at first they suffered heavy losses, but after a couple of weeks of fighting they had turned the situation around and made even more territorial gains in both Egypt and Syria. The UN called a ceasefire to end the war. Over the following years US Secretary of State Henry Kissinger carried out 'shuttle diplomacy' between the belligerents. In 1974 this resulted in Israel handing back the additional Syrian territory it had gained in 1973 (although not the Golan Heights, which they had captured in 1967, and still hold). In the 1978 Camp David accords, Israel agreed to hand back the Sinai peninsular to Egypt – which they eventually did in 1982 – and to negotiate autonomy for the Palestinians in the West Bank and the Gaza strip. This goal has still not been satisfactorily achieved.

What is the PLO?

The Palestinian Liberation Organisation was founded in 1964 as a co-ordinating council for various Palestinian guerrilla groups that organised terrorist attacks upon Israel with the eventual aim of destroying it and expelling the Jewish population. It was dominated by Fatah (*Harakat al-Tahrir al-Watani al-Filastini* –

Liberation Organisation of the Palestinian Nation), whose leader Yasser Arafat also led the PLO from 1967 until his death in 2004. The organisation, which was initially controlled by Egypt, gained autonomy and recognition after Israel occupied the West Bank in the Six-Day War. It was then no longer a terrorist group operating out of Jordan (which until 1967 controlled the West Bank), but came to be seen by many as a legitimate resistance movement aiming to free the million Palestinian Arabs in the West Bank who had been brought under Israeli military occupation.

The UN officially recognised the PLO as the representative of the Palestinian people by allowing Arafat to address its General Assembly in 1974, much to the consternation of Israel. In 1988 Arafat publicly renounced terrorism on behalf of the PLO, and recognised Israel's right to exist. At the Oslo Peace Accords in 1993, Israeli Prime Minister Yitzhak Rabin recognised the PLO for the first time, and in 1994 Arafat became president of the Palestinian Authority (PA), an interim administration set up to govern most of the Palestinian territories. At the Annapolis Conference in 2007, new PA president Mahmoud Abbas agreed with Israeli Prime Minister Ehud Olmert to work towards a two-state solution, in which an independent Palestine would exist alongside Israel.

What is Hamas?
Hamas, an acronym for *Harakat al-Muqawamat al-Islamiyyah* (the Islamic Resistance Movement), is a Palestinian militant group and political party who refuse to recognise the state of Israel and aim to destroy it. For them, the two-state solution is not an option. Formed in 1987 during the first intifada (a series of Palestinian uprisings against Israeli occupation), Hamas gained popular support by building schools and hospitals,

emerging as a radical alternative to the increasingly corrupt and inefficient moderates in Fatah. Meanwhile its militant wing, the Qassam brigades, carried out frequent suicide and rocket attacks on Israeli targets. In January 2006 Hamas were the surprise winners of Palestinian parliamentary elections, which caused sanctions to be imposed on their new government by Israel and its Western allies. A violent power struggle with Fatah ensued from 2006–7 that resulted in Hamas taking control of the Gaza strip in May 2007. In June Palestinian President Mahmoud Abbas declared a state of emergency, dissolved the Hamas government and assumed control of the West Bank by presidential decree, appointing a Fatah Prime Minister, Salaam Fayyad, in place of Hamas' Ismail Haniyeh. Hamas refused to recognise these actions and remained in power in the Gaza strip while Israel blockaded it, closing its six border crossings in an effort to weaken Hamas' control. Only the most essential humanitarian basics were allowed in. Feeling the squeeze, Hamas started firing rockets into Israel in 2007, and after a broken ceasefire Israel eventually launched a devastating three-week military assault against them in December 2008 that left around 1,300 Palestinians and 13 Israelis dead. Israel's blockade of Gaza is still in place at the time of writing, with restrictions or complete bans on the entry of materials needed for reconstruction, sanitation, agriculture and industry.

What is going to happen next?

Hamas are still in charge in Gaza and are not co-operating with the Fatah-led PA in the West Bank. While this political division lasts, the prospect of an independent Palestinian state seems unlikely. Meanwhile in Israel, the election in February 2009 of Likud's Binjamin Netanyahu as prime minister cast further doubt that a two-state solution would be achieved in the near future, despite Barack Obama's efforts to achieve one through diplomacy. In the past Netanyahu has been opposed to a two-state solution, and although he agreed to recognise a Palestinian state in June 2009 under pressure from Obama, this was under the improbable conditions that Palestine recognises Israel as the state of the Jewish people and that Palestine is demilitarised. He also refused Obama's plea to put a halt to Israeli settlements in the West Bank in an attempt to please the right-wing parties with whom he went into coalition to gain a majority in the Knesset (Israel's parliament). These are the ultra-Orthodox Shas party and the far-right Yisraeli Beiteinu (Israel Our Home) party, whose leader, former nightclub bouncer Avigdor Lieberman, was made foreign minister. This dominance of right-wing politicians in Israel's government could hamper the renewed US efforts at brokering a peace and increase discrimination against the Israeli Arabs, who make up one fifth of Israel's population and are people of Palestinian origin whose ancestors remained in Israel post-1948.

Why does the US give so much military aid to Israel?

The US has played a key role in making the IDF (Israel Defence Force) one of the most technologically advanced militaries in the world. The Americans started supplying Israel with arms in the 1960s, and from 1976 onwards gave it more military aid annually than any other country (until Iraq overtook it in 2003). A US Report for Congress on Foreign Aid to Israel in 2008 stated that 'US military aid for Israel has been designed to maintain Israel's qualitative edge over neighbouring militaries, since Israel must rely on better equipment and training to compensate for a manpower deficit in any potential regional conflict.' The US supported the creation of Israel in 1948 and is home to a strong pro-Israel lobby composed of influential

Jewish Americans and evangelical Christians who believe that Israel's rebirth is the fulfilment of biblical prophecy. The US and Israel have reasons to be allies; they are both democracies with shared security interests in the Middle East including concerns over Syria, Iran and Islamic extremism. Bill Clinton put it bluntly when he said that 'America and Israel share a special bond. Our relationship is unique among all nations. Like America, Israel is a strong democracy, a symbol of freedom, and an oasis of liberty, a home to the oppressed and persecuted.' During the Cold War the US also supplied arms to Saudi Arabia, Lebanon and Jordan as a way of countering Soviet influence in the Middle East, and today supports its Arab allies in the region (such as Saudi Arabia and Egypt), either with military aid or arms sales. Israel, however, will always be the priority, and in 2008 the US stepped up its military aid package to Israel, pledging an average of $3 billion per year for the next ten years.

'In Israel, in order to be a realist you must believe in miracles.'
DAVID BEN-GURION, *the first Prime Minister of Israel*
(1948–53, 1955–63)

IVF

What does it stand for?
In Vitro Fertilisation – the fertilisation of human eggs in a
laboratory environment (literally 'in glass'), as opposed to
inside the body (*in vivo*). IVF births are known colloquially as
'test-tube babies', although fertilisation actually takes place in
petri dishes.

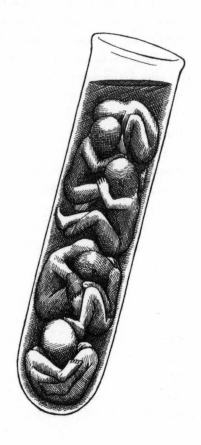

What does IVF treatment involve?
The prospective mother undergoes a cycle of hormone injections in order to stimulate multiple ovarian follicles (the egg-producing cells). When the eggs have matured and are ready to be released, the woman undergoes an egg-retrieval operation, a 20-minute procedure during which an ultrasound-guided needle pierces the vaginal wall to reach the ovaries. The eggs are then isolated in the laboratory and incubated together with the prospective father's semen in a culture media (a gel used to grow cells in) for around 18 hours. The resulting embryos are then left to grow to the 6–8 cell stage (sometimes bigger) before being selected for transfer to the uterus via a plastic catheter. Multiple embryos are often transferred to improve the chances of implantation in the womb and subsequent pregnancy.

Who can benefit from IVF treatment?
Although originally developed specifically to enable women with blocked Fallopian tubes to become pregnant, scientific advances have adapted and developed IVF techniques to treat several types of infertility. This includes most forms of male infertility, such as low sperm count: a method known as Intra-Cytoplasmic Sperm Injection enables the sperm to be injected directly into the egg.

What are the risks?
The main risk is that more than one of the embryos will develop successfully in the womb, causing potential complications for the mother or babies. Because of these risks and the financial strain that multiple births place on health services and families, some countries place regulations on the number of embryos that can be transferred into the womb

during IVF treatment. In the UK, two embryos is the normal limit for women under 40, whereas Belgium only allows one embryo for women under 36. In the US, there are guidelines advising a maximum of two embryos, but no legislation exists to enforce this. In January 2009, 33-year-old Californian Nadya Suleman, an unemployed single mother who had already had six children via IVF, gave birth to octuplets, which all survived. 'It's going to be difficult,' admitted her grandmother.

What does it cost?
A lot. Each cycle of IVF treatment in the UK costs around £5,000 and is restricted on the NHS (see **NHS**). A cheaper alternative treatment, IVM (In Vitro Maturation) is currently being pioneered in which immature eggs are retrieved from the ovaries and then grown in the laboratory before being fertilised.

When was the first successful IVF baby born?
In Vitro Fertilisation of human eggs was first achieved by the American team of Robert Rock and Miriam Menkin in 1944, although embryo transfer into the womb was not attempted. On 25 July 1978, after 12 years of joint endeavour by Britons Robert Edwards and Patrick Steptoe, former cheese factory worker Lesley Brown gave birth to the first ever test-tube baby, Louise Joy Brown. Since then over 3 million have been born worldwide. The history of IVF can be traced back as far as the 1890s, when Walter Heape successfully transferred embryos between rabbits.

What are the attitudes of the major world religions towards IVF?
The Roman Catholic Church is opposed to IVF treatment as it
holds that sexual intercourse is the only acceptable means of
procreation in the eyes of God, and that infertility is a call
from God to adopt children instead. In 1949, Pope Pius XII
condemned any fertilisation of human eggs outside the body,
declaring that those who do so 'take the Lord's work into their
own hands'. On 25 July 1968, exactly a decade before the birth
of Louise Joy Brown, Pope Paul VI issued a statement
forbidding the use of the contraceptive pill and making
explicit the necessary link between intercourse and
procreation. The Eastern Orthodox Church is also against IVF,
whereas the Anglican Church permits it.

Other religions have differing attitudes; in Hinduism, the
destruction of an embryo is considered murder, meaning that,
strictly speaking, all fertilised embryos must be implanted into
the womb. In Buddhism, there is debate over the status of
embryos and whether discarding them amounts to destroying
human life (to which the religion is fundamentally opposed).
In Judaism, IVF is not only acceptable but encouraged for
infertile couples due to the Torah's imperative to 'be fruitful
and multiply'; according to the Talmud (rabbinic literature)
the soul does not enter the embryo until it is 40 days old,
making embryo rejection before this time limit permissible. In
Islam, IVF is permitted, but the two major sects differ over
their attitudes to sperm or egg donation; in Sunni countries it
is banned, whereas Shi'ites have generally allowed it since the
Ayatollah Khamenei issued a ground-breaking fatwa on the
subject in 1999.

Early theories
In 1873 Harvard doctor Edward Clarke speculated in his book *Sex in Education* that having a college education is one cause of sterility in young women.

Kashmir

Where on earth is Kashmir?
Kashmir is sandwiched between India, Pakistan, Afghanistan and China. The region is currently divided between India and Pakistan in a territorial dispute that has caused several wars between the two countries, and is the source of ongoing political tensions. Kashmir has been fought over for centuries, its geographical importance inviting invasions from Afghans, Mughals, Sikhs and the British.

When was Kashmir unified?
The area used to be composed of 22 small independent states, known as the Panjab Hill States, before they were conquered by the Sikh Raja Ranjit Singh and unified as the state of Jammu in 1820. Over the next couple of decades the Raja of Jammu, Gulab Singh, expanded the territory through various conquests of neighbouring regions, before helping the British East India Company defeat his fellow Sikhs in the First Anglo-Sikh War of 1845–6. In recognition of this, the British acknowledged him as the Maharaja of the Princely State of Jammu and Kashmir at the Treaty of Amritsar in 1846; this new state encompassed various areas diverse in their religion and ethnicity. The princely state remained part of the British Indian Empire until the British left in 1947, and Partition split the country into Pakistan and India (see **Pakistan**). At this point all 565 Indian princely states had to decide whether to join either India or Pakistan, or, in special cases, make a bid for independence.

What did the Maharaja eventually decide?

It was expected that Kashmir, with its 77% Muslim population, would cede to Pakistan (the new state intended for Indian Muslims), but the last Maharaja of Kashmir, Hari Singh, hesitated to do this and tried to avoid joining either country. This provoked an invasion by Pashtun tribesmen from Pakistan calling themselves Azad Kashmir ('free Kashmir') in October 1947, shortly after Partition had occurred. Hari Singh asked India to intervene to help repel this attack, which it agreed to do in return for Kashmir's accession to India. Singh signed the accession papers, relinquishing power over communications, defence and external affairs, with an understanding that once the fighting was resolved a plebiscite would be held to determine Kashmir's fate. The Indian army consequently airlifted in troops to fight against the Azad Kashmir forces, which were later reinforced by the regular Pakistani army.

What happened then?

As the war continued through 1948 the UN arrived and insisted that once the fighting was over there would be a plebiscite so that the Kashmiri people could determine their own fate. Despite renewed calls over the years this plebiscite has never been held, and to this day the events surrounding the act of accession are hotly disputed. While India claims the accession was legal, Pakistan argues that it occurred under duress and that Kashmiris were never given the chance to decide for themselves; they also claim that the Maharaja had no right to call in the Indian army as his position had been created by the British, who no longer held sway over the region. The First Indo-Pakistani War ended on the last day of 1948 with the Ceasefire Line being established through Kashmir, demarcating the Indian and Pakistani-held areas that remain more or less unchanged to this day (the Ceasefire Line was redesignated as the 'Line of Control' in 1972). The Indian state of Jammu and Kashmir, which includes the heavily Muslim Kashmir Valley, consists of around two-thirds of it, while Pakistan's third is poor, rugged and sparsely populated; it consists of Azad Jammu and Kashmir (AJK) and the Federally Administered Northern Areas (FANA).

Is that the only territorial dispute in the region?

No. In the 1950s the Chinese military started building a strategic road through Aksai Chin, the eastern part of Ladakh in Indian-controlled Kashmir, an inhospitable and unpopulated area of the Tibetan plateau in which the exact border between China and India had never been properly agreed upon. India's discovery of this road led to the Sino-Indian war of 1962, which the Chinese won. China still controls Aksai Chin and the Trans-Karakoram Tract, a smaller area which was ceded by Pakistan in 1963 but which is still claimed by India.

What's happened since 1948?

Pakistan and India have fought two further wars over Kashmir, both of which were inconclusive, in 1965 and 1999. In 1989 there was a violent uprising in the Indian-administered Kashmir Valley, which is heavily Muslim, with some groups demanding independence for the entire region, and others for union with Pakistan. Twenty years on, violence still prevails in the valley and, to a lesser degree, in Jammu, with multiple splinter groups and a defiant strain of Islamic fundamentalism swelling the ranks of the militants. The numbers of casualties from this fighting has dropped in recent years, but still remain high: in 2001 there were 4,500 deaths, including a thousand civilians, while in 2006 there were 900 casualties, nearly 300 of whom were civilians. Pakistan still feels that as the majority of

Kashmir's population is Muslim the state should join them, or that the Kashmiri people should be allowed to decide. India, meanwhile, makes continual claims that Kashmir is an 'integral part' of it, and that Kashmir's Muslim majority boosts its credentials as a secular state that is tolerant of all religions.

Salman Rushdie on Kashmir

Rushdie is 'more than half Kashmiri', and his novels *Midnight's Children* and *Shalimar the Clown* are partly set in Kashmir. In 1999, Rushdie wrote in the *New York Times*: 'For more than 50 years, India and Pakistan have been arguing and periodically coming to blows over one of the most beautiful places in the world, Kashmir, which the Mughal emperors thought of as Paradise on earth. As a result of this unending quarrel, Paradise has been partitioned, impoverished and made violent. Murder and terrorism now stalk the valleys and mountains of a land once so famous for its peacefulness that outsiders made jokes about the Kashmiris' supposed lack of fighting spirit.'

Cashmere jumpers

'Cashmere' is the ancient spelling of Kashmir. The wool used to make cashmere jumpers, cardigans and scarves comes from Cashmere goats, which can be found in Kashmir, as well as Afghanistan, China, India and Pakistan.

Kosovo

Where is it?

Kosovo is a self-declared nation (disputed by some) bordering Serbia, Albania, Macedonia and Montenegro in the Balkan region of south-eastern Europe. Having been swallowed up in turn by the Bulgarian, Byzantine and Serbian empires, Kosovo was subsumed into the vast Ottoman Empire in the mid-15th century, and there it remained until 1912 when Serbia, which had become independent during the 19th century, once again took control of Kosovo. As the Ottoman Empire waned, other Balkan nations broke free, and in the aftermath of the First World War the Kingdom of Serbs, Croats and Slovenes was created; in 1929 this underwent a change of name and became Yugoslavia. Following the Second World War, six republics were declared within Yugoslavia – Croatia, Bosnia and Herzegovina, Macedonia, Montenegro, Serbia (in which Kosovo was an autonomous region) and Slovenia.

What happened then?

Around 90% of Kosovo's estimated 2 million people are of Albanian origin, and 6% are Serbs. Throughout the 20th century the Albanian majority called for greater autonomy. This eventually came in the form of the 1974 Yugoslav constitution, which guaranteed it as an autonomous region of Serbia with the same self-government and status enjoyed by the other republics in Yugoslavia. Importantly, however, it wasn't given the right to break away completely.

Ethnic cleansing

When Slobodan Milosevic became president of Serbia in 1989 he introduced a new constitution which effectively scrapped the autonomy of Kosovo. This fuelled tensions in the region that persisted throughout the 1990s, with the Albanian population calling for independence. When peaceful protests against Serbian rule had no effect, the Kosovo Liberation Army formed in the mid-90s and began attacking Serbian police and politicians, provoking serious reprisals. Internationally brokered peace talks between Serb and Albanian negotiators in February and March 1999 failed when Milosevic refused to accept the proposed autonomy deal, provoking a NATO aerial campaign beginning with the bombing of strategic targets in Kosovo and Serbia. Milosevic responded with a campaign of 'ethnic cleansing' which killed around 10,000 ethnic Albanians and forced 850,000 more to leave their homes. This persisted for nearly 80 days before international peacekeepers intervened and Serbian forces retreated. Around 200,000 Serbians and other ethnic minorities also fled their homes during this period.

The road to independence

With an uncertain future, Kosovo was placed under United Nations administration in 1999. In late 2007, talks on Kosovo's status between the Serbian government and the Kosovo Albanian leadership, mediated by the EU, the US and Russia, failed to come to a consensus. This prompted Kosovo unilaterally to declare itself an independent country in February 2008 – to the joy of the Albanian population and the anger of Serbia.

Yugoslavia's last years

In the 1990s Yugoslavia was on its last legs as Croatia, Slovenia, Macedonia and Bosnia and Herzegovina all declared their independence. These declarations were met with resistance and led to fighting over disputed territories by Milosevic's Serb forces. In 1992, war in Croatia created hundreds of thousands of refugees, while in Bosnia, Muslims and Croats were victims of ethnic cleansing committed by Serb forces. In 1997 Milosevic became president of the Federal Republic of Yugoslavia, which by this time retained only two of the original republics – Montenegro and Serbia. Milosevic remained in charge until 2000 when he was deposed and arrested. Yugoslavia officially existed until 2003 when a new union of Serbia and Montenegro was formed. Three years later, in June 2006, Montenegro also declared its independence.

Hope for a brighter future?

This declaration of independence hasn't passed without criticism and controversy. Although more than 40 countries, including the US, the UK and the bulk of Europe, have recognised Kosovo's independence, Serbia and its ally Russia still refuse to do so. Russia is concerned that worldwide acceptance of Kosovo's independence might trigger other calls for independence, including from its own autonomous regions. Kosovo has since made a number of moves to assert its status: adopting a new constitution, opening embassies, creating its own army and choosing a national anthem. As these were put in place, however, Kosovo's case for independence was referred to the International Court of Justice (ICJ) for consideration. The

KOSOVO

ICJ is due to give a non-binding ruling on the legality of
Kosovo's independence, which could take years, but Kosovo's
Foreign Minister has said he expects a decision by April 2010.

Passing judgement
Milosevic was the first serving head of state to be charged with
crimes against humanity. At the time of his death in prison
from natural causes, the prosecution had finished but the
defence hadn't, so no verdict was ever given.

> 'There is no doubt that of the evil that stalked the Balkans for
> the best part of a decade one way or another, one of the primary
> authors was Slobodan Milosevic.'
>
> LORD PADDY ASHDOWN, *former high representative*
> *to Bosnia and Herzegovina*

> 'He was systematically killed by all the years he spent in The
> Hague and this is a great loss for Serbia, the Serbian people and
> the Socialist Party of Serbia. It is of major importance for the
> future of our country that through his defence and the fact he
> died without being convicted, Milosevic had managed to defend
> national and state interest.'
>
> IVICA DACIC, *Socialist Party of Serbia*

Microfinance

What is it?

Microfinance is the provision of financial services, such as savings accounts, small loans (microcredit), insurance and fund transfers to the very poor. It is an expanding network of practices which aims to provide opportunity for some of the billion people in the world living on less than one dollar a day.

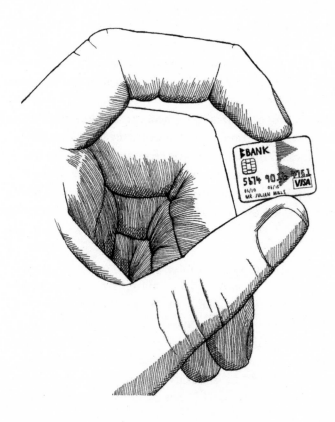

Can't they just go to the bank?

Banks in the developing world have not traditionally offered their services to the very poor because of the high administrative costs of managing accounts and processing loans, as well as the lack of collateral that could be claimed in the event of loan defaults. In the past, poor people have not had the means to make their savings grow and have had to use local moneylenders for loans, paying high rates of interest. Increasingly, Microfinance Institutions (MFIs) are catering for their financial needs instead.

What sort of financial needs are these?

Much the same as in the developed world, only on a smaller scale. Loans might be needed to invest in materials, livestock, machinery or skills in order to generate income (microenterprise), or in unforeseen circumstances such as family illness or crop failure where extra cash is needed quickly. Deposits are required to put aside money for things like education, retirement or home renovation, as well as the opportunity to earn interest. Health and natural disaster insurance is also in demand in the developing world, while fund transfers are often needed to send money to relatives at home or abroad.

How do MFIs ensure loans are repaid?

By relying on forms of social pressure. There are two main models: the first was established by Bangladesh's Grameen Bank, a pioneering microfinance provider founded by economics professor Mohammad Yunus in 1983 (he was awarded the Nobel Peace Prize in 2006). The bank's key initiative was that of 'solidarity lending': any person requiring a loan must apply for it with four other people whose job it is to oversee the repayments, although the responsibility to repay the loan rests solely with the individual. Before being granted the loan, the borrower must also agree to the 'Sixteen Decisions' – commitments to hygiene, education, childcare, health, sensible farming techniques and other forms of socially responsible behaviour. No collateral is needed, and no contract is signed; 97% of Grameen Bank's borrowers are women and its loan repayment rate is 95–98%, which is higher than many commercial banks. The other major microfinance model is village banking, invented by John Hatch of FINCA International (the Foundation for International Community Assistance) in 1984. Capital is provided by MFIs or NGOs to groups of 20–30 villagers, usually women, who meet once a week under supervision to take out loans or make deposits. In this model, all members of the group are guarantors for each others' loans.

Positive Equity

While many microfinance initiatives are run by NGOs or non-profit organisations, this is not always the case. Kenya's Equity Bank has risen to become the country's third most profitable bank, with over 50% of the national market. It achieved this by targeting so-called 'Bottom-of-the-Pyramid' customers (the 'watchmen, tomato-sellers and small-scale farmers', according to its Chief Executive Officer James Mwangi), and providing them with loans of as little as $7. To ensure debts are repaid, the bank employs 'social pressure' methods similar to those described above, sometimes even requesting women's matrimonial beds as collateral, on the basis that the shame suffered would be too great if these symbolic objects were removed. Equity Bank's huge success flew in the face of conventional lending policies and has since caused multinational players such as Barclays and BNP Paribas to enter the microfinance arena.

What does the future hold?

The increasing availability of mobile phones in the developing world is enabling microfinance to flourish in countries with low-density populations; Mongolia's Xacbank, for example, is planning a mobile-banking scheme which will include 300,000 people. The internet is also playing its part: several websites now exist on which individuals can lend money to borrowers in the developing world via international organisations. The first of these online platforms, Kiva.org, was given a ringing endorsement by Bill Clinton in his latest book *Giving: How Each of Us Can Change the World*.

'This is not charity. This is business: business with a social objective, which is to help people get out of poverty.'

MOHAMMAD YUNUS, *founder, Grameen Bank*

'Microfinance is an idea whose time has come.'

KOFI ANNAN, *UN Secretary-General 1997–2007*

MRSA

What does it stand for?
Methicillin-Resistant Staphylococcus Aureus.

What is it?
Also known as 'the superbug', MRSA refers to antibiotic-resistant strains of bacteria that form part of the Staphylococcus aureus family – common bacteria that one in three people carry in their noses or on the surface of their skins without being troubled. If, however, the bacteria do find their way into a person's body through a cut or wound, this can lead to an infection.

What infections does MRSA cause?
Most infections caused by the bacteria are skin infections such as boils and abscesses, but if the bacteria gets into the bloodstream this leaves most of the body susceptible – causing anything from lung, bone-marrow or heart-lining infections to joint problems, septicaemia (blood poisoning) or internal abscesses.

How did it build up resistance?
Doctors first described Staphylococcus aureus in the 1880s, recognising its role as the most common culprit in infecting surgical wounds. Penicillin worked effectively against most strains when it came into use in the 1940s, but gradually strains began to evolve that were able to protect themselves by making an enzyme that broke down the penicillin, and by 1959 between 90 and 95% were resistant. In response, scientists developed methicillin, but it was only a year after methicillin was

introduced that MRSA was first reported in England. The superbug remained fairly uncommon until the mid-1990s when certain strains hit hospitals across the UK. MRSA is linked to the deaths of around 1,500 people a year in Britain.

Why is it such a problem in hospitals?

For two main reasons. First, people in hospital are already weak and therefore more susceptible to disease, and second, hospitals unfortunately provide ideal conditions for the superbug to spread. Opportunities for infection include person-to-person contact, surgical wounds or intravenous drips which enable MRSA to get into the bloodstream.

So how is it treated and prevented?

While some common antibiotics don't work when they come up against MRSA, there are others, such as Linezolid or Vancomycin, which do. Minor infections can be treated by draining pus. As a way of preventing infection, antiseptic lotion and shampoo as well as antibiotic cream are applied to the skin, hair and cuts of patients who are about to undergo surgery.

Is there a cure?

Not yet, but scientists are hopeful. Destiny Pharma, a pharmaceutical company, have claimed that a drug called XF-73 has been developed which kills five of the most deadly strains of MRSA. Researchers say that the drug could be used in hospitals by 2011.

Leslie's cash

Actress Leslie Ash, best known for playing Deborah in the television comedy *Men Behaving Badly*, was awarded a record sum of £5 million in damages after contracting Methicillin-

Sensitive Staphylococcus Aureus (MSSA), a variant of MRSA, at Chelsea and Westminster Hospital in London. An epidural needle is said to have caused the infection. This led to nerve damage to her spinal column where there was an abscess that caused her to lose both feeling and the ability to move her legs. Ash, who underwent a lot of physiotherapy, is now able to walk with the aid of a walking stick. The compensation, which was awarded in January 2008, reflects the potential past and future earning losses she suffered as a result of contracting the infection.

NATO

What does NATO stand for?
The North Atlantic Treaty Organisation – an alliance of
countries committed to goals contained in the North Atlantic
Treaty, signed on 4 April 1949.

Which countries are members?
Belgium, Bulgaria, Canada, Czech Republic, Denmark, Estonia,
France, Germany, Greece, Hungary, Iceland, Italy, Latvia,
Lithuania, Luxembourg, Netherlands, Norway, Poland, Portugal,
Romania, Slovakia, Slovenia, Spain, Turkey, the United
Kingdom and the United States – 26 in total.

What are its goals?
NATO's primary goal is to safeguard the freedom and security
of its members by political and military means. The
organisation also works to preserve democracy, individual
liberty, the rule of law and to resolve disputes peacefully. The
North Atlantic Treaty came about as a result of the Cold War –
the tense relationship between the superpowers of America and
the former USSR, and their respective allies. The perceived
threat of the Soviet Union and the ideological aims of the Soviet
Communist Party prompted countries in Western Europe and
North America to sign it.

Does NATO have its own armed forces?
Yes. Forces and equipment are provided by all member
countries. Control remains with the individual countries until
such time as NATO needs them, for example, to carry out a
peacekeeping mission. NATO, however, does possess and

operate some of its own equipment, including an early-warning radar aircraft.

Where have NATO forces been deployed?
NATO forces were involved in ending the conflicts in Bosnia and Kosovo as well as the civil war in the former Yugoslav republic of Macedonia. They still have a presence in Kosovo and are also currently working in Afghanistan and Iraq.

How are decisions made by this group of countries?
All decisions are taken by collective agreement.

Being Blunt
James Blunt was a NATO peacekeeper in Kosovo, before leaving the army to pursue a career as a singer/songwriter. In 2006, Blunt returned to Kosovo where he performed a concert for the troops stationed there; how much they enjoyed it is unclear.

'I think to be in NATO for the countries of our region, it means more guarantees for us, it means more responsibility for our common security, but it means fulfilment of all standards of the civilised world, like protection of human rights and democratic mechanisms.'

ALEKSANDER KWAŚNIEWSKI, *Polish president (1995–2005)*

'I bear solemn witness to the fact that NATO heads of state and of government meet only to go through the tedious motions of reading speeches, drafted by others, with the principal objective of not rocking the boat.'

PIERRE ELLIOTT TRUDEAU, *Canadian Prime Minister (1968–79)*

Neuroscience

What is it?

Neuroscience is an umbrella term for a group of scientific disciplines which investigate the nervous system and brain. Of its many branches and specialist fields, perhaps of most interest to the non-scientist is cognitive neuroscience, the field that attempts to understand the workings of the human mind by measuring the brain's neuronal activity (neurons are the core cells of the nervous system, which transmit information as electrochemical signals). Cognitive neuroscience has developed

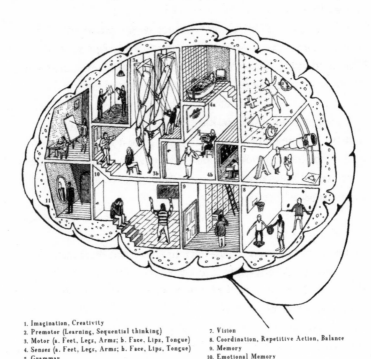

1. Imagination, Creativity
2. Premotor (Learning, Sequential thinking)
3. Motor (a. Feet, Legs, Arms; b. Face, Lips, Tongue)
4. Senses (a. Feet, Legs, Arms; b. Face, Lips, Tongue)
5. Grammar
6. Spacial Sense, Symbols
7. Vision
8. Coordination, Repetitive Action, Balance
9. Memory
10. Emotional Memory
11. Conscience, Inhibitions

rapidly in the last decade and is providing insights into the nature of our consciousness, emotional behaviour and social interaction, and has even proposed neurobiological bases for complex notions such as morality or religious belief. The 21st century will see neuroscientists attempting to understand a whole host of mental mysteries, including the nature of subjective experience, memory, language, sleeping, dreaming and imagination.

The workings of the brain

Thanks to recent technological advances such as functional MRI (Magnetic Resonance Imaging) and EEGs (Electro-encephalograms), neuroscientists can accurately map brain activity and see what happens where. Motor movement and primitive impulses such as rage, love, fear and appetite are processed by the 'reptilian brain', or brain stem, the oldest part of the brain in an evolutionary sense. On top of this is the limbic system, or mammalian brain, which deals with more complex emotions, senses, some memory functions, aspects of identity and new knowledge. The outermost layer of the brain, and its most highly evolved part (larger in humans than in other species), is the neo-cortex, which enables reason, speech and complex social behaviour.

Is the brain a muscle?

Not exactly, but there is evidence to show that it can improve with use. A University College London study of black-cab drivers in 2000 showed that they had a larger posterior hippocampus (the part of the temporal lobe used for encoding long-term memory) than normal, owing to the years spent memorising 'the knowledge'. The swelling was more pronounced in cabbies who had been in the job the longest. As well as beefing up, the brain can also adapt; in blind people, for example, the areas of the sensory cortex normally used for visual processing can be 'colonised' by auditory functions, enhancing their sense of hearing.

Is there a difference between the brain and the mind?

Most neuroscientists would agree that 'brain' and 'mind' are just two ways of talking about the same thing. There is a strong dualist tradition in Western culture, which claims that the mind is somehow independent from the body and brain, but neuroscience suggests otherwise, and aims to explain all of the mind's activity in terms of neuronal firing.

What does the conscious mind do?

Evidence suggests that far more of the brain's processes occur below the level of consciousness than was previously thought. If we move a hand, for example, we unconsciously send a signal to move the appropriate muscles 0.2 of a second *before* we consciously do so. The conscious mind seems to conduct high-level planning and keeps track of day-to-day experiences such as places, objects and people around us. But it is not clear that consciousness is located in any specific part of the brain, or indeed that it is one coherent thing.

Does neuroscience have medical implications?

Yes. Both neurology and psychiatry, the medical fields addressing diseases of the nervous system and mental illness, respectively, have been influenced by neuroscientific research. Schizophrenia is one area that is already better understood as a result. When schizophrenics experience hearing 'voices', we now know these voices are just as real to the sufferer as actual voices; scans show their brains' auditory areas to be active, behaving as though they were processing a real sound from the auditory nerve.

What were the beginnings of modern neuroscience?

Cognitive neuroscience's recent development as a coherent field of study owes much to the work of the Estonian Jaap Panksepp, whose influential book *Affective Neuroscience* was published in 1997. However, it is possible to trace the roots of the discipline back to the 19th century, when two noteworthy case studies provided scientists with early clues that specific parts of the brain performed different behavioural and cognitive tasks. In 1848 an American railroad construction foreman, Phineas Gage, was injured in a rock-blasting accident by an iron bar, 109 cm long and 3 cm in diameter, which entered his skull at the side of his face and passed clean through his brain, coming out at the top of his head. Amazingly, he survived and was able to walk and talk again only a few minutes later. However, the accident changed his personality so profoundly that his friends judged him to be 'no longer Gage'; he was, according to his doctor, 'fitful, irreverent, indulging at times in the grossest profanity … obstinate, yet capricious and vacillating'. Leading Portuguese neuroscientist António Damásio refers to Gage's case as 'the historical beginnings of the study of the biological basis of behaviour'. In 1861, the pioneering French neurologist Paul Broca studied a stroke victim who could understand language but could no longer speak, except for the word 'tan'. After the patient's death, Broca dissected his brain and found damage to the left frontal lobe, which he concluded was the part responsible for language formation. Sigmund Freud also made early investigations into neuroscience, publishing the influential monograph *On Aphasia* in 1891.

Lobal warming

One of the most fascinating areas of neuroscientific research is into temporal lobe epilepsy, a chronic condition that, in acute cases, can cause the sufferer to experience paranormal phenomena, fainting, ecstatic religious visions and hypergraphia (an overwhelming urge to write). Many artists and writers are known or suspected to have suffered from it, including William Blake, Edgar Allan Poe, Vincent van Gogh, Fyodor Dostoyevsky, Gustave Flaubert, Lewis Carroll and Sylvia Plath. The condition has also been known to induce orgasms, but only in women.

NHS

What is it?

The National Health Service, or NHS, provides free healthcare for UK residents. It is the largest service of its kind in the world. Over 1.5 million people work for the NHS, more than any other employer in the UK. Only three employers worldwide have a larger workforce – the Chinese People's Liberation Army, Indian Railways and Wal-Mart. Last year, the NHS's budget stood at

over £90 billion, and it deals with an average of 463 patients every minute.

How did it come about?

The idea of accessible healthcare for everyone gathered steam in the first half of the 20th century. One early proposal for a 'state medical service' was written in 1909 by Beatrice Webb (an economist who founded the *New Statesman* magazine), followed by various others in the 1920s and 30s. In 1942 during the Second World War, Sir William Beveridge issued his influential Beveridge Report, which called for a welfare state and National Health Service to attack the 'five giants of Want, Disease, Ignorance, Squalor and Idleness'. By 1944 Health Minister Henry Willink had produced a White Paper on the subject. However, a change of government the following year saw new Health Minister Aneurin Bevan scrap much of Willink's paper and start afresh. Bevan felt Willink had 'run away from so many vested interests that in the end he was left with no scheme at all', and introduced new policies such as bringing all hospitals into public ownership. He also proposed stopping the buying and selling of GPs' practices, and introduced the idea of doctors receiving a basic salary as part of their pay, which was fiercely opposed by the British Medical Association. A former BMA official said Bevan's plans were 'the first step, and a big one, towards National Socialism as practised in Germany … under the dictatorship of a "medical Führer"'. A compromise was reached on the question of salary, with Bevan agreeing that consultants could get a state salary while continuing to treat private patients in nationalised hospitals. In agreeing to this Bevan stated he was forced to 'stuff their mouths with gold'. After this compromise, the NHS was finally established in July 1948.

Controlling the beast

The NHS is administered by the Department of Health, which is run by the Secretary of State for Health. Although it is one service, it is run separately in England, Northern Ireland, Scotland and Wales, with the lion's share of NHS employees – over 1.3 million – working in England. There is, unsurprisingly, a seemingly endless bureaucratic structure. The NHS service in England, for instance, is managed by ten Strategic Health Authorities as well as numerous NHS trusts, including Primary Care Trusts, Mental Health Service Trusts and Ambulance Service Trusts, all with different responsibilities for ensuring it runs efficiently. Managers warned in June 2009 that the NHS faced huge budget cuts after 2011 due to the debts the government will incur in its bank bail-out scheme (see **Credit Crunch**).

What is primary/secondary/tertiary care?

Primary care refers to healthcare provided by General Practitioners (GPs), who are the first point of contact for patients. GPs, also known as family doctors, cover the widest possible scope of healthcare and can refer patients to consultants if their needs are more specialised. Secondary care refers to the activity of consultants, based in hospitals, who focus on particular areas of medicine – for example, cardiology, urology or dermatology. It takes eight years of postgraduate training to become a consultant, compared to the five it takes to qualify as a GP. Tertiary care is even more specialised, and refers to areas of medicine that are not commonly catered for in every hospital – such as plastic surgery, neurosurgery and specialist cancer care.

How is healthcare regulated?

By various agencies including the Healthcare Commission, an independent body which monitors the NHS and private healthcare in England, and the Medicines and Healthcare products Regulatory Agency (MHRA), which is in charge of checking that medicines and medical equipment work effectively. One of the better known agencies is the National Institute for Health and Clinical Excellence (NICE), which gives guidance in England and Wales on which new drugs and relevant treatments should be made available on the NHS. It is in the unenviable position of having to make cost/benefit analyses of new drugs and treatments, and as such is often in the news for decisions that appear cold-hearted.

No magic tooth-fairy in sight

In April 2006 the government introduced new contracts to reform dentistry in the NHS, which were aimed at solving what was seen as a 'drill-and-fill' treadmill. But they have been heavily derided, with vehement criticism from the British Dental Association. Dentists have quit the NHS because of these contracts, and hundreds of thousands fewer people have been to an NHS dentist since they were introduced. A year after the contracts began the consumer watchdog *Which?* called NHS dental healthcare in England a 'postcode lottery', with huge variations in availability in different areas of the country.

'In a world which frequently appears to be a selfish one, the dedication and devotion to duty that one finds in those who operate the NHS is a wonderful reminder of humane values. Over the last 60 years, countless people working within the NHS have given us cause to be proud of what people can do for one another.'

ALEXANDER MCCALL SMITH, *author of*
The No. 1 Ladies' Detective Agency *series*

North Korea

In brief

North Korea (the Democratic People's Republic of Korea or DPRK) is a single-party communist state considered by many to be the world's most repressive totalitarian regime. Since the collapse of its ally the USSR in 1991, the DPRK has doggedly pursued an isolationist policy while watching its southern neighbour, the Republic of Korea (ROK), grow into one of the

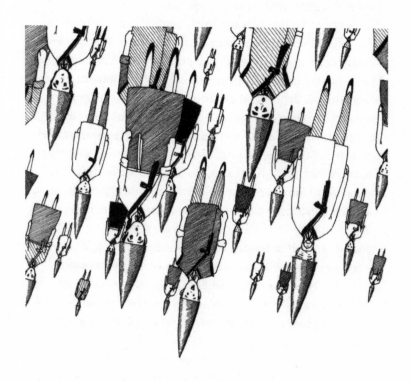

economic powerhouses of Asia. North Korea professes itself to be *Juche*, or self-sufficient, despite the fact that for decades it has relied on foreign aid to feed its starving population and support its barely functioning infrastructure. There have been tentative signs that a reunification of Korea might be on the horizon, which would finally consign this bizarre Orwellian relic of the Cold War era to the dustbin of history. Recently, however, North Korea's expanding nuclear weapons programme has seriously undermined these peace prospects.

How did it separate from South Korea?
The Korean peninsular was a single unified country from the 6th century right up until the defeat of Japan in World War II. The Japanese had annexed the country as part of their empire in 1910 but were expelled in 1945, leaving Korea's fate in the hands of the victors, the US and the Soviet Union. As a temporary measure, they split the country in two along the 38th Parallel, agreeing to occupy their respective halves until an independent government could be established to rule the whole peninsular. Unsurprisingly, this didn't happen, because the Soviets sponsored a Communist provisional government in the North while the Americans backed an anti-Communist administration in the South. By 1948 it was clear that no political compromise could be reached to reunify Korea, and the occupying superpowers pulled out, leaving two separate states behind them. Hardly any Koreans had been in favour of the division in 1945, but by 1948 North and South were sworn enemies, each laying claim to the whole peninsular. These tensions soon erupted into the Korean War (1950–3), which saw the superpowers weigh in once more on either side. The USSR and China came to the aid of the North while the US (joined by several other members of the newly created UN) supported the

South. The war ended in stalemate, with up to 3 million people dead and the border back where it started. It remains to this day the most heavily militarised national boundary in the world, with a large US military presence stationed on the southern side. North Korea still considers itself to be at war with the US, and is in a state of constant paranoia about an imminent American invasion.

Who is North Korea's leader?
Officially, the 'Great Leader' and 'Eternal President' of the DPRK is still Kim Il-Sung, even though he died in 1994. He was the founder of the *Juche* ideology and led North Korea as an absolute dictatorship, complete with forced labour camps and secret police, from its inception in 1948. On his death, his son, the 'Dear Leader' Kim Jong-il, took over; he remains head of state to this day, although he is widely believed to have suffered a stroke in 2008 and may not survive much longer. The bouffant-haired Kim is a movie fanatic, spicy-food lover, composer of 'revolutionary operas' and an expert golfer (according to his aides, who report that he shot 11 holes-in-one in his first ever round). He is also estimated to have around $4 billion stashed in a Swiss bank account. He is thought to have named his youngest and favourite son, Kim Jong-un, as his successor in January 2009.

What's it like to live there?
Daily life in the DPRK is dominated by a Stalin-esque cult of personality to the two Kims; they are mythologised and discussed incessantly by the state-run media, oversized statues and images of them overlook public spaces, and children are trained to love them from their first day at school. Every day at 7 a.m. the nation awakes to loudspeakers blaring 'Ten Million

Human Bombs to Kim Il-Sung', a hymn celebrating the willingness of the population to martyr themselves for the Great Leader (despite the fact he's dead). North Korean living standards are generally poor, even in the showpiece capital Pyongyang, owing to economic stagnation, meagre food rations, a crumbling healthcare system and frequent energy shortages. Informal social activities outside the workplace or family circle are discouraged. Mobile phones and internet are restricted and freedom of speech is severely limited. Foreign television and other media are forbidden; until recently it was possible to incur the death penalty for listening to South Korean radio. All these restrictions have resulted in a population who are effectively banned from leaving the country and know virtually nothing about the outside world. Many believe what they are told: that they are living in a socialist paradise. Nevertheless, thousands attempt to cross the border into China every year. This is a dangerous journey which, if unsuccessful, ends in imprisonment or execution, and if successful, leads to repatriation by Chinese officials or a life of slavery and exploitation: 95% of women who complete the journey successfully are sold into the Chinese sex trade.

What about the nukes?
Despite floods, famine and disease ravaging his country, Kim Jong-il has persisted in prioritising military concerns above all others. His policy of *songdun*, or 'military first', has produced a million-strong standing army, one of the largest in the world, and a nuclear weapons programme that is seriously troubling to the international community, particularly the US and Japan. North Korea first conducted an underground nuclear test in 2006, followed by a much larger one in May 2009, as well as long-range missile tests in the previous month. Official state

media claimed that this was in fact the launch of a satellite put into orbit to transmit revolutionary songs, but then in June changed its tune, announcing that it would use nuclear weapons in a 'merciless offensive' if provoked. Barack Obama has condemned these actions as 'provocation', but remains committed to finding a diplomatic solution to the growing threat. North Korea was on the US list of states that sponsor terrorism due to its past history of providing weapons and training to rogue states, such as Libya and Zimbabwe, as well as revolutionary networks such as the PLO (see **Israel/Palestine**); it was only removed from this list in 2007 as a bartering tool in ongoing nuclear disarmament negotiations. These negotiations, known as the Six Nation talks, were instigated in 2003; over the last few years Kim Jong-il has played a deft game of cat and mouse with the other nations involved (Russia, China, the US, Japan and South Korea), by turns agreeing to their demands for disarmament in return for aid, only to unveil new nuclear plans, tests or capabilities shortly afterwards. According to US estimates, North Korea has extracted enough plutonium to build six to eight nuclear bombs, although it is unclear how close they are to being able to weaponise it (see **Nuclear Weapons**). If North Korea don't use their own plutonium, the concern is that it'll get into the hands of terrorists instead.

'Korea is an independent and sovereign state, but the South is still controlled by the imperialist interests and the US troops. If any South Korean citizen tries to visit North Korea crossing the big concrete wall, he'll be killed by the American soldiers. The "Security Law" in South Korea forbids to any South Korean citizen to talk or read about the North or else he'll be punished with jail or even death penalty.'

The DPRK's official website, www.korea-dpr.com

Northern Ireland

When was Northern Ireland created?
Ireland was partitioned in two – Northern Ireland and Southern
Ireland (now the Republic of Ireland, or Eire) – under the 1920
Government of Ireland Act.

Which counties are in Northern Ireland?
This Act stated that the parliamentary counties of Antrim,
Armagh, Down, Fermanagh, Londonderry and Tyrone, and the
parliamentary boroughs of Belfast and Londonderry, should
make up Northern Ireland. The remaining 26 counties formed
Southern Ireland.

How and why did partition come about?
It was thought that partition would satisfy both nationalists,
who wanted Irish Home Rule (increased self-government),
and unionists, who were against this. On Easter Monday 1916,
a rebellion known as the Easter Rising occurred in Dublin; it
was the latest in a long history of Irish revolts against British
rule, which had held sway over Ireland in some form since the
Normans invaded in 1171. Rebels took over strategic
buildings, including the General Post Office and a biscuit
factory, proclaiming an independent Irish Republic, but they
were defeated after five days of fighting. Fifteen of the leaders
were executed, which fuelled support for the rebels and
caused deep anger against British rule. After this uprising,
Home Rule bills introduced in the UK parliament were
defeated, driving Ireland to the brink of civil war. Then
Walter Long – a former leader of the Ulster Unionist Party
who chaired the British cabinet's Committee of Ireland –

came up with the idea of creating two Irish home rule territories, which resulted in partition and the creation of Northern and Southern Ireland.

What happened next?
In December 1921 the Anglo-Irish Treaty was signed by the British government and negotiators of the Irish Republic. The Irish Free State was established by this agreement and was made up of the 26 counties of (southern) Ireland. Northern Ireland was given the option of not being part of this Free State, which it took.

Did conflict cease after Northern Ireland was created?
No. Conflict continued between the unionists (or loyalists), who wanted Northern Ireland to remain part of the UK, and nationalists (or republicans) who believed it should become part of the Irish Free State (later the Republic of Ireland).

What is the religious make-up of Northern Ireland?
Protestants in Northern Ireland make up around 53% of the population and Catholics 44%, according to a recent census. Protestants are predominantly unionists, while most Catholics are nationalists. Many Protestants trace their lineage back to English and Scottish 'Planters', who arrived in Ulster in the early 17th century to colonise land that had been confiscated from Gaelic clans as part of James I's scheme to pacify the country.

Was Northern Ireland given a guarantee that it would remain part of the UK?
Yes. In 1949 the UK parliament passed the Ireland Act, which guaranteed that 'in no event will Northern Ireland or any part

thereof cease to be part of His Majesty's dominions and of the United Kingdom, without the consent of the Parliament of Northern Ireland'. This Act followed the Republic of Ireland Act passed in Ireland the previous year, which declared that (southern) Ireland was officially a republic.

What were 'The Troubles'?

'The Troubles' refers to a period of unrest and violence in Northern Ireland from the late 1960s until the late 1990s. One of the most infamous events during this time was Bloody Sunday (30 January 1972), when troops from the British army's Parachute Regiment shot dead 13 Catholic protestors after a civil rights march in Londonderry, which had been banned. Throughout this period bomb and gun attacks were carried out by paramilitary groups, with the Irish Republican Army (IRA) targeting protestant and British targets, and their loyalist equivalents, such as the Ulster Freedom Fighters, attacking Catholics. Meanwhile British forces, who had first been deployed in 1969, tried to maintain control. In 1981, ten Republican inmates at the British Maze prison in Belfast went on hunger strike, starving themselves to death in protest at being treated like ordinary criminals instead of prisoners of war. This caused rioting in Catholic areas and an upsurge in the killings as well as increased sympathy from abroad for the republican cause.

What is the Good Friday Agreement?

After several years of negotiations and a ceasefire from paramilitary groups, the Good Friday Agreement was signed in April 1998. Broadly, British and Irish governments recognised that Northern Ireland will remain part of the UK while there remains a desire from the majority who live there. The agreement dealt with a number of complex issues, including the early release of terrorist prisoners and the decommissioning of paramilitary weapons. It also established a new democratically elected Northern Ireland Assembly (see **Devolution**). A referendum on the agreement was held in both Northern Ireland and the Republic of Ireland in May 1998 to gauge support: 71.2% of people in Northern Ireland and 94.39% in the Republic of Ireland voted in favour. In August of that year a republican splinter group, the Real IRA, killed 28 with a car bomb in the town of Omagh in County Tyrone. They failed in their attempt to derail the peace process and received condemnation from republicans and unionists alike.

A new era?

Difficulties remained in the years afterwards, with unionists calling on the IRA to honour the agreement by scrapping their weapons and ending punishment beatings, and with republicans claiming that unionists were being unreasonable in their demands for photos of the decommissioned weapons, and were using this as an excuse to avoid a power-sharing deal. In 2007, however, a new power-sharing government was formed with Ian Paisley, leader of the Democratic Unionist party, and Martin McGuinness, former IRA commander and leading Sinn Féin figure (a republican party in favour of a united Ireland), taking office as First and Deputy First Minister respectively. There have been occasional incidents disruptive to the peace – such as the March 2009 murder of two British soldiers at Massereene army base in Antrim – but so far both sides have expressed determination not to let such events signal a return to the Troubles.

Smellfast
The Parliament Buildings in Northern Ireland are located in the
Stormont area of Belfast. During World War II there were fears
that it was an obvious target for bombing because of its exposed
position on a hill. Consequently, a mix of bitumen and cow
manure was painted on the building, turning the white stone
black, and ash and clinker (residue from burnt coal) were used
to disguise the roads leading there.

Nuclear Weapons

Which states possess nuclear weapons?
The US, Russia, the UK, France and China (the 'nuclear club')
are the five states permitted to possess nuclear weapons under
the terms of the Nuclear Non-Proliferation Treaty. India,
Pakistan and North Korea also have them, and it is an open
secret that Israel has them too, although it won't confirm or
deny anything. Iran might have them soon (see **Iran**).

Have nuclear weapons ever been used?

Yes, the US used atom bombs to destroy the Japanese cities of Hiroshima and Nagasaki in August 1945, effectively ending the Second World War. The largest bomb ever to be detonated was the 50-megaton Soviet 'Tsar Bomba' in a test in 1961; this was about 250 times more powerful than 'Fat Man', which destroyed Nagasaki. Today's nuclear weapons can be launched from land, sea or air, and vary in their destructive capability and purpose; the neutron bomb, for example, is designed to cause huge amounts of casualties without much damage to infrastructure.

What is nuclear fission?

Nuclear fission is the key reaction behind nuclear energy creation and nuclear weapons. It occurs when neutrons bombard the unstable atoms of radioactive fissile material (e.g. Uranium-235), causing the atom to split, releasing energy and freeing neutrons which cause further atoms to break up and a chain reaction to ensue. In nuclear-energy plants, fission is a slow and controlled process, being used to heat water and create steam, which in turn drives turbines to create electricity. In nuclear weapons the concentration of fissile material is much higher, causing extremely fast and uncontrolled reactions which lead to explosive devastation.

How do you make a nuclear weapon?

The most important thing you need is a critical mass (sufficient quantity) of fissile material to create a chain reaction. Fissile material can either be enriched uranium (mostly U-235) or plutonium (Pu-239). Plutonium is created from uranium in nuclear reactors, so either way, you'll need to start by getting hold of some uranium. This occurs naturally as uranium ore, most of which is mined in Canada, Australia or Kazakhstan.

You'll need quite a lot, though: it takes 25,000 tonnes of typical uranium ore to produce 50 tonnes of metal, and of this, only about 1% will be Uranium-235, the fissile isotope you require (the remaining 99% will be Uranium-238, which is radioactive but doesn't break up under neutron bombardment). Grind and leach the ore to extract uranium oxide powder (known as yellowcake) then convert it into uranium hexafluoride gas by reacting it with a few other substances. Use a gas centrifuge to separate the U-235 from the U-238 and you'll end up with two substances: a tiny amount of enriched uranium (your fissile material), and a huge amount of depleted uranium (a high-density, weakly radioactive metal used for military purposes in armour plating or armour-piercing weapons). Enriched uranium of the type used in nuclear reactors to create nuclear energy contains between 3 and 20% U-235, whereas weapons-grade uranium is between 80 and 90% U-235. You need around 50 kg of this stuff to make one nuclear bomb.

If you want to use plutonium, you'll need to collect a year's worth of spent uranium fuel rods from a nuclear reactor. These will give you about 10 kg of plutonium – enough for one nuke – after an extremely expensive extraction process which also creates a huge amount of radioactive waste. Once you've got your fissile material, you need to weaponise it – this means finding ways of compacting it and incorporating it into a bomb or a missile along with conventional explosives which will trigger the nuclear reaction. Missiles are better because they can be launched from land or stealthily by submarines, whereas bombs have to be dropped from planes, which could get shot down. Plutonium is easier to launch than enriched uranium at the tips of missiles, because the critical mass required (10 kg rather than 50 kg) is a lot less. Either way, employ rocket scientists who know what they're doing.

What is a 'nuclear deterrent'?

This is just a euphemism for nuclear weapons themselves. The idea of deterrence, or Mutually Assured Destruction (MAD), was the key strategy of the Cold War, when the US and the USSR stockpiled nukes in a bid to convince one another that launching a nuclear strike was a bad idea because of the massive and inevitable retaliation it would provoke. Deterrence forms the basis of British nuclear weapons policy today; at any given time there is always a British nuclear submarine on patrol somewhere in the ocean, poised to launch a retaliatory strike at a nuclear aggressor. So if the British Isles get completely annihilated, at least we can be sure we'll get our own back, even if we're not around to see it happen. 'Nuclear deterrent' is just one of many disingenuous names associated with Weapons of Mass Destruction, as nuclear (as well as chemical, biological and radiological) weapons are otherwise known when convenient. For example, from 1986 to 2005 the US possessed a missile which could deploy ten different warheads at once, each of them twenty times more destructive than the Hiroshima bomb. They named it the Peacemaker.

What is the Nuclear Non-Proliferation Treaty (NPT)?

This is an agreement between nuclear weapons states and non-nuclear weapons states that was opened for signature in 1968. Every country in the world has now signed it except for India, Pakistan and Israel; North Korea signed but then withdrew in 2003. The NPT states that only the five states in the 'nuclear club' are allowed to possess nukes. These states promise not to 'assist, encourage or induce' other states in obtaining them, while making efforts to decommission their own weapons with a view to disarming completely at some unspecified point in the future. All the other countries promise not to 'receive, manufacture or acquire' nuclear weapons. Meanwhile, all signatories of the treaty are allowed to develop nuclear technology for peaceful purposes (i.e. producing nuclear energy).

In practice, the NPT is fraught with tensions and problems. The nuclear states are very keen on non-proliferation (i.e. making sure no one else gets their hands on the weapons) but not so bothered about honouring their own disarmament pledges. This angers non-nuclear weapons countries who feel that they're getting a raw deal. India, Pakistan and Israel saw this coming a long time ago and opted out completely, pointing out that they couldn't understand what qualified some states to be allowed nukes and others to be denied them. The nuclear energy aspect of the NPT is also highly problematic, because the uranium-enrichment process necessary for the development of nuclear energy is also an early stage in the development of nuclear weapons. Mohammed El Baradei, Director General of the International Atomic Energy Agency, has called this the 'Achilles heel' of the NPT and estimates that 35–40 states with nuclear-energy programmes could have the technology to develop nuclear weapons if they wanted to. For years Iran has been enriching uranium for what it claims are 'peaceful purposes', but the international community are pretty sure that's a lie (see **Iran**).

Are the nuclear states ever going to disarm?

Unlikely. Although they have decommissioned weapons gradually over the years, it would not be in their interests to disarm completely. Nuclear weapons maintain the balance of power between these states and ensure their global hegemony. Even if they all agreed to disarm, it would be practically impossible to get them all to do so at exactly the same time.

There would therefore be huge and dangerous fluctuations in the balance of power during the process of disarmament. Besides, it is almost inevitable that states would secretly stash a few nukes away to gain an advantage later, or out of fear that others would do the same. It is, however, in the interests of the 'nuclear club' to keep *talking* about disarming in order to stop non-nuclear weapons countries from reneging on their non-proliferation commitments and creating their own nuclear arsenals.

Why do some people oppose disarmament?
Some oppose disarmament because they argue it encourages other states to develop their own nuclear weapons. They claim that as the large arsenals of the nuclear club are diminished, the strategic value of creating a small arsenal elsewhere is increased.

Does anyone oppose non-proliferation?
Yes. Amongst others, international relations scholar Kenneth Waltz has argued that the proliferation of nuclear weapons is in fact the safest option for global security. If nuclear weapons are here to stay, he claims, everyone should have them, and this would prevent full-scale war ever erupting between countries – as it was prevented during the Cold War.

What is the Trident programme?
Trident is Britain's only type of nuclear weapon, a US-provided submarine-launched ballistic missile. In March 2007 the House of Commons voted to renew the Trident system, including the nuclear submarines that launch them, in a process which will take around 17 years and cost £15–20 billion. The issue of whether or not Britain should give up its nuclear weapons programme has provoked much debate. Tony Blair and the

Tories defended the programme, saying it would be essential for Britain's protection in an uncertain future. Opponents consider it irrelevant in the post-Cold War world and argue that it is ineffective in combating terrorist threats which they see as a greater threat to national security than other nuclear powers. They also say the money could be better spent on other things and claim, perhaps rather wishfully, that by disarming, Britain would be setting an example to other nuclear countries to do the same.

Doh!

Nuclear submarines are well-known for being silent and undetectable, but in January 2009 this seems to have worked rather too well when a British submarine and a French one, each carrying more destructive potential than the entire campaign of World War II, grazed past each other in the depths of the Atlantic Ocean. Fortunately the damage was minimal and there were no serious consequences. Vice Admiral Tim McClement described the collision as an 'astonishing coincidence'.

Organic Food

What is it?

In general, organic food is produced without the use of pesticides, artificial fertilisers, additives, human waste, ionising radiation or biotechnology. Organic livestock are reared humanely and without the routine use of antibiotics or growth hormones. Organic farming uses methods such as crop rotation to sustain soil health and productivity, conserve water and

maintain ecosystems. However, there is no fixed definition for organic food as governmental regulations vary from country to country. In Cuba, for example, food may be genetically modified and still certified as organic, while, in the US, there are yet to be organic standards agreed upon for fish, pet food or nutritional supplements.

Why is it more expensive than non-organic food?
Conventional farming often relies on monocultures (the planting of a single crop), and so benefits from the cost advantages of mass production, the use of machinery and centralised processing and transportation systems. Organic food, however, is produced on a smaller scale and is usually more labour intensive (organic growers, for example, often weed vegetables by hand rather than use pesticides) which creates higher costs. In the case of meat, dairy and eggs, it is more expensive to meet the pasturing, housing and feeding requirements of organically farmed animals than their conventionally farmed counterparts.

Is it healthier?
There is currently no evidence to suggest that organic food is more nutritious than conventionally farmed food, according to a July 2009 report by the Food Standards Agency, though an EU study, due to be published later this year, may find higher levels of antioxidants. Some people buy organic food to limit their exposure to the pesticides used in conventional farming, though most experts agree that the quantities of these are small enough not to pose health risks.

Does it taste nicer?

The Soil Association, the UK's most influential campaigning organisation for organic food, claims that 'many people buy organic food because they believe it tastes better than non-organic', and goes on to mention the 'fuller flavour some people experience'. Tests have offered little evidence that this is the case.

Is it more sustainable?

This is a matter of widespread controversy. For agriculture to be considered sustainable, it has to balance environmental concerns with human needs, while still remaining profitable. According to the International Federation of Organic Agriculture Movements, organic farming 'relies on ecological processes, biodiversity and cycles adapted to local conditions, rather than the use of inputs with adverse effects'. It 'combines tradition, innovation and science to benefit the shared environment and promote fair relationships and a good quality of life for all involved'.

However, organic methods have been criticised as unsustainable by experts such as Dr Norman Borlaug, a Nobel-prize winning agronomist who developed high-yield conventional farming techniques in the 1960s (the 'Green revolution'). Borlaug claims organic farming is not a viable means of feeding the world's growing population because a) it is low-yield, and there is not enough farmland available to produce the required amount of food, b) marginal areas and rainforests would have to make way for organic farmland, and c) to produce organic nutrients for crops, huge amounts of manure are needed, which itself requires further land on which to raise cattle. He argues that high-yield techniques combining chemical fertilisers with biotechnology are the only answer to the problem of feeding 8 billion people by 2025.

However, other evidence (from ongoing studies such as the Sustainable Agriculture Farming Systems Project at the University of California, Davis) suggests that organic farming can produce equal yields to conventional techniques in the developed world, and even higher yields in the developing world. Organic crops also appear to be more resilient to the kind of severe weather that seems likely to intensify in the future as a result of climate change, and to hit poor tropical countries the hardest (see **Climate Change**). The pro-organic lobby argue that the many large farms in the developing world that grow monocultures of luxury crops for export (e.g. tobacco, sugar cane, cotton) should be replaced by small family-run farms that grow a variety of crops, including subsistence crops to feed the local people. Supporters of this idea claim that this is a much more sustainable solution, as it is better for the environment, more profitable and makes small communities more self-sufficient.

'Cancer has been the curse of my family. I am challenging these evil genes by natural means. I am convinced that by eating biological foods it is possible to avoid the growth of tumours.'

GWYNETH PALTROW, *Oscar-winning American actress*

Pakistan

When was it founded?

Pakistan ('Land of the Pure') was founded in 1947 after the Partition of India. Muhammad Ali Jinnah is regarded as the father of the nation; he was leader of the Muslim League in India from 1934, and supported the 'Two-Nation Theory' – the idea that Indian Muslims needed their own nation because of their irreconcilable differences with Hindus. The Muslim League's intentions to form an independent state were formally declared in the Lahore Resolution of 1940. When the British pulled out of India in 1947, they left behind them the Mountbatten Plan (named after the last Viceroy of the British Indian empire, Lord Louis Mountbatten), which became the blueprint for the division of the country. Partition involved the relocation of 14.5 million people, and religious violence in the process caused the deaths of between 200,000 and 1 million. The Indian Muslims' new homeland was in two separate areas: West Pakistan, in the western half of Punjab in the north-west of India, and East Pakistan, in the eastern half of Bengal in the east of India. Its capital city and government were in West Pakistan, initially in Karachi before switching first to Muzaffarabad in 1949, and then to Islamabad in 1960.

What happened to East Pakistan?

It was renamed East Bengal in 1956. Its people, culturally distinct and more numerous than the West Pakistanis, felt they were being exploited economically and dominated politically by the West Pakistan-based government. Their grievances fuelled an independence movement which gathered force in 1970 and led to the declaration of the nation of Bangladesh in March

1971. India came to the aid of Bangladesh, defeating Pakistan in a war in December 1971 which guaranteed the new nation's survival.

Has Pakistan fought other wars with India?
Yes, all of which concerned the disputed territory of Jammu and Kashmir (see **Kashmir**). The first was from 1947–8, following Partition, and resulted in Pakistan capturing 45% of Kashmir and the Line of Control being established through the middle of the state. Other inconclusive wars over the region occurred in 1965 and 1999, as well as several skirmishes in the 80s and 90s. In 1998 Pakistan announced its nuclear weapons capability to the world and to India, which had gone nuclear in 1974. The possibility of a nuclear war between the two countries was raised in the 1999 Kargil conflict in Kashmir and in a tense military standoff in 2001–2. The most recent source of tension was the Mumbai attacks of November 2008, in which ten armed members of the Pakistan-based Islamic militant organisation Lashkar-e-Taiba killed 173 and injured 308. This group and others, such as Jaish-e-Mohammad, draw their support from numerous madrassas (religious seminaries) in Pakistan and aim to expel India from Kashmir altogether. Although often accused, the Pakistani government has always denied funding such groups in order to destabilise India.

Who runs Pakistan?
Pakistan has had a turbulent political history, torn between military dictatorship, democracy and Islamic rule. Of these, military rule has been predominant, with the military running the country directly for three distinct periods (1958–71, 1977–88 and 1999–2008) and exercising considerable clout in political affairs in intervening times; this contravenes the

supreme law of Pakistan set out in the 1973 Constitution, which requires federal parliamentary democracy based on Islamic principles. An uncomfortable precedent for authoritarian rule was set as far back as 1954 when the Supreme Court upheld Governor-General Ghulam Muhammad's dismissal of the civilian government, citing the 'theory of necessity'. Pakistan's most recent military leader, General Pervez Musharraf, stood down in 2008 following calls for his impeachment. He was replaced by Asif Ali Zardari, head of the democratic centre-left PPP (Pakistan People's Party). He is the widower of former prime minister and PPP leader Benazir Bhutto, a hugely influential figure in Pakistani politics who was assassinated in 2007. Zardari is a controversial figure because of his vast wealth, which many claim was acquired corruptly, a charge also levelled against his late wife. With little political experience, he faces a tough job in attempting to stabilise a desperately divided country. Pakistan's most popular politician, Nawaz Sharif of the Pakistan Muslim League, stands in opposition to Zardari. Twice Prime Minister in the 90s, Sharif was Musharaf's bitterest rival and was exiled for eight years when the general seized power in a bloodless coup in 1999.

What has happened in Pakistan since 2001?
General Musharaf was a key ally of George W. Bush in his War on Terror, deploying the powerful Pakistani military to attack Taleban and suspected al-Qaeda militants in their post-9/11 hideouts in the Federally Administered Tribal Areas, rural regions on the Afghan border which are only nominally controlled by Pakistan. The US also used Pakistan as a base from which to supply their forces in Afghanistan. However, Musharaf and the military were extremely unpopular with many Pakistanis, and after 2001 the country became a hotbed of

Islamic fundamentalism, with frequent suicide bombs and terrorist attacks aimed at military and civilian targets. The Taleban, although initially an Afghan movement, attracted a strong Pakistani following, which aided the existing militants and spread across the North West Frontier Province (NWFP), where they intended to set up an Islamic state controlled by Sharia law (see **Islam**). In February 2009 they succeeded in establishing Sharia law in one region, Swat, as part of a peace deal with the local government. Islamic extremism in Pakistan has been fuelled partly by its promotion in certain madrassas, religious seminaries which offer free board and lodging to their students. From 2006–7 Islamic militants from the Red Mosque and adjacent Jamia Hafsa madrassa in Islamabad engaged in violent protests against Musharraf's government, which culminated in a siege of the mosque complex and the deaths of the militants. Madrassas have been a popular choice for many poor parents whose children otherwise would have no prospects because of the low priority placed on education by the government, whose budget goes mainly towards military spending and servicing the country's vast national debt.

And as if that wasn't bad enough …

Pakistan is also blighted by sectarian violence between Sunni and Shi'a factions (Pakistan is 77% Sunni, 20% Shi'a). While overwhelmingly Muslim, Pakistan is ethnically and linguistically very mixed, like its neighbour Afghanistan. Various tensions exist between the Punjabis (who at 44% of the population constitute the largest group), the Sindhis, Mojahir, Baloch and Pashtun. The Pashtun, concentrated in the NWFP, are one of several minority groups who for years have complained of neglect by the central government. A nationalist insurgency by the Baloch people in Balochistan, Pakistan's poorest and largest province, has been running for years, and has been put down brutally by the military amid accusations that India are funding the insurgents in order to destabilise the country.

Itching to play
Pakistan is a nation of cricket lovers, and one of its biggest stars is the 'Rawalpindi Express', fast bowler Shoaib Akhtar, who set a world record in 2003 by bowling faster than 100 mph. Shoaib is no stranger to controversy, having been banned for ball tampering, involved in drugs scandals, and sent home from the Twenty20 World Championship squad in 2007 for hitting a teammate with a cricket bat in a dressing-room spat. In 2009 he had to sit out the same competition because he needed treatment for an attack of genital warts.

Pandemic

What is the difference between an epidemic and a pandemic?
It's not very scientific: an epidemic is an outbreak of a disease
that rapidly infects an unusually large number of individuals in
one or several communities, while a pandemic is the same but
on a global scale.

Have there always been pandemics?
Today's world provides ideal conditions for diseases to spread
swiftly, with global travel and more people than ever living in close
proximity in cities, but pandemics are far from a new
phenomenon. The first pandemic we know about travelled from
Ethiopia to Egypt and Libya before hitting Athens in 430 BC; the
Greek historian Thucydides described symptoms including
'unnatural and fetid breath', diarrhoea and vomiting. Of those it
didn't kill, some were left with no memory while others lost body
parts such as fingers and toes, and in four years the disease
claimed the lives of one third of the Athenian population and its
armed forces. One of the worst recorded pandemics is the Black
Death, which lasted from 1347 to 1351 and killed an estimated 25
million people in Europe – around a quarter of its population at
the time. The population took until the beginning of the 16th
century to recover to the level it had been before the plague struck.

Besides flu, have many other diseases caused pandemics?
Yes, quite a few. Smallpox was an infectious disease with
symptoms that included very high temperature, back pain and a
rash which quickly covered the body. It emerged over 3,000
years ago but was finally eradicated in 1980 after a massive
global vaccination programme that began in 1967.

A recurring pandemic is cholera, a water-borne disease which causes a severe infection in the small intestine, leading, unless treated, to a quick death. There have been seven cholera pandemics in the last two centuries and recent outbreaks in Iraq, India, Vietnam, Zimbabwe and South Africa.

HIV/AIDS is the most recent pandemic of a new disease to have struck. The human immunodeficiency virus (HIV) infects cells in our immune systems, which are either destroyed or damaged, leaving a person less able to fight off other infections or diseases. Depending on whether the sufferer is treated with anti-retroviral drugs, HIV can take over 15 years to develop into its advanced stage, AIDS (acquired immunodeficiency syndrome). The HIV virus can be transmitted by sexual intercourse, sharing contaminated needles and the transfusion of contaminated blood, or between a mother and her baby either during pregnancy, in childbirth or through breastfeeding. According to UNAIDS, 2 million people died of HIV-related deaths and a further 2.7 million became infected in 2007 alone. There is no cure for HIV and it has claimed around 25 million lives since emerging in 1981.

How do we know a flu pandemic has officially begun?
According to the World Health Organisation (WHO), there are three conditions which have to be met for a flu pandemic to start: 1) the emergence of a new virus, 2) the virus causes serious illness, and 3) the virus spreads easily and sustainably among humans. Five years ago the WHO introduced the following six phases of alert to indicate the likelihood of a pandemic: Phase 1 – the flu exists only in animals, and not humans; Phase 2 – the first human case is diagnosed; Phase 3 – a few humans are becoming infected, but not transmitting widely to one another; Phase 4 – the flu is being transmitted

PANDEMIC

significantly from human to human at community level; Phase 5 – human-to-human transmission in at least two countries; Phase 6 – pandemic declared: the virus has spread to another country in a different region and is being transmitted from human to human there.

How many flu pandemics were there in the 20th century?

Three. The most severe of these was the 1918–19 Spanish flu (which didn't actually start in Spain) that took more than 50 million lives. As Spain was neutral in World War I there was no media censorship, and consequently the pandemic was reported there more than in other countries, prompting allied nations to call it 'Spanish' flu. Worldwide, 2 million people died from the Asian flu pandemic of 1957/8 and a further million were killed globally by the Hong Kong flu pandemic, which struck in 1968/9.

What recent flu threats have there been?

H5N1, better known as bird flu, first appeared on the radar in 1997 after passing from birds to humans. It has taken 257 lives since 2003 and caused over 300 million birds to be culled across the world. Although it continues to infect both animals and humans it doesn't infect humans easily, and it is difficult for one person to pass it on to another. Nonetheless scientists continue to monitor this virus in case it becomes more contagious.

The latest threat is swine flu, or H1N1, which began in Mexico in April 2009. It caused global panic over the following months as thousands of confirmed cases cropped up in Europe, North and South America and Asia. In June 2009 the World Health Organisation declared swine flu the first global flu pandemic in 40 years. The decision to raise the alert status to level 6 was made after the confirmation of over 27,000 cases and

141 deaths. The symptoms of swine flu are similar to those of ordinary flu – cough, sore throat, fever, body aches, chills and fatigue.

So how do I protect myself?

The easy answer is to get yourself vaccinated. However, if it's a new virus there won't be a vaccine available and it may take up to half a year to make one. While effective anti-viral drugs (such as Tamiflu) exist, they only slow a virus down rather than getting rid of it entirely. They also come with possible side effects, such as nausea and vomiting. Try, then, to avoid catching the disease: make sure your personal hygiene is up to scratch and don't socialise. If things are looking really bleak, book a flight to a tropical island and see out the last days of mankind in style.

Philanthropy

What is it?
Philanthropy is the act of helping others, usually by giving money (from the Greek *philanthropos*, 'man-loving').

How much do Britain's big earners donate?
Despite the credit crunch (see **Credit Crunch**), the 2009 *Sunday Times* Giving List shows that Britain's leading philanthropists

put even more money into worthy causes than the year before. The top hundred philanthropists channelled over £2.8 billion between them, up 8% on 2008. Christopher Cooper-Hohn, a hedge-fund manager, topped the list with recent donations of £462.5 million.

What about the rest of us?

Around 56% of the UK's population donate regularly to charity, a figure which hasn't changed much in recent years. In the 2007/8 financial year, £10.6 billion was donated to charities by the UK population, an increase of over 8% on the year before, after taking inflation into account. Donors in the UK give an average of £33 a month, up from £29 in 2006/7.

Mr Nasty turns Mr Nice

When music mogul and X-Factor judge Simon Cowell appeared on Oprah Winfrey's talk show, he ended up writing a cheque for £80,000 to a couple whose three-year-old daughter had cancer, in order to clear their mortgage. Cowell, notorious for being TV's nastyman, said: 'I never knew that doing good could feel so good.' Winfrey is a leading philanthropist herself, setting up The Oprah Winfrey Foundation in 1987 to support women, children and families both in America and around the world. More recently, Winfrey's global efforts include her Leadership Academy Foundation, created after a conversation with Nelson Mandela in 2000, which contributed more than $40 million towards the creation of a school for girls in South Africa.

The Gates' guide to giving

In the late 90s Bill Gates, co-founder of Microsoft, read in an article that rotavirus, a disease he had never heard of which affects the stomach and intestine, was killing half a million children every year. This prompted him and his wife to set up the Bill and Melinda Gates Foundation, launched in 2000, whose work includes researching a cure for HIV/AIDS, fighting malaria epidemics and improving the state of some of America's high schools. By 2005 they had endowed the foundation with over $28.8 billion for global health and learning programmes. Warren Buffett then pledged $37 billion of his fortune to the foundation the following year, saying: 'I am not an enthusiast of dynastic wealth, particularly when the alternative is six billion people having that much poorer hands in life than we have, having a chance to benefit from the money.'

What about the kids?

Anita Roddick, founder of the Body Shop, gave £54 million to her charitable foundation, which gives away around £2.5 million a year to organisations such as Amnesty International. Roddick, who died in 2008 at the age of 64, said: 'I told my kids that they would not inherit one penny.' Before Roddick died, her daughter Sam, who runs the erotic boutique Coco de Mer, said: 'If my mum had said to me, "I'm not leaving the money to you but I've decided to give it all to a distant cousin," then I would have found that offensive. But giving it all to charity is different. You can't argue about someone giving their money away, can you? They've already given us everything in terms of love and support.' Roddick's decision is by no means exceptional. Baron Hilton, the hotel magnate and grandfather of socialite Paris Hilton, vowed to leave 97% of his $2.3 billion fortune to the Conrad N. Hilton Foundation, which was set up by his father. Since its inception, the foundation has ploughed hundreds of millions of dollars into areas such as providing housing for the mentally ill and increasing people's access to clean water.

Lend us a tenor

Life was looking good for Alberto Vilar, a former refugee from the Cuban revolution who rose to run a $10 billion company, Amerindo Investment Advisors, with his business partner Gary Tanaka. He was known as a generous benefactor, channelling many millions into cultural and other causes. However, after the dotcom bubble burst in 2002, Vilar and Tanaka clocked up debts, leading them to siphon money from their clients. Vilar, an opera lover, then had to renege on pledges he had made to institutions including the Royal Opera House, who removed his name from what had previously been called the Vilar Floral Hall. After being arrested and put on trial for stealing money from investors he was convicted in November 2008 of all twelve charges he was facing.

Pirates!

In this day and age?

Absolutely. According to the International Maritime Bureau there were 293 piracy incidents reported worldwide in 2008, an increase of 11% from the previous year. Piracy incidents can consist of anything from boarding a vessel and stealing some valuables to stealing the entire cargo and ransoming it or, in

some cases, making off with the entire ship. Unlike Bluebeard and his contemporaries, modern-day pirates do not tend to use violence indiscriminately: of the 889 crew members taken hostage in 2008, only 11 were killed and 21 reported missing (presumed dead). Some pirates belong to organised criminal networks, some claim to be political rebels acting on grievances, and many are simply small-time bandits trying to get rich quick.

Where?
Any lawless coastline where ships carrying valuable cargoes pass within reach of desperate men. Nowhere is this more true than the waters off Somalia, which in 2008 became the undisputed piracy hotspot of the world with a record 111 incidents and 42 successful hijacks, a trend which continued into 2009, with 29 successful hijacks from 114 attempts by the end of May. The East African country has not had a functioning government since 1991, and for its impoverished and hungry population the huge volume of maritime traffic navigating one of the world's busiest shipping lanes nearby offers a tempting opportunity. In 2008 Somali pirates made roughly $50 million from their attacks, which included the ransoming of the *Sirius Star*, a Saudi supertanker carrying $100 million worth of oil, and the MV *Faina*, a Ukrainian ship transporting 33 ex-Soviet tanks and other weaponry including ammunition containing depleted uranium. Naval vessels have been sent by the US, India, Russia, China, Japan and the EU (the first mission of its kind) to escort ships en route to or from the Suez Canal. In February 2009 the countries in the immediate area also agreed to collectively patrol the volatile Gulf of Aden, where many of the attacks take place.

Where else?
The Malacca straits, a 500-mile-long sea passage between
Malaysia, Singapore and Indonesia were until recently the most
pirate-infested waters in the world. More than 50,000 ships and
half the world's oil pass annually through the waterway, which is
only 2 miles across at its narrowest point. Much of the coastline
consists of heavily forested inlets which provide an ideal hideout
for pirates, whose attacks used to be so frequent that in 2005 the
straits were classified as a war zone by the maritime insurance
arm of Lloyd's, one of the world's largest insurance companies.
Malaysia, Singapore and Indonesia responded with a security
crackdown that has so far been successful, although experts fear
that pirates are merely lying low for the moment. The Gulf of
Guinea, off Nigeria and Cameroon, is increasingly under threat
from pirates, many of whom target the lucrative oil-export
industry in the Niger delta area. The South China Sea and the
Caribbean (yes, still) are other notorious waters.

What should I do if pirates attack my ship?
Make sure you and your crew are prepared in case the worst
happens. If you haven't hired a private security firm to protect
your ship, it's best not to fire guns at approaching pirates
because they're bound to have more weapons than you and
you'll only come off worse. When they get within 300 metres,
unleash the sonic blaster on them – a dish-shaped gadget which
directs an extremely loud and debilitating 'beam' of sound. This
should hopefully put them off, or at least deafen them a bit, and
it's a technique that worked well in 2005 for the crew of luxury
cruise liner USS *Seabourn Spirit*, who used one to deter Somali
pirates firing grenade launchers and machine guns. If that
doesn't work, prepare to deploy the heavy-duty fire hoses – to
blast the blighters back into the sea as they're trying to climb

aboard. If it's dark when the pirates attack, make sure you've got some searchlights handy so you can temporarily blind them, or at least keep track of them while you're hosing them down. Some might succeed in scrambling up the sides, so let's hope you've got a Secure-Ship™ 9,000-volt electrifying fence installed to frazzle them when they reach the top. If they do manage to get on board, the game's up – do exactly what they say. Don't try and be a hero. Let them steal from your cabin, sleep in your bunk and use your computer to look up internet porn. Laugh at their jokes. Don't ask to phone your family too often. If they let you talk to a journalist, make a big thing about how well you're being treated. Just read a book and wait until someone pays the ransom money.

How do I commit an act of piracy?
We wouldn't advise this, but Somali pirates are doing pretty well at the moment so here's how to do it. Assemble a group of between 2 and 16 men – the poorer and hungrier the better – and arm them with knives, machine guns and rocket-propelled grenades. You'll need to arrange a pirate mothership to get you and your men out into the shipping lane; these can easily be found in the port of Mogadishu, Somalia's ruined capital. If there are any previously captured yachts hanging around, bring one with you – they can be useful for hiding in and sending out fake distress signals to lure passing vessels into a fiendish trap. If not, get hold of some rope ladders, grappling hooks and a couple of motorised skiffs and wait with the mothership until a large tanker passes. Make sure your men are jacked up to the eyeballs on *khat* – a local plant whose leaves can be chewed as a stimulant – this will make them euphoric and outlandishly confident that their mission will be successful. Approach the ship at high speed in the skiffs, and as you get near, brandish

your weapons and make it quite clear that you mean business. Board the ship, take the crew hostage, find the relevant documents and contact the owners to begin ransom talks. The owners will employ a seasoned negotiation specialist who'll gradually barter you down, so make sure you start off with truly ridiculous demands (say $15 million). The negotiation process will probably take around two months, so in the meantime take the ship into the pirate port of Eyl in Puntland where you can resupply with food, weapons and personnel, find an accountant to take care of the figures and feed your hostages in special hostage restaurants. Once you've got hold of the money – you'll probably end up with $1–2 million – pay your men and embark on an irresponsible spending spree. Just be aware that local Islamist warlords al-Shabab ('the Lads') might be expecting half of your money.

The fourth emergency service?
'We don't consider ourselves sea bandits. We consider sea bandits those who illegally fish in our seas and dump waste in our seas and carry weapons in our seas. We are simply patrolling our seas. Think of us like a coast guard.'

SUGULE ALI, *Somali pirate*

Russia

Just how big is it?

Russia is the largest country on earth, covering over 17 million square kilometres, about seventy times bigger than the United Kingdom. It spans 11 time zones, stretching from the Black Sea in the West to the Bering Strait in the East, close to Alaska.

End of the Empire

In 1917, a communist revolution in Russia put an end to the Romanov dynasty that had ruled for over three hundred years. In 1905, unarmed protestors had taken to the streets and been fired on by troops in what would become known as Bloody Sunday, but revolutionary fervour that year was quelled when the regime created a parliament (duma) and a constitution. Yet the impact of World War I on the country and its people, as well as renewed repression from the regime, brought about another revolution, and this time Tsar Nicholas II was executed alongside his family. A shaky provisional government was established, but civil war ensued between Vladimir Lenin's communist Bolsheviks (Reds), and the loosely allied anti-Bolsheviks (Whites), with the Reds eventually emerging victorious.

Back in the USSR

After the Reds' victory, Lenin established the world's first communist state in the form of the Union of Soviet Socialist Republics (USSR), which survived for most of the 20th century until its collapse in 1991. Initially the USSR was made up of four Union Republics, but over the following decades they were divided, and eventually numbered fifteen: Armenia, Azerbaijan, Belorussia (now Belarus), Estonia, Georgia, Kazakhstan, Kirghizia (now Kyrgyzstan), Latvia, Lithuania, Moldavia, Russia, Tadzhikistan, Turkmenistan, Ukraine and Uzbekistan.

From Cold War to collapse

After a brief, uneasy truce to defeat Hitler in the Second World War, the US and the USSR began the Cold War, a long period of rivalry and subterfuge between the two nations and their allies that lasted until the Soviet Union's collapse in 1991. As well as economic, political and social tensions, there was also a very public arms race that brought the world to the brink of nuclear war – most notably during the Cuban missile crisis (see **Cuba**). After Stalin's death in 1953, a degree of freedom was ushered in by Nikita Khrushchev, who toned down the severe dictatorial nature of his predecessor's regime. He was followed by Leonid Brezhnev and his formidable eyebrows, who adopted a more conservative approach; on his death Mikhail Gorbachev took charge, introducing reforms known collectively as *glasnost* (openness) and *perestroika* (restructuring).

But by the late 1980s the Soviet Union was showing signs of severe strain. In August 1991, while Gorbachev was on holiday in the Crimea, a coup organised by hard-line members of the Communist Party, military and KGB tried to remove him from power. Although it failed after a few days, partly because of divisions within the military and the KGB, the coup left Gorbachev's position untenable and the Soviet Union beyond repair. Independence movements swiftly took advantage and soon Lithuania became the first Soviet Republic to break free, followed by Estonia and Latvia. Ukraine, Belorussia (Belarus) and Moldavia (Moldova) then followed. Soon there were 15 new states, each of which began their independence in economic turmoil.

What happened then?

Boris Yeltsin became the first democratically elected president of the new Russian Federation. During Yeltsin's time in office he pushed through a series of economic reforms, including privatisation and free trade (see **Free Trade**). Although the end result was a much freer economy, the number of people living in poverty increased, and a large gap began emerging between the wealthy and poor. In 1998 there was a disastrous financial collapse, and a year later Yeltsin was replaced by the former secret service member Vladimir Putin.

What about the future?

After the financial collapse Russia, fuelled by its abundance of energy supplies, began to enjoy a period of sustained economic growth, and has since reasserted itself as a regional power. In January 2009, for instance, Russia cut off gas supplies to Ukraine, ostensibly because of unpaid debts, though many saw it as a way of voicing disapproval at Ukraine's moves to cosy up to the European Union and NATO. In August 2008, it gave military assistance to the breakaway region of South Ossetia in Georgia (see **Georgia**). However, after a buoyant period for Russia's economy, the country now faces a more difficult time ahead. In May 2009, a year into his Presidency, Dmitry Medvedev was feeling the strain of the global financial crisis, as unemployment in Russia nudged 10% and inflation stood at 15%.

Dealing with this crisis alongside Medvedev is his mentor Putin, who many see as the man calling the shots. A survey of over one thousand Russian citizens in April 2009 found that 27% thought Putin, who is prime minister, held real power compared with just 15% for President Medvedev; 40% of those questioned thought they shared power equally. There is speculation that Putin wants to regain the presidency in 2012, an idea fuelled by recent amendments approved by the Duma extending the presidential term to six years and the parliamentary term to five. As this couple try to lead Russia forward in the next few years their relationship, and in particular Putin's actions, will be keenly observed.

Stalemate

Garry Kasparov, the former World Chess Champion, has been a thorn in the side of the government in the last few years. After retiring from the game in 2005, with some calling him the greatest ever player, he formed Other Russia, a coalition made up of a broad range of opponents to the government. Kasparov, a fierce critic of Putin, even put himself forward for the Presidency, but had to withdraw his candidature after alleged interventions from his opponent. His criticisms led to him being thrown in jail for five days in 2007 for organising an 'unsanctioned' rally against the regime he calls undemocratic. He remains an active voice against the present government.

Who are the oligarchs?

An oligarchy is a system of government in which power is held and retained by a small, elite group of people. In recent years the word oligarch has been used to describe billionaire tycoons from Russia and other former Soviet states, where the boundary between business and politics is somewhat porous. Some of them started in the late 1980s as entrepreneurs trading in black-market goods during Gorbachev's *glasnost* period of partial market liberalisation, while others took advantage of the chaotic transformation from communism to capitalism following the collapse of the Soviet Union in 1991. Government officials, their close friends or relatives, and criminal bosses were able to acquire state assets very cheaply during privatisation.

Famous oligarchs include Chelsea Football Club owner Roman Abramovich, who launched his business career by selling deodorants, tights, toothpaste, dolls and plastic ducks;

industrial magnate Alisher Usmanov ('the hard man of Russia'), who owns a 14.58% stake in Arsenal Football Club, and oil tycoon Mikhail Khordokovsky, who in 2004 was the richest man in Russia, with an estimated $15.2 billion to his name. The following year, however, Khordokovsky was found guilty of tax evasion and fraud, and he lost his fortune because his company, Yukos, had its assets frozen, causing a collapse in its share price. Khordokovsky began an eight-year jail sentence in 2005, and within a month had written a political essay from his cell calling for a return to socialism in Russia. He currently resides in Siberian forced labour camp YaG-14/10, and was denied parole in 2008, partly for refusing to attend prison sewing classes.

'Let's drink to all the Russian gas'

Gazprom, which is 50.002% owned by the Russian government, is the largest gas company in the world with reserves worth an estimated $182.5 billion, and is at the centre of Russia's gas wars with Europe. The EU depends on Gazprom alone for a quarter of its gas, and several Eastern European countries are wholly dependent on it for their supply. The company has its own professional football team, FC SOYUZ Gazprom-Izhevsk, who are currently in the Russian second division. Until recently the club's president, Vladimir Tumayev, used to appear as a substitute striker on a fairly regular basis, and in 2005 he scored a goal in his last game at the age of 58. Tumayev, who is a director of Gazprom subsidiary Spetsgazavtotrans, is clearly a man of many talents, as he also wrote and performed a rousing corporate anthem for Gazprom which hymns the company's successes – it can be found under 'Gazprom Song' on YouTube.

Social Networking

What is it?
'Social networking' is a term for the recent profusion of websites
that create online communities around shared interests or
activities, and allow users to share information with each other
– from photos to favourite books to the minutiae of what
they're thinking, feeling or doing.

How do I get started?

Most of these websites are open to all and easy to join. You usually need to set up a profile, perhaps explaining a little bit about yourself. But take note: while you may want people to know the 'real you', it is important to decide who you want to associate yourself with. If you wish to be online 'friends' with work colleagues, it may be prudent not to boast in your profile that your main skill is being able to undress in less than five seconds. You may also want to check the privacy settings so that you are comfortable with who can access your page and personal information. With all of this information available at the click of a button, many companies have taken to scanning people's profiles on these sites to get a more true-to-life idea of job applicants than they might admit to on their CVs.

Why do people join these sites?

For many reasons. Schoolchildren may use such sites to stay in touch and compare answers to maths questions, whereas 20- and 30-somethings juggle their social lives online. One of the reasons online social networking has caught on is the ease with which connections are made. As with all new and trendy products, the big bucks have rolled in – in 2005 media tycoon Rupert Murdoch bought MySpace for $580 million, while a Russian technology investment firm bought a 2% stake in Facebook in May 2009 for $200 million, therefore valuing the whole company at $10 billion. Public relations firms and communications strategists all over the world are scrambling over themselves to tap into this trend, perhaps having been spurred on by one rather successful politician.

SOCIAL NETWORKING

Obamamania
One aspect of Barack Obama's much-praised election campaign
was an awareness of the power of the internet. Obama, who has
been referred to as 'the first online social-networking president',
raised an astonishing $500 million online over the course of his
21-month campaign. This sum wasn't reached because of a few
wealthy and computer-savvy Democratic backers; rather, 3
million supporters made 6.5 million donations online, most of
which were for $100 or less. His new-media strategy also
allowed him to harvest over 13 million email addresses. Obama
can also be found on sites such as Facebook, where he has
almost 6.5 million supporters.

Some of the big players
MySpace: The first social networking site to have truly global
reach, MySpace is perhaps most famous for giving budding
musicians the chance to post their latest efforts online. The site's
success stories include Lily Allen and the Arctic Monkeys.

Facebook: Founded in 2004 and originally only for students
from Harvard University, this site soon reached the point where
over a million people per week were signing up. In 2008 it
became the most popular social-networking site in the UK and
has made founder Mark Zuckerburg a billionaire. After nearly
100 groups had been set up on the site demanding a return of
the chocolate bar Wispa, Cadbury obliged.

Twitter: A site that enables you to send short messages – known
as 'tweets' – of 140 characters or fewer to other members of the
site that choose to 'follow' you. Twitter applications can be
downloaded to your mobile phone so you can keep your
devoted fans regularly updated about every detail of your life,

from what you think of the new England manager to what brand of toilet paper you are using. Twitter proved it wasn't merely of use to the vain and self-obsessed in June 2009, when the world's media gained unique access via 'tweets' to the pro-Mousavi demonstrations in Iran following the controversial presidential elections.

Counterfeit Kates
One downside to social networking came to public attention just before the Oscars in February 2009 when British actress Kate Winslet bore the brunt of 'Fakebooking'; internet nuisances set up false accounts in her name and posted rude comments about Angelina Jolie, one of Winslet's rivals for the Best Actress award.

Pri-mates
In 2002 anthropologists Russell Hill and Robin Dunbar calculated that the average size of a 'social network' – the number of people with whom we maintain social relationships at any one point in our lives – is 150. This figure resulted from a study of people's Christmas card-sending habits, but it correlated with an earlier prediction that the pair had made after studying the social networks of non-human primates and their corresponding brain sizes. The bigger our brains, the more friends we can juggle.

Sri Lanka

Where is it?

Sri Lanka (meaning 'sacred island' in Sanskrit) lies off the coast of southern India. The Portuguese colonised the island in the early 16th century, followed by the Dutch, who replaced them in the mid-17th century, and then the British from 1796. Around 74% of the Sri Lankan population today are Sinhalese, mostly Buddhist, whose ancestors first came to the island in the 6th century BC. Estimates for the mainly Hindu Tamil population range from 9–18%. Tamils began migrating to Sri Lanka in the 3rd century BC from south-eastern India (what is now the state of Tamil Nadu); their descendants are known as Sri Lankan Tamils, and live mainly in the northern and eastern provinces of the island and in the capital, Colombo. In the early 19th century a second wave of Tamils (known as Indian Tamils) arrived under orders from the British to work on tea and coffee plantations in the central highlands. A variety of other ethnic groups, including Parsis from Western India and Sri Lankan Moors (Muslim descendants of Arab traders) make up the remaining population. Islam and Christianity are significant minority religions (each followed by roughly 7% of the population).

Why did ethnic tensions escalate?

Following independence in 1948, the government began introducing a series of nationalist policies which aimed to assert the new independent identity of Ceylon (as the country was then known) and shrug off the legacy of the colonial era. These policies prioritised the Sinhalese people, their language and religion (Buddhism) at the expense of Tamils and other minorities. The Sinhalese felt that the Tamils had been given an unfairly privileged position under the British; most of the English language schools had been located in the Tamil-dominated north of the island which meant that many high-profile civil service jobs requiring knowledge of English went to Tamils.

In 1956 a new government led by Solomon Bandaranaike set about changing this with the controversial Sinhala Only Act, which made Sinhalese the only official language in Sri Lanka and forced thousands of Tamil civil servants to resign because they couldn't speak it. In 1959 the world's first female Prime Minister, Srimavo Bandaranaike, took over from her husband following his assassination by a Buddhist monk, and continued his nationalist policies, although Tamil was restored as an official language in 1960. Nationalism ebbed and flowed over the next decade as the United Party snatched victory in 1965 and undid Bandaranaike's policies, only for her to wrest back power in 1970 and reintroduce them. In 1972 the country changed its name to Sri Lanka and became a republic, ending its status as a dominion with an allegiance to the British crown. Although Buddhism was not made the official state religion, the constitution said it 'shall be the duty of the State to protect and foster Buddhism', which did nothing to calm the bitterness between Sinhalese and Tamils. Ethnic tensions continued to escalate until civil war broke out in 1983, fought between the Sri Lankan army and the Tamil Tigers.

Who were the Tamil Tigers?

The Tamil New Tigers were formed in 1972 and changed their name four years later to the Liberation Tigers of Tamil Eelam, or LTTE (Eelam is the native Tamil name for Sri Lanka). More commonly known as the Tamil Tigers, this separatist organisation, labelled a terrorist group in 32 countries, fought for an independent Tamil state in north and east Sri Lanka until its eventual defeat at the hands of government forces in May 2009. The group was notorious for using women in suicide attacks and pioneering the use of the suicide-bomb jacket. The Tamil Tigers were linked to over 200 suicide attacks and assassinations of senior figures, including the former Indian Prime Minister Rajiv Gandhi in 1991, and the president of Sri Lanka, Ranasinghe Premadasa, two years later. Sri Lanka's civil war caused the displacement of over a million people and the deaths of 80–100,000 between 1983 and 2009. The war was brought to a temporary halt in 2002 when a ceasefire was declared following successful negotiations mediated by the Norwegian government.

How long did the ceasefire last?
This 2002 ceasefire offered hope as both the government and the Tamil Tigers agreed to put an end to the bloodshed. A number of agreements were hammered out during six rounds of talks, with the Tigers ending their insistence on an independent Tamil state, and both groups exploring ways in which power could be effectively devolved. In April the following year, however, the Tigers pulled out, and violence gradually returned. Elections in November 2005 saw Prime Minister Mahinda Rajapakse become president, promising voters to take a tough stance against the Tigers. Attacks increased, and the government officially brought the ceasefire to a close in January 2008.

What is the human rights situation in Sri Lanka?
Both the Sri Lankan government and the Tamil Tigers have been embroiled in accusations of human rights breaches

ranging from abductions to torture. The Tigers have also been
condemned for swelling their ranks with child soldiers (in 2004
alone they recruited 1,466 child soldiers with an average age of
14, according to UNICEF), and for using Tamil civilians as
human shields during their final stand in May 2009. The island
is also regarded as an extremely dangerous place for journalists
to work. One recent victim was Lasantha Wickramatunga,
editor of the *Sunday Leader*, shot and killed in Colombo in
January 2009.

Tigers lay down their arms
Events in early 2009 signalled progress for the government as
they won control of the towns of Mullaitivu and Kilinochchi,
home to the Tigers' military and administrative headquarters.
By April the Tamils were in an increasingly weak position as
senior commanders had been killed and government troops
had them surrounded in the country's north-east. In May 2009
the Tigers agreed to lay down their arms after Velupillai
Prabhakaran, the long-standing leader of the rebels, was killed,
and the last remaining ground they controlled was lost. The Sri
Lankan government was subject to an international outcry as
claims emerged that over 20,000 Tamil civilians were killed
during their final offensive to defeat the Tigers.

Sri Lankan refugee goes M.I.A.
Mathangi 'Maya' Arulpragasam (better known by her stage
name M.I.A.) is a Sri Lankan Tamil musician, as well as a
fashion designer and artist. Born in Hounslow in 1975, she
moved to Sri Lanka with her parents at the age of six months
before returning to Britain as a refugee from the civil war at the
age of ten. Her father, Arul Pragasam (whose nickname 'Arular'
is the title of M.I.A.'s first album), was one of the founders of

the Eelam Revolutionary Organisation of Students, a militant group with links to the Tamil Tigers. M.I.A. turned heads in February 2009 when she gave birth to her first child only days after performing at the Grammys ceremony in Los Angeles.

Stem Cells

What are stem cells?
Cells are the basic units of the body; most adult cells can't normally replicate, and have a specific role that can't be changed. A stem cell, however, is a jack of all trades, and can divide indefinitely, becoming either a new type of cell (a muscle cell or a nerve cell, for example) or another stem cell.

Where are they found?
Stem cells are found in embryos as well as adult organs and tissue. Embryonic stem cells are generally seen as the most valuable, as they can divide into almost any other type of cell. These can be harvested from young embryos of around five days old which have developed from human eggs fertilised in the lab (see **IVF**). Those found in an adult organ or tissue, however, can divide only into other cell types found in that organ or tissue: they are more a localised emergency service for when cells are damaged in that particular part of the body. Stem cells also occur in tissues in the foetus, as well as in umbilical cord blood, baby teeth and amniotic fluid.

What is all the fuss about?
The excitement surrounding stem cells is that they could be used as an ambulance for the body, treating a broad range of debilitating conditions from Alzheimer's to Parkinson's, diabetes to spinal-cord damage, and potentially lead to cures for them. If someone has suffered an injury to their brain, for instance, stem cells could be coaxed by scientists into replenishing the damaged cells.

Could this sort of treatment be dangerous?
There are worries over whether stem-cell therapy may have a
negative impact. One of stem cells' main benefits – their ability
continually to divide – is also a potential downside. There is a
danger of tumours forming if stem cells keep replicating into
more stem cells, instead of dividing into the specialised cells
that the body requires. Doctors will also need to ensure that
stem cells don't develop into the wrong type of tissue cells.
Another fear is that stem cells could pass viruses on to the
patient being treated; if the patient's immune system is already
weak, their body may struggle to cope with any virus or disease
that is passed on. Sometimes nutrients from animal sources may
be used by scientists to cultivate stem cells in the lab; here the
worry is that diseases from these sources may go unnoticed and
consequently be passed on.

Can human embryonic stem cells be used for research in the UK?
Yes. Stem cells from human embryos can be used for research
until they are 14 days old. The Human Fertilisation and
Embryology Authority is the watchdog that assesses all research
on a case-by-case basis. Embryonic stem cells have not yet been
used to treat people; however in January 2009 the world's first
human trial using embryonic stem cells for medical treatment
was approved by the US Food and Drug Administration. One of
the goals of this trial is to assess the safety of injecting embryonic
stem cell-derived cells into humans.

Is embryonic stem-cell research controversial?
Very much so. Embryonic stem-cell research attracts strong
opposition, mainly from religious and anti-abortion groups.
When cells are removed from an embryo this prevents the
embryo from developing any further. Opponents see this as

immoral, arguing that life begins at conception, and that to destroy an embryo is to destroy a human life. Stem cells from adults do not provoke the same objections; however, as outlined above, these cells are much less adaptable, and therefore less useful. Soon after becoming president of the United States, Barack Obama signed an executive order to end a ban on federal funding for most stem-cell research, which had been put in place by George W. Bush. 'As a person of faith, I believe we are called to care for each other and work to ease human suffering. I believe we have been given the capacity and will to pursue this research – and the humanity and conscience to do so responsibly,' Obama said.

Supercells

Christopher Reeve, the actor immortalised for his role as Superman, was a leading advocate of embryonic stem-cell research. In 1995 he became paralysed from the neck down after he was thrown from his horse during an equestrian event, fracturing the top two vertebrae in his neck and damaging his spinal cord. He went on to become a tireless campaigner for stem-cell research, even testifying at a Senate hearing on its federal funding, before dying of heart failure in 2004 at the age of 52.

Stocks and Bonds

What is a stock?

A stock is a piece of ownership (equity) in a public company –
more commonly referred to as 'shares' in the UK. The more
shares you buy, the greater the stake in the company you own,
and the more say you have in how it's run. Shareholders usually
make money by buying shares at one price and then selling
them later for more. However, the value of shares can go down

as well as up, so shareholders risk losing part or all of their investment.

Many companies also issue dividends to their shareholders in return for investing in their business. Dividends are a proportion of the company's post-tax profits and are usually issued every three months. New companies tend not to issue dividends, reinvesting the money instead in order to drive their own growth.

There are two types of shareholders: ordinary shareholders form the majority – they hold common shares which entitle them to vote at shareholder meetings and receive dividends. Preference shareholders receive fixed dividends and take priority over ordinary shareholders in their entitlement to a company's assets if it goes bust.

Shares can be bought in three ways: directly from a company, on an online trading platform or via a stock broker, who will give investment advice in return for a fee. This might include analysis of a stock's growth rate and dividend, and take into account the client's reasons for investing and their ability to shoulder risk.

When a company issues new stocks, it sells them directly to investors in what is known as the primary market. Once bought up, they can then be traded among other investors, in the secondary market. Stock exchanges provide facilities for brokers to trade stocks of companies that are listed on that particular exchange. The stock exchanges with the highest annual turnover are both in New York (NYSE and NASDAQ – National Association of Securities Dealers Automated Quotations), followed by Tokyo, Frankfurt, London and Shanghai. Stock prices fluctuate according to wider trends in the markets and can therefore act as markers of economic health in a particular area or sector. Stock market indices exist to compare stock prices quickly and easily: the most famous (such as the Dow Jones, S&P 500, FTSE 100 and Nikkei 225) list the largest companies on a nation's largest stock exchanges.

What are bonds?
Unlike stocks, bonds do not represent part ownership of a company; they are a form of debt or IOU. Companies and governments who need to borrow large sums of money split this up into smaller debts which are issued as bonds. These have a specific date of maturity on which the issuer must repay the loan, and a fixed rate of interest called a coupon, which is paid out to the bondholder every six months or year during the bondholding period (although some bonds have floating interest rates based on an underlying index).

The interest rate of the bond will depend on three factors:

1. Its duration – the longer the period, the higher the interest. This is to acknowledge exposure to risk (in case the bond issuer goes bust during this time), and also to take potential inflation into account.
2. The credit rating of the issuer, set by ratings agencies; companies with lower credit ratings must pay out more interest to their creditors to reward the greater risk that they are taking by lending their money.
3. General interest rates. Bond issuers must set their interest rates higher than general interest rates in order to tempt people to move their money from deposit accounts to the riskier area of bonds.

Once the bond has been issued, the bondholder is not obliged to keep it until the date of maturity. Bonds can be traded, like stocks, in the secondary market, and it is possible to make losses or gains this way. Some corporate bonds are floated on stock exchanges but the majority change hands directly in 'over the counter' trades.

The value of a bond in the secondary market fluctuates according to several factors. First, a change in general interest rates has an inverse effect on the value of bonds. For example, if general interest rates go down, so will interest rates for new bonds, which will make the higher interest rate of your bond, set at an earlier point in time, more attractive to a buyer. The value of your bond therefore rises, and you can sell it for more than you bought it. A second factor is inflation, which also has an inverse effect on the value of bonds with fixed interest rates. If inflation is increasing, the value of the fixed payouts diminishes over time. This makes the bond less attractive as a proposition in the secondary market, and its price goes down as a result. Third, with corporate bonds, the performance of the company affects its bond price. If a company is not generating enough cash comfortably to repay its creditors, ratings agencies might decide to downgrade it to below investment grade (BBB), which will cause bond prices to fall as the risk of lending money to it increases.

Which are better to invest in, stocks or bonds?
Stocks tend to carry greater reward as well as greater risk (although high-yielding, risky bonds known as 'junk' bonds do exist). If the economy is doing well, and companies are making profits, there are often higher gains to be made in stocks than with fixed-interest-rate bonds. If the economy is slowing down, however, share prices and dividends fall, and bonds can be attractive for their fixed returns. If regular income from the investment is important, bonds are a better bet as coupon payments are generally higher than stock dividends. Also, if a

company goes bankrupt, it is the bond holders who are paid first.

> 'One of the funny things about the stock market is that every time one person buys, another sells, and both think they are astute.'
>
> WILLIAM FEATHER, *American author and publisher (1889–1981)*

Tax

What are taxes?

Taxes are unbelievably boring, so let's not go into too many details. They are the government's way of raising money to pay for public services, which include education, health, defence, social security and emergency services.

What are the main types of tax in the UK?

Income tax – on the money you earn in employment or self-employment. It's been a fixture in the UK since William Pitt the Younger introduced it in 1798 to help fund the Napoleonic War effort. There are different bands depending on your salary. Currently, earnings up to £37,400 are taxed at 20%, and anything above that at 40%. The first £6,475 of your earnings comes tax-free.

National Insurance Contributions – originally introduced in 1948 to provide funds for welfare benefits, NICS are what the government raises sneakily while promising not to raise income tax. Employers and employees must pay NICs, and there are different rates depending on whether you are employed or self-employed. Also known as 'the tax that dare not speak its name'.

VAT (Value Added Tax) – a tax on goods and services exchanged in business transactions, paid for by the consumer. A French invention, VAT was introduced in the UK in 1973. The normal VAT rate of 17.5% was reduced to 15% by Chancellor Alistair Darling for the whole of 2009 in a bid to boost the economy by encouraging consumers to spend more. Certain things are exempt from VAT, such as health services, rent, insurance, stamps, books, newspapers and most food (including meat, ready meals, cakes and biscuits, but excluding snack food, restaurant meals, chocolate-covered biscuits and hot takeaways). In 1991, the courts had to ponder whether the Jaffa Cake was a chocolate-covered biscuit (VAT-rated) or a cake (VAT-exempt). In the end they went for cake. And in 1994, the owners of Blackpool Pleasure Beach tried to get their 'Big One' rollercoaster classed as a form of public transport in order to exempt it from VAT. The VAT tribunal initially agreed, but the decision was later overturned.

Council tax – this contributes to local government revenue, helping to pay for things like rubbish collection and recycling services, social housing benefits, police and fire services, leisure centres, parks, flood defences and CCTV installation. How much you pay depends on where you live – council tax on a £200,000 property in Richmond, Surrey currently costs £2,662 per year, compared to £1,146 in Westminster. Council tax replaced the unpopular Poll Tax in 1993.

Business Rates – the business equivalent of Council Tax.

Excise Duties – taxes levied on alcohol, tobacco and gambling (sometimes called 'vice taxes') and other things such as road fuel.

Corporation Tax – taxes on the annual profits that companies make.

Other taxes – these include road tax, the TV licence (which pays for the BBC), Stamp Duty or Stamp Duty Reserve Tax (charged on purchase of shares), Stamp Duty Land Tax (charged on all purchases of property or land over £175,000), Capital Gains Tax (on profits from sales of capital assets such as shares), and Inheritance Tax, paid by the personal representatives of a deceased person with an estate (total combined value of property, money, possessions and investments) worth more than £312,000.

What is the Budget?

This is the Chancellor of the Exchequer's annual fiscal plan for government revenue and spending, outlining which taxes are going to be raised or lowered. Usually announced in early March, in 2009 it was delayed until late April for reasons relating to the recession. Alistair Darling's 2009 budget, designed to combat the effects of the recession, was optimistic in its forecast that the UK's economy would grow by 1.25% in 2010, despite the IMF's predictions that it would continue to shrink by another 0.4% (see **World Bank/IMF**).

Famous tax evaders

Al Capone, Luciano Pavarotti, O.J. Simpson, Wesley Snipes, Sophia Loren, Chuck Berry and Boris Becker have all been found guilty of tax evasion, while Geoffrey Chaucer, Thomas Paine, Robert Burns and Richard (Dick) Whittington all worked as customs officers at some stage of their careers.

Notable tax havens

Andorra, the Bahamas, Barbados, Bermuda, the Isle of Man, Liechtenstein and Monaco (amongst others) have little or no taxation, and therefore attract people seeking to reduce their tax bills by emigrating there. The OECD (Organisation for Economic Co-operation and Development) is demanding that these 'offshore' countries be more transparent in exchanging information about tax exiles and others who have opened bank accounts or registered companies there, some of whom are thought to be tax evaders. Andorra, Liechtenstein and Monaco are the three countries the OECD lists as being unco-operative in sharing this information.

One for you, nineteen for me

George Harrison wrote the song 'Taxman' (the first track on the Beatles' 1966 album *Revolver*) as a protest against the 95% top tax rate that multi-millionaires such as the band had to pay under Harold Wilson's Labour government of the time.

Tibet

Where is it?

Tibet, sometimes described as 'the roof of the world' due to its average altitude of 14,000 feet, is a vast plateau north of the Himalaya mountain range. At 12,500 feet, Lhasa is one of the highest capital cities in the world (nearly three times higher than Ben Nevis, the highest mountain in the British Isles). The indigenous Tibetan people have a language and distinct culture

stretching back thousands of years, and are mainly Buddhist. Tibet has been ruled as an independent country, divided into different countries, and ruled over by China at various stages throughout its long history. It has been a Chinese province since 1959 but is well known as a disputed territory thanks to the high profile of the Dalai Lama (Tibet's spiritual leader and political leader-in-exile) and several international campaigns which have drawn attention to the oppression of the Tibetan people at the hands of the Chinese.

What is the historical background?

Tibet and China both lay claims to historical sovereignty over the region, and offer differing interpretations of history to back up their assertions. China argues that its government has exercised sovereignty over Tibet for over 700 years since the Yuan dynasty, while Tibet contends that it was independent for centuries prior to that (since its unification by the Emperor Songzen Gampo in the 7th century) and that subsequent Chinese rule has been far from constant. One much-debated period was between 1912 (when the 13th Dalai Lama declared independence) and 1949, during which time Tibet essentially ran itself while China faced wars both at home and abroad. Some argue that Tibet was independent during this time, with its own foreign affairs bureau and its neutral stance in the Second World War. China, however, denies that this amounted to independence, pointing out that Tibet wasn't officially recognised by any major Western power at this time.

What happened next?

Soon after Chairman Mao took charge of the newly formed People's Republic of China in 1949, he ordered troops into Tibet to impose his country's authority over the region. In 1951 Tibet was forced to sign the 'Seventeen Point Agreement' which effectively ceded control to China. Although Buddhism could still be practised and autonomy exercised, the agreement allowed Chinese military and civil headquarters to be set up in Lhasa. This agreement caused bitter resentment, fuelling a Tibetan resistance movement that was encouraged by the CIA.

In 1959, Chinese soldiers brutally suppressed a revolt against Chinese rule, forcing the Dalai Lama to flee to Dharamsala in northern India with his government (the Central Tibetan Administration) and 90,000 Tibetans. The Dalai Lama and the CTA have been based there in exile ever since, while China has ruled Tibet as an 'autonomous region' (so-called despite the fact that any local legislation must first be approved by the central government in Beijing). There have been criticisms from around the world over China's handling of Tibet, for example in its destruction of thousands of Buddhist monasteries during the Cultural Revolution, and human rights abuses including the torture of political prisoners, 'patriotic re-education' of monks and nuns and suppression of Tibetan culture.

Free Tibet

Free Tibet, the movement for full independence, has gained strong international momentum with support from human rights groups and celebrities such as Richard Gere, Steven Seagal and Radiohead, while recent international protests focused on disrupting the torch rally in the lead-up to the Beijing Olympics in 2008. Demonstrations (said to be the most serious for 20 years) also broke out in Tibet itself; these were violently suppressed by Chinese troops. The Dalai Lama advocated strongly for Tibetan autonomy, but not independence, until his semi-retirement from the political cause in December 2008. His 'middle way' for Tibet envisaged a democratic, internally

autonomous region whose defence and foreign affairs were
handled, at least in part, by China, and which enjoyed the
economic benefits that being part of China entailed.

The first Dalai Lama – and the last?

The first Dalai Lama ('Ocean of Wisdom') was Gyalwa Gendun
Drup (1391–1474), student of Tsongkhapa, a Tibetan Lama
(Buddhist spiritual teacher) who founded the *Gelugpa* sect,
which grew to become the region's main Buddhist tradition.
After Gendun Drup's death a young boy, Gendun Gyatso, was
identified by the High Lamas as his reincarnation, and so began
the tradition of the Dalai Lama being reborn in another body.
High Lamas find the reincarnation of the Dalai Lama through a
dream, by following smoke if a Dalai Lama is cremated, or by
visiting the Tibetan Holy Lake, Lhamo Lhatso, for a sign. They
then use a series of tests to ascertain whether the boy, born at a
similar time to the last Dalai Lama's death, is the true
reincarnation. One such test is to present the infant with some
of the last Dalai Lama's possessions. If he picks them from a
collection of other random odds and ends, this indicates that he
may be the true heir.

The current and 14th Dalai Lama is Tenzin Gyatso, born in
July 1935, who was identified as the 13th Dalai Lama's
reincarnation at the age of two. He has served as Tibet's leader
since 1950 (longer than any other living head of state, including
Queen Elizabeth II). His successor, however, has not yet been
chosen; indeed, in the 1970s the Dalai Lama said he thought he
would be the last to hold the position. Since then however, he
has indicated that his successor might be born outside of Tibet,
and recently said that the next Dalai Lama should no longer
have political responsibility; this, he thought, should go instead
to a democratically elected leader of the Tibetan people. The

Chinese have sought to strengthen their grip on Tibet by nominating a Panchen Lama (second in seniority to the Dalai Lama) who they hope will one day play a role in choosing a Beijing-friendly Dalai Lama. Although this Chinese-nominated Panchen Lama is not generally recognised as such by Tibetans, who have nominated a rival Panchen Lama of their own, fears remain that the Chinese will try to capitalise in some way if the role of Tibetan leader is still vacant when the current Dalai Lama passes away.

Seven Years in Tibet
This 1997 film tells the true story of Heinrich Harrer (Brad Pitt) and Peter Aufschnaiter (David Thewlis) who leave Austria in 1939 on an expedition to the Himalaya. They are subsequently arrested by the British after news arrives that Germany has invaded Poland, and held in a prisoner-of-war camp. They escape and eventually find themselves in Lhasa, where Harrer becomes a friend and teacher of the Dalai Lama. The film is based on Harrer's memoir *Seven Years in Tibet*. Pitt and Thewlis are permanently banned from China because of their involvement with the film.

UK Elections

How often are general elections held and who decides when they happen?
General elections are not fixed, but must occur before the end of the parliamentary session, which lasts a maximum of five years. The governing party can decide when to call the election, and will do so at a time that maximises their political advantage. The next general election is to be held on or before 3 June 2010. Traditionally, general elections happen on a Thursday – the last time it took place on a different day of the week was on Tuesday, 27 October 1931.

How many MPs are there?
There are currently 646 MPs, each of whom occupies a seat in the House of Commons and represents a geographical area known as a constituency. At the last General Election in 2005, Labour won 356 seats, the Conservatives 198 and the Liberal Democrats 62, with other parties sharing the remainder. The next general election is likely to yield very different results.

What is the voter turnout in general elections?
In 2005, 61.3% of the electorate (the body of people with the right to vote) came out to vote, a slight rise on the all-time low of 59.4% in 2001; 2005, however, saw the lowest ever percentage of the electorate voting for the winning party. Labour won 35.3% of the vote, but this translated to only 21.6% of the electorate, or roughly a fifth of the UK's eligible voting population. Turnout for European Parliament elections in the UK is one of the lowest in Europe, with only 34.7% of the electorate showing up in 2009 (compared to the EU average of

43.1%). This was worse than the 38.5% who showed up in 2004, but an improvement at least on the woeful 24% of 1999.

When did women get the vote?
In 1918, for women over the age of 30, and in 1928 this was reduced to the age of 21.

When was the voting age reduced to 18?
In 1969, for both men and women.

What is a hung parliament?
For a party to hold a majority in the House of Commons it needs to win more than 50% of the seats available (at least 324, at present). If no party wins an outright majority, this results in what is known as a hung parliament (also known by the Lib Dems as a balanced parliament). If this occurs, either a minority government is formed, a coalition government is negotiated and then formed, or parliament is dissolved and another general election called in the hope that the outcome will be more decisive.

What is a minority government?
A government in which the ruling party or coalition does not have an overall majority of seats in parliament. Minority governments are generally weak because they can be brought down easily by a vote of no confidence (see **UK Political System**). The last minority government in Westminster was formed by Labour leader Harold Wilson after the February 1974 election, in which he narrowly defeated Edward Heath's Conservative party by 301 seats to 297 (Wilson called another General Election in October that year and won a tiny majority of 3). Scottish National Party (SNP) leader Alex Salmond

currently heads a minority government in Scotland after his party defeated Labour by 47 seats to 46 (out of 129 seats) in the Scottish Parliamentary Elections of 2007. Neither the SNP nor Labour were able to negotiate a coalition government with other parties in order to gain a majority, so a minority government was formed.

What is a coalition government?

A coalition government is made up of two or more parties in co-operation with one another. When coalition governments are being negotiated, smaller parties can suddenly become very important by holding the balance of power and becoming 'kingmakers' in deciding which of the larger parties to side with. It is often speculated whether the Liberal Democrats would form a coalition government with Labour or the Conservatives in the event of a hung parliament, or whether they would agree to support specific aspects of a minority government in return for certain concessions. The last coalition government in the UK was Winston Churchill's brief 'caretaker government' following the end of World War II in 1945. In February 1974, Edward Heath at first refused to resign as prime minister following his narrow defeat to Labour's Harold Wilson while he tried unsuccessfully to get the Liberals to form a coalition with his Conservative Party.

How are MPs elected?

In every constituency, candidates from different parties (or independent candidates) compete against one another for election as that constituency's Member of Parliament. In general elections a Single Member Plurality or 'First-Past-the-Post' (FPTP) system is used, which simply means that the candidate with the highest number of votes wins their constituency's seat.

In the past this method has been criticised as being unrepresentative, particularly by the Lib Dems, because it favours the largest two parties (Labour and Conservative) while penalising the smaller ones; if, for example, a smaller party were to consistently gain 20% of the vote in every constituency (and therefore a fifth of the overall vote), they would not win any seats because there would always be a more popular party in each constituency. At the 2005 general election, the Liberal Democrats won over a fifth (22.1%) of the nationwide vote but gained less than a tenth of the seats available (62 out of 646) because they lacked concentrated support. Meanwhile Labour won only 35.3% of the vote but had the support where it mattered, winning 356 seats, a majority of 66 and a third term of government. Advocates of First-Past-the-Post contend that the strength of the Westminster system actually resides in this two-party bias, as it allows one party to govern the country with strong and uncompromised leadership while the other forms a healthy opposition. It also provides a 'constituency link' between voters and their MPs – all voters have a directly accountable MP who is in some sense 'theirs', who they can vote out if their views are not being represented.

What is Proportional Representation?

Proportional Representation (PR) refers to a number of electoral systems which attempt to represent, to a greater or lesser degree of proportionality, the number of votes a party wins with the number of seats it gains in parliament. The simplest of these is Direct Representation, which does away with constituencies altogether and allocates a party's seats according to its share of the vote. If this had been used at the 2005 election (and everyone had voted the same way, which isn't necessarily the case given that voting systems themselves can influence the way people vote), Labour would have won 219 seats, the Conservatives 200 and the Liberal Democrats 138, resulting in a hung parliament. Although, for some, Direct Representation is the fairest electoral system possible, it severs the link between MPs and specific regions by scrapping constituencies, and in being fully proportional it would award seats to extreme and undesirable parties such as the BNP, who would have won four seats in 2005 under such a system. Many other forms of Proportional Representation have been devised, all with their own strengths and weaknesses, including Single Transferable Vote (used in the Australian Senate and Republic of Ireland) and closed or open Party List (used by most of continental Europe, South Africa, Israel, Russia and in European Parliament elections). In general, Proportional Representation systems rarely produce outright majorities for one party, which makes coalition governments made up of two or more parties the norm. It is harder for coalition governments to make bold decisions on a particular issue because they are usually compromised in some way, and they are also harder to kick out of office at an election.

Apart from general elections, what other elections happen in the UK?
Quite a few, which bewilderingly involve six different electoral systems. There are elections to the Welsh National Assembly, Scottish Parliament, Northern Ireland Assembly, European Parliament, local government elections (which elect councillors to run local services), mayoral elections (since their introduction by the 2000 Local Government Act) and by-elections. By-elections take place in individual constituencies outside general elections to elect a new MP in case of the 'resignation, expulsion, elevation to the peerage, bankruptcy, lunacy or death of the sitting Member'.

What is the Electoral Commission?

This is an independent body set up by the UK parliament to oversee, regulate and publicise the democratic process. It sets standards for elections and observes them, conducts boundary reviews for local government, ensures that party and election financing rules are followed, updates electoral registers and provides guidance for electoral administrators.

Things can only get better

In 1998 Lord Jenkins was commissioned to come up with an improved electoral system for the UK. His solution, explained in the Jenkins Report, was named 'Alternative Vote Top-Up', a mixture of FPTP and PR, in which everyone has two votes (one for a constituency candidate and one for a party). The Labour government, who commissioned the report, thanked Lord Jenkins before deciding that the current system, which had helped them to a landslide victory in 1997, would probably do for the moment. Since then, electoral reform has faded from the political agenda in the UK.

UK Political System

What system of government operates in the UK?
The UK is a parliamentary democracy with a constitutional
monarch, or sovereign. The monarch is the head of state and the
prime minister the head of government. The people are
represented by members of parliament (MPs).

What is the difference between government and parliament?
The government, also known as the executive, is in charge of
running the country, implementing policy and drafting laws.
Executive power is in the hands of the prime minister and the
cabinet (a body of senior ministers chosen by the prime
minister, most of whom are secretaries of state with specific
responsibilities (portfolios) such as health, education or
defence). The members of the executive are also members of
parliament (or, less commonly, lords). Parliament's role is to
examine and challenge the government's work and to debate
and pass laws – it is the highest legislative (law-making) body in
the UK. It consists of two chambers: the House of Commons
and the House of Lords. The House of Commons is the more
important; its 646 MPs are elected by the people in general
elections at least every five years. Government is answerable to
parliament; in order to survive, a government must retain the
confidence of a majority in the House of Commons. If the
House votes to indicate that it has no confidence in the
government, the government would call a general election.
James Callaghan was the last prime minister to be brought
down by a vote of no confidence in 1979.

Is there a constitution in the UK?

There is no single written constitution (set of rules about government) in the UK – unlike, for example, the US (see **US Political System**). The UK constitution is a combination of statute law (written legislation created by parliament), common law (law made by judges) and European law, as well as some unwritten sources such as parliamentary conventions and royal prerogatives (special types of authority and immunity usually exercised by ministers rather than the Crown). Because the UK constitution comprises statute law, it is constantly evolving, reformed by each new Act of Parliament that is passed. The most important idea of the constitution is that of parliamentary sovereignty – parliament's supremacy over the executive and judicial branches of government and its power to create, change or abolish any law.

How are new laws made?

Proposals for new laws begin in either of the houses (but more often in the Commons) as bills. There are various types of bill, including public bills, which affect everyone in the country and are usually put forward by government ministers, private members' bills, proposed by MPs or lords who are not in government, and private bills, proposed by (and affecting) only specific companies or organisations. A bill must go through several stages of reading and debate in the house in which it is introduced before being passed on (if successful) to the second house, where a similar process occurs. Once the second house has made any amendments and passed the bill, it returns to the first house, where these amendments are examined and considered.

Once both houses have agreed upon a final text, which may involve a bit more toing and froing, the bill eventually

progresses to the Queen, who grants her royal assent, enabling
the bill to become law as an Act of Parliament. Government bills
are often circulated in draft form for consultation by
committees before being proposed formally in parliament.
These draft bills may have their basis in white or green papers –
documents proposing policy changes issued by the government
in order to invite feedback and debate (green papers often
suggest alternative policy options whereas white papers are
usually more firm in their recommendations).

Who are the Lords and what do they do?
The House of Lords is the unelected second (or 'upper')
chamber of parliament. There are around 750 lords, 630 of
whom are life peers (appointed for life by the Queen on the
recommendation of the prime minister). Hereditary peers
(lords whose titles were automatically passed down through the
generations of their families) were abolished by the 1999 House
of Lords Act, although 92 of them were internally elected to
remain, pending further reform; 26 bishops of the Church of
England (the established Church of the State) and up to 12 Law
Lords (senior judges) make up the remaining membership of
the house.

The lords have a legislative function, proposing, debating and
amending laws, but they cannot veto bills passed by the
Commons; they can only delay them from being pushed
through for a year. The lords' power of veto was abolished by
the 1911 Parliament Act, which gave them two years' delaying
power, later reduced to one year by the 1949 Parliament Act.
The only laws passed without the assent of the lords since 1949
are the 1991 War Crimes Act, 1999 European Parliamentary
Elections Act, 2000 Sexual Offences (Amendment) Act and the
2004 Hunting Act. The House of Lords also has a judicial

function, with its 12 Law Lords comprising the Appelate Committee of the House of Lords, the highest court in the land. However, the judicial function of the house will cease in October 2009 when a separate Supreme Court will assume this purpose. Reform of the House of Lords is a subject of ongoing debate, with some calling for abolition of the remaining hereditary peers, while others (such as Secretary of State for Justice Jack Straw) demand that it become a democratically elected chamber like the House of Commons.

How powerful is the Queen?

In theory, the Queen can use the royal prerogative, a set of special powers possessed by the sovereign alone which do not require parliamentary consent in order to be exercised. These would let her dismiss ministers and governments (including those of other states of which she is monarch), dissolve parliament, choose the new prime minister, refuse royal assent to new laws, pardon convicted criminals and command the army. In practice, however, it is unrealistic that she would ever exercise these powers, because to do so would provoke a constitutional crisis. The last time royal assent was denied was when Queen Anne vetoed the Scottish Militia Bill in 1708, and the last dismissal of a government by the monarch was in 1834, when William IV dismissed Lord Melbourne's Whig government and replaced it with Sir Robert Peel's Tories.

The powers of the royal prerogative are still important, however, because some have now passed to the prime minister and his executive, who can use them to take action without consulting parliament. As a result the government can (amongst other things) declare war, make treaties, change criminal sentences, recognise foreign states and refuse to issue passports whenever it likes. In 2005 Home Secretary Charles Clarke used the royal prerogative to deny passports to two British men freed from Guantánamo Bay, and in 2000 Northern Ireland Secretary Peter Mandelson used it to grant an early prison release to James McArdle, the IRA man responsible for the Docklands bombing of 1996, under the terms of the Good Friday Agreement (see **Northern Ireland**).

What are political parties?

Most members of the Commons and the Lords belong to a political party – an organised group of people with similar ideas on how to run the country. The largest party in the Commons (usually) forms the government, while the second largest forms the opposition, with its own leader and shadow cabinet, which examines and criticises the activities of the government as well as coming up with alternative policies. Parliamentarians who do not hold positions in government or opposition (the vast majority of MPs) are known as backbenchers, because they sit behind the government and opposition who sit opposite one another on the front benches in the House of Commons. They can voice their opinions with relative freedom as they are not constrained by government or opposition policy. Each party has its own Chief Whip – a person in charge of imposing party discipline and ensuring votes are cast a certain way – who must work hard to keep the backbenchers in the party line. At the start of every week the Chief Whip issues a letter ('the whip') to every MP in their party outlining the schedule for the coming week. Next to any debate in which votes will be cast in parliament is the sentence 'Your attendance is absolutely essential,' underlined one, two or three times depending on the importance of the vote (a one-, two-, or three-line whip). MPs can be thrown out of their party for defying a three-line whip.

What do MPs do?

Members of parliament divide their time between their constituency, parliament and working for their party. In their constituency, they might attend functions, make visits and meet constituents to find out what issues need to be raised in parliament. They need to be present in parliament to vote on legislation, attend debates and take part in committees which examine specific issues in detail. In May 2009 the expenses scandal brought to light another favourite pastime of MPs: spending extravagant sums of money on gratuitous things and then charging it to the taxpayer as part of their second home allowance (which they were allowed because of their need to travel frequently between their constituency and Westminster). Tory Sir Peter Viggers notoriously spent £1,645 on a floating island for his ducks (part of a total £30,000 he claimed in gardening expenses), while Labour's John Prescott claimed for a set of mock Tudor beams for the front of his house as well as two new toilet seats in the space of two years. Some other MPs found it hard to make up their mind which was their main home and which was their second home, 'flipping' between the two and claiming expenses on both. The expenses system is under independent review and is likely to be reformed.

'I've done nothing criminal, that's the most awful thing, and do you know what it's about? Jealousy. I've got a very, very large house. Some people say it looks like Balmoral.'

Tory MP ANTHONY STEEN *explains away his Totnes constituents' anger over an £87,729 claim for work on his home and estate over a period of four years (May 2009)*

UN

What is it?

The United Nations (UN) is an international organisation established on 24 October 1945 to help stabilise relationships between countries after the Second World War. Its purpose is to maintain peace and security; to develop friendly relationships between countries, to help solve global problems and to promote human rights. The organisation supports countries in

a number of ways, from clearing landmines, helping relief efforts in the aftermath of disasters and intervening as peacekeepers in conflict situations. There are currently 16 UN peacekeeping missions going on worldwide, involving a total of 114,000 people.

Why was it established?
After World War I, the League of Nations was set up to promote international co-operation and peace. This organisation achieved some successes, notably helping resolve disputes between Sweden and Finland, and Greece and Bulgaria. But around two decades after being established the League faded away after being powerless to stop Italy's invasion of Abyssinia (now Ethiopia) and Japan's invasion of Manchuria. Benito Mussolini, Italy's prime minister, quipped that 'the League is very well when sparrows shout, but no good at all when eagles fall out'. The UN was established after World War II as a successor to the League.

How do countries become members?
They have to accept the UN Charter, which sets out both the rights and obligations of member countries. In 1945, this Charter was signed by 51 countries. There are now 192 members – almost every country in the world. The only non-members of the UN are the Vatican City (Holy See), which is an official observer state; Palestine, also an observer with special 'non-member entity' status represented by the PLO; Taiwan, which the UN considers part of China; Western Sahara, a 'non-self-governing territory' whose status as a sovereign state is in dispute between Morocco and the Sahrawi Arab Democratic Republic; and the Cook Islands and Niue, which are represented at the UN by New Zealand.

Who is the boss?
Ban Ki-moon, a South Korean diplomat, is the current UN secretary-general. He came to the job with the nickname 'the slippery eel' in honour of his reputation for dodging tough questions from journalists. Another nickname, given to him during his time at the Korean foreign ministry, was 'Ban-chusa', which means the bureaucrat. Shortly after being elected the eighth secretary-general, he demonstrated his charismatic side at a dinner for UN correspondents by singing 'Ban Ki-moon is coming to town' to the tune of the familiar Christmas jingle.

Does it have its own army?
No. However, many UN peacekeepers are armed, and are soldiers who belong to the armed forces of their native countries. There have been over 60 peacekeeping operations since 1948, including missions in Haiti, Sudan, the Democratic Republic of Congo, Kosovo, Georgia and Lebanon. Well over 100 countries have contributed soldiers and military officers, police and civilians to help these peacekeeping efforts.

How is it funded?
Funds for the UN are mainly sourced by contributions from member countries. The amount of money countries contribute depends on their means. The latest two-year budget stands at $3.8 billion.

What is the structure of the UN?
The UN Charter established the General Assembly, the Security Council, the Economic and Social Council, the Trusteeship Council, the Secretariat and the International Court of Justice.

General Assembly – the main deliberative, policymaking and representative arm of the organisation, composed of all 192 members.

Security Council – has responsibility for maintaining international peace and security and is made up of five permanent members (China, France, Russia, the UK and the USA) and ten non-permanent members, elected by the General Assembly for two-year terms, five of which change each year. The five permanent members each have the power of veto and can therefore block any action proposed by the other members. The Security Council issues resolutions in reaction to situations in which peace is threatened. A resolution might do a number of things, for example alter the mandate of a peacekeeping mission, impose sanctions on a country, or establish international guidelines on nuclear non-proliferation (see **Nuclear Weapons**). Many of these resolutions are issued under Chapter VII of the UN Charter ('Action with Respect to Threats to the Peace, Breaches of the Peace, and Acts of Aggression') which makes them legally binding. Other resolutions issued under Chapter VI ('Pacific Settlement of Disputes') are not generally considered legally binding. The Security Council issues a resolution if at least 9 of its 15 members have voted in favour of it, and none of the permanent members have used their power of veto.

UN Economic and Social Council – co-ordinates economic, social and related work of specialised UN agencies.

Trusteeship Council – set up to help 'trust territories' move towards independence or self-government. These were territories placed under the administration of one or more countries for various reasons, such as having become detached from a country after a conflict. (It suspended operations when Palau, an island nation in the Pacific ocean which was the last trust territory, achieved independence in 1994).

Secretariat – responsible for carrying out the organisation's day-to-day work.

International Court of Justice – settles legal disputes brought to its attention by countries. It also provides advice on legal questions from UN organisations.

How about other UN organisations?

There are a number of funds and programmes, specialised agencies and other related organisations within what is referred to as the 'United Nations System'. The funds (for example the United Nations Children's Fund – UNICEF) and programmes (such as the World Food Programme – WFP) are subsidiary bodies of the General Assembly, while agencies such as the World Health Organisation (WHO) or the Educational, Scientific and Cultural Organisation (UNESCO) are linked to the UN by special agreements – they report to either the Economic and Social Council or the General Assembly. There are also related organisations such as the World Trade Organisation (WTO), who have their own legislative bodies and budgets. (For the UN Millennium Development Goals, see **Aid**.)

How effective is the UN?

The UN has been credited with many achievements since it was set up over 60 years ago. These include distributing over 2 million tons of food every year, helping to eradicate smallpox, aiding the transition to democratic rule in, for example,

Namibia, Nicaragua, El Salvador and Guatemala, and helping
East Timor achieve its independence in 2002. It has also been
criticised, however, particularly for its ineffective peacekeeping
missions; the UN has admitted responsibility for failing to
prevent the Rwandan genocide in 1994 in which around
800,000 were killed, and doing nothing to stop the Srebrenica
massacre in 1995 in which 8,000 Bosnian Muslims were
murdered by Serbian soldiers. More recently the UN has been
condemned for the failure of UNAMID and MONUC, its
missions in Darfur and the DR Congo, to protect civilians
adequately from the fighting (see **Darfur** and **Congo**).

Has it been caught up in controversies?

Yes. In 1996 an Oil for Food Programme, administered by the
UN, was set up so that Iraq could buy supplies such as food and
medicine with the proceeds from oil sales, which were
regulated. However, this programme became mired in
controversy, with accusations of widespread corruption. The
final report from an independent inquiry, which came out in
September 2005, described extensive manipulation by Saddam
Hussein which led to nearly two billion dollars being made by
his regime through illicit kickbacks and surcharges. The Iraqi
regime was far from the only guilty party; over 2,000 companies
were involved in illicit payments. The report was highly critical
of the UN's role and called for reform.

White House, red face

The United Nations may not seem like the most terrifically
inspired of names, but US President Franklin D. Roosevelt was
so excited when he came up with it on New Year's Day 1942 that
he sped in his wheelchair to Winston Churchill's guest room in
the White House to announce his brainwave, only to find him in

the bath. Churchill is said to have reassured an embarrassed FDR that 'The Prime Minister of Great Britain has nothing to hide from the President of the United States.'

US Elections

Who can vote?
All US citizens who are 18 and above are eligible to vote.
Originally the US Constitution limited voting to white men over
the age of 21, but subsequent changes – including the Fourteenth
and Fifteenth Amendments of 1868 and 1870 and the Voting
Rights Act in 1965, which gave blacks and other minorities the
right to vote, and the Nineteenth Amendment, passed in 1920,
which gave women the right – made suffrage universal.

How is a president elected?

Unlike the UK, where an election is called by the prime minister and voters cast their ballots a little over three weeks later, the process of electing an American president is a long, complicated and multi-layered system. Here's how it pans out:

The primaries

Beginning in January of an election year, primaries are the first stepping stone presidential candidates must successfully negotiate. At this stage there are a number of candidates for each party, each of whom hopes to win their party's nomination.

In order to determine the preferred candidate for a party each state holds either a primary or a caucus. At primaries people cast their votes in secret at the ballot box: some primaries are 'open', meaning anyone can vote, but others are 'closed', meaning only people registered to the party can vote. The procedures for caucuses are more complicated and differ depending on which state you are in, but in most of them locals hold meetings anywhere from homes to schools and debate the pros and cons of the candidates. At Republican caucuses, secret ballots are usually used for voting, but at Democratic ones the process can seem a bit like a school disco, with people breaking off in clusters through the room in order to show support for different candidates.

The level of support for a candidate from voters at the primaries and caucuses determines the number of 'pledged delegates,' allocated in each state depending on the size of the population, that go on to represent them at the party conventions.

Iowa holds the first caucus and New Hampshire the first primary. 'Super Tuesday' is (unsurprisingly) a Tuesday when a large number of states all hold their primaries or caucuses. At the last election this took place on 5 February 2008, when 24 states voted. The remaining primaries and caucuses carry on until June.

Party conventions

In order to get the nomination from a party at the national convention in the summer, a candidate must have the support of the majority of delegates. Although candidates have normally wrapped up their party's nomination before this point, it is at these conventions that they are formally endorsed as a presidential candidate. If, however, rival candidates are supported by a similar number of pledged delegates, the unpledged delegates – who are essentially party elders, from senators to former presidents – may play an important role. These unpledged delegates (called super-delegates by the Democrats) are free to vote however they wish, and are the final decisive factor.

More campaigning

After the gruelling primary campaigns, the nominated candidates from each party must go head-to-head in the race for the White House. They travel across the country, spend millions on advertising, appear in debates on television and do anything else in their power to court voters.

Election Day

The general election always takes place in November. The election is not decided by popular vote but by the electoral college system, established in the Constitution. Essentially this system works as follows: there are 538 electoral college votes across all 50 states and the District of Colombia (better known as Washington DC, the capital of the United States). The number of electoral votes in a state is determined by adding up its number of representatives and senators (see below). For example, in Texas there are 32 representatives and two senators, giving the state 34 electoral votes.

All of the ballots from US citizens in a state are counted up. Whichever candidate has the most votes gets all of the electoral college votes for that state, no matter how narrow the result. In Texas, even if a candidate scrapes victory by a couple of thousand votes, he or she will walk away with all 34 electoral college votes.

In order to win the presidential election a candidate must rack up 270 electoral college votes. Winning the most votes overall won't necessarily spell victory for a candidate; in 2000 Al Gore won 48.38% of the vote compared with 47.87% for George W. Bush – but Bush became president because he won 271 electoral college votes.

Whoever emerges victor after this arduous battle becomes the president-elect until inaugurated as president in January.

How often are representatives and senators elected?

Unlike the presidential election, which takes place every four years, senators are elected to the Senate every six years and representatives to the House of Representatives every two years. In order to decide which candidates are on the ballot for the general election, most states hold primary elections, though sometimes the candidate has no opposition. A candidate automatically gets on the ballot paper for a primary if he/she represents a major political party. Minor parties have their own rules for deciding candidates, while if a candidate is running as an independent they simply nominate themselves. Both independent and minor party candidates must comply with certain state requirements to make it on to the general election ballot.

For Representative elections all eligible voters who live in the congressional district for which the candidate is standing can cast a vote, whereas with Senate elections every eligible voter in the state can cast their ballot.

There are three prerequisites for candidates wishing to stand in an election. They must be a certain age by the time they take office (at least 30 for a Senator and 25 for a Representative), a US citizen (at least nine years for a Senator and seven for a Representative) and a resident in the state he or she represents.

What is gerrymandering?

Gerrymandering, or redistricting, is the manipulation of electoral district boundaries for the political advantage of the party in power. State legislatures are responsible for defining the boundaries of their own constituencies, and it is an accepted part of the political process that they will change them to favour their own party. The population of each district must be maintained as equal, and limiting the political influence of a particular ethnic group is prohibited by the Voting Rights Act of 1965, but otherwise it is perfectly legal. Traditionally, gerrymandering took place after the national census at the beginning of each decade. However, a ruling by the Supreme Court in 2006 approved nearly all of a controversial mid-decade redistricting plan pushed through by the Republican state government of Texas in 2003. This ruling effectively means that other state legislatures will be able to redraw their boundaries as often as they like.

The most common redistricting techniques are known as 'packing' and 'cracking'; packing is done by herding opposition party voters into the same district so that they win it easily but cannot influence the outcome of other districts, whereas cracking spreads an opposition group over several districts, splitting them into ineffective minorities. Usually both techniques are combined in order to maximise wastage of the opposition's votes. Computer software is used to analyse vast amounts of data and redraw the electoral boundaries as favourably as possible for the party in power.

There are those who think that gerrymandering is undemocratic on the grounds that it violates the principle of fair competition. The winners of district elections become members of the House of Representatives, the chamber of US government intended by the framers of the US Constitution to be most responsive to changes in public opinion ('a numerous and changeable body', in the words of James Madison, 'father' of the Constitution). However, gerrymandering has polarised districts to the extent that nowadays most seats in the House (around 400 out of 435) are not seriously contested but determined by the state legislatures who decide where the district boundaries should be.

Advocates of gerrymandering say that constituencies are there to be manipulated, and that in some cases it can help to better represent the opinions of minority groups. Opponents have suggested various measures to make elections more competitive, such as using fixed districts, devising algorithms or precise rules to determine the shape of districts, or changing the voting system altogether.

The word gerrymandering comes from Elbridge Gerry, a Governor of Massachusetts who approved the redistricting plans proposed by his Democratic-Republican party in 1812. These included one extremely convoluted district shaped like a salamander. Although this wasn't the first instance of redistricting, the hybrid *gerrymander* was coined afterwards to describe the practice.

Who would get your vote?

In the blue corner are the Democrats, who are seen as centre-left liberals. Broadly, they are pro-abortion, against the death penalty, cautious about the use of guns, divided over gay marriage and in favour of government playing a central role in the economy. Past Democratic presidents include Franklin D Roosevelt, Harry Truman, John F. Kennedy and Bill Clinton. Their symbol is a donkey.

In the red corner are the Republicans (also known as the GOP or 'Grand Old Party') who are regarded as centre-right conservatives. Broadly, they are anti-abortion (also referred to as pro-life), against gay marriage, in favour of the death penalty, lenient in their approach to gun ownership and in favour of big business and small, non-interventionist government. Past Republican presidents include Richard Nixon, Ronald Reagan and George Bush Sr and Jr. Their symbol is an elephant.

'As people do better, they start voting like Republicans – unless they have too much education and vote Democratic, which proves there can be too much of a good thing.'

KARL ROVE, *the strategist credited with George W. Bush's*
rise to the presidency

US Political System

How did the United States gain its independence?
During the 1760s and early 70s, tensions arose between the King
of Great Britain & Ireland, George III, and his subjects in the 13
British colonies on the east coast of America. The settlers there
were loyal to the Crown, but became angry when the King
demanded money from them to help him recover from the Seven
Years' War, which had involved all the major powers of Europe.
The strain between the King and the colonies grew and in 1775

the British invaded, sparking the American Revolution and War of Independence. It was at this time that a young planter from Virginia called Thomas Jefferson, who would go on to become the third American president, sat in a bricklayer's house in Philadelphia and drafted the Declaration of Independence, a document that announced the severance of links with Great Britain and proclaimed independence for the new United States of America. After some rejigging of the declaration by Congress, a group that represented the 13 colonies, this seminal document was completed on 4 July 1776, a date still recognised and celebrated as the country's Independence Day.

How did the Constitution come about?

Making this bold declaration of independence was all very well in theory, but there was also a need to set up governments for each state, as well as establish a central government which could act on a national level. A few months before the declaration, therefore, it was decided by Congress that each of the 13 colonies should plan how their own states would be governed, which they did by 1780. As for a central government, the first effort at a constitution was the Articles of Confederation, but problems with it led representatives from the states to meet and discuss a better solution. They came up with a framework involving three branches of national government – executive, judicial and legislative – all of which had different responsibilities to ensure that one person or group didn't hold too much power. After long periods of negotiation Congress successfully ensured that a new central government could represent states collectively on a national level, but without compromising their individuality. This framework was codified as the Constitution, which remains Supreme Law in the country to this day.

A Bill of Rights?

One of the sticking points during the long discussions over the Constitution was about the lack of a Bill of Rights – essentially laws that outline and protect basic rights. This was resolved by the first Federal Congress, which added ten amendments to the Constitution, including giving citizens the right to bear arms and protecting them 'from unreasonable search and seizure' (see **Civil Liberties**).

How does the federal government work?

The federal government is the country's national government. It is divided into three branches:

Executive Branch – the US president heads the executive branch of government as well as being head of state and commander-in-chief of the armed forces, a role which combines the responsibilities of the British monarch and the prime minister. The president must ensure that the country's laws are adhered to, which he does with the help of 15 executive departments – including the Department of Agriculture, Department of Defense and the Department of Housing and Urban Development. They are headed up by members of the cabinet, all of whom are referred to as Secretary, except the Head of the Justice Department, who is known as the Attorney-General. There are also many other agencies that fall within this area of government that carry out specific duties, such as the Office of National Drug Control Policy.

Legislative branch – the US Congress, made up of both the House of Representatives and the Senate, is responsible for making new laws and for changing current ones. The reason why there are two bodies goes back to a disagreement during the drafting of the Constitution. While some representatives from the larger states were pushing for states to be represented according to their population size, the smaller states argued against this, saying that each one must get the same number of votes. This dispute resulted in the 'Great Compromise', which satisfied both the large and small states by creating two bodies: a House of Representatives and a Senate. In the House, the number of Representatives who come from each state (currently 435) depends on the size of their population. In contrast, the Senate has an equal number of seats for each state. There are now 100 senators, two for each of the 50 states. The vice-president – currently Joe Biden – is always president of the Senate, while the leader of the House of Representatives, known as the Speaker, is elected by fellow Members of the House. The current speaker is Democrat Nancy Pelosi, the first woman ever to serve in this role. They are, respectively, second and third in line to the presidency. Congress is the only arm of government with the authority to declare war, and is also responsible for keeping tabs on the running of government through investigative committees.

How are laws made?
Passing legislation is a lengthy process. Any member of Congress can introduce a bill, which is then passed on through various subcommittees and committees who debate it. Upon agreement it is then sent to the House and the Senate, who have differing procedures for thrashing it out. Once they both have their respective versions of the bill, agreed by majority, the two versions are woven together by a conference committee. Only then is it sent to the president, who signs it – thereby making it law – or returns it to Congress. In the event that the president does veto a bill, it can still become law if at least two-thirds of both the House and the Senate vote in its favour.

Judicial branch

A Chief Justice and a varying number of Associate Justices (eight at the time of writing) make up the Supreme Court, the highest court in America. The president appoints these Justices, but they have to be confirmed by the Senate. They don't have fixed terms; instead, they serve until they die, retire or are impeached and convicted by Congress. The Constitution gave Congress the power to set up lower courts, which it has done in the form of district courts, mainly focused on federal cases, and courts of appeal, which handle appeals passed on from the district courts. After district and appeals courts, cases may end up in the Supreme Court. The lower courts must follow interpretations of the law as decided by the Supreme Court.

How are the States governed?

Like the federal government, the 50 state governments are also made up of executive, judicial and legislative arms. An elected governor runs the executive branch. (One of the most internationally recognised governors is the Austrian-born former bodybuilder and Hollywood actor, Arnold Schwarzenegger, who was elected as California's 38th Governor in 2003.) The legislative arm makes state laws as well as holding other responsibilities including signing off on the budget. Every state except Nebraska has an upper and lower house that make laws. As with the national model, appeals from state courts also end in supreme courts. Then there are the local governments, split into counties and municipalities (towns and cities), which look after such things as police departments and public transport.

Before they were president …

Between them, American presidents have had a wide variety of careers before taking on the top job. Jimmy Carter (1977–81) and George Washington (1789–97) were both farmers; Lyndon Johnson (1963–69) taught at a school in South Texas; James Garfield (1881) was a preacher and Ronald Reagan (1981–89) acted in 53 films over two decades. Barack Obama was a community organiser and a lawyer before becoming Illinois State Senator, US Senator and finally the 44th President of the United States.

World Bank/IMF

When were they established?

In July 1944, when representatives from 44 Allied countries gathered at a conference in Bretton Woods, New Hampshire, to come up with a plan for getting world economies back on their feet after World War II. The key players in the Bretton Woods talks were the economists Harry Dexter White, head of the American delegation, and John Maynard Keynes, head of the British.

White and Keynes had markedly different ideas on the best way forward; Keynes proposed a global bank called the International Clearing Union, with its own currency, the bancor, which could be exchanged with national currencies at fixed rates. This was designed to foster economic growth and maintain an equilibrium in the balance of trade between nations by placing a responsibility on countries with trade surpluses to increase imports from those with trade deficits (see **Free Trade**). White, on the other hand, proposed that rich countries should pool money into an International Stabilisation Fund, from which other countries could borrow. His system placed no limits on the amount of trade surpluses a country could accumulate through its exports, and placed the responsibility for restoring the balance of trade on countries with trade deficits. White's plans prevailed due to the greater financial clout of the US Treasury and the powerful position it would be likely to hold as the world's major creditor after the war.

The Bretton Woods talks resulted in a new global financial system and two major new institutions, the International Monetary Fund (IMF) and the International Bank for

Reconstruction and Development (IBRD). They also gave the US supremacy over this global system by granting it special veto powers in these new institutions, and by establishing the US dollar as the pre-eminent global currency. Whereas before, the value of national currencies had been dictated by their relationship to gold (the 'gold standard'), from this point on currencies were 'pegged' to the US dollar (which was backed separately by gold); this meant that most large international transactions were conducted in dollars and increased the purchasing power of the currency. The Bretton Woods monetary system collapsed in 1971, but the IMF and IBRD (by then the World Bank) survived.

What does the World Bank do?
The World Bank actually comprises two institutions, the International Bank for Reconstruction and Development (IBRD), which currently has 186 member states, and the International Development Association (IDA), which has 168. The IBRD is the principal lending arm of the World Bank, and was founded in 1945 to fund economic reconstruction in the post-war years; it now lends money to developing countries at favourable rates. The IDA was founded in 1960 in order to provide no-interest financial loans, grants and technical expertise to some of the world's poorest countries. In 2008, $23.6 billion was channelled into around 280 World Bank projects, which ranged from promoting HIV/AIDS awareness to improving the delivery of healthcare to funding social development, sanitation, and poverty reduction schemes.

What does the IMF do?
The IMF is what resulted from Harry Dexter White's idea for an International Stabilisation Fund. Founded in 1944, it monitors

the macroeconomic policies of its member states and examines how they affect exchange rates and the global financial system in general. The IMF provides advice to governments experiencing economic turbulence, issues loans, technical assistance and training, and instructs debtor countries on how to manage their loans. There are 186 member countries in the IMF, the newest of which is the Republic of Kosovo, which joined on 29 June 2009.

What do the critics say?

The World Bank and IMF faced criticism in the past for supporting military dictatorships that welcomed American or European corporations, such as Indonesia (1967–98), Brazil (1964–85) or Argentina (1976–83). More recently they have come under fire from the anti-globalisation movement and affiliated lobby groups and NGOs, who have questioned the ethics of their development projects and the various stringent conditions, known as structural adjustments, that they place on debtor countries for lending them money.

One outspoken critic is the journalist George Monbiot, who claimed in November 2008 that the IMF does more harm than good by exposing vulnerable countries to harmful foreign corporations: 'The countries the Fund instructs must place the control of inflation ahead of other economic objectives; immediately remove their barriers to trade and the flow of capital; liberalise their banking systems; reduce government spending on everything except debt repayments; and privatise the assets which can be sold to foreign investors. These happen to be the policies which best suit predatory financial speculators. They have exacerbated almost every crisis the IMF has attempted to solve.' The IMF and World Bank have also been criticised for the way they are run – the countries which contribute the most money have the most say in their decision-making processes – and for always appointing an American to be president of the World Bank.

When did the IMF get it wrong?

In 1997 Asian economies were shaken by a financial crisis that saw currencies plummet and stock markets devalue. The IMF was criticised for its handling of the crisis, which had a severe impact on Thailand, Indonesia, Malaysia, the Philippines and South Korea. One criticism was of the Fund's 'one-size-fits-all' policy of urging countries to hike up interest rates to keep a lid on inflation. Another criticism attacked the IMF's recommendation to Indonesia that it shut 16 of its 220 banks. These closures were supposed to restore confidence in the banks but all they did was cause panic as Indonesians rushed to withdraw their money, in turn prompting foreign investors to pull out. One of the IMF's fiercest critics in recent years has been Nobel-prize-winning economist Joseph Stiglitz, who in 2000 wrote about the IMF's handling of the Asian crisis: 'I was chief economist at the World Bank from 1996 until last November [1999], during the gravest global economic crisis in a half-century. I saw how the IMF, in tandem with the US Treasury Department, responded. And I was appalled.'

The Asian crisis is not the only time criticisms have been levelled against the IMF – the Fund's policies in Bolivia and Russia, for instance, have also been condemned – and over the years the IMF has accepted that in some instances its approach has been wrong. In 2004, for example, it admitted that its activities in Argentina over the previous decade had set in motion the crisis that began in 2001. The Argentinean President, Nestor Kirchner, responded: 'The IMF has to bear in mind that it is publishing this *mea culpa* 10 to 15 years after the events and that the damage it's left us with in Argentina is 15 million people or more living in poverty.'

How about the World Bank?
One of the areas in which the World Bank has attracted controversy is its loans for mining, oil and gas projects. Critics contend that these loans do little to fulfil the bank's mandate of alleviating poverty, instead creating pollution and fuelling violent conflicts over mining in, for example, Peru and the Democratic Republic of Congo (see **Congo**). Another recent criticism of the Bank concerned its handling of a project in Chad where it part-funded an oil pipeline linking the country with Cameroon. The Bank ignored warnings that the project should be postponed until corruption in the country had been addressed and it had built up its ability to run the project. In signing up, the Chadian government agreed that 72% of the oil royalties would be spent on healthcare and education. When it became clear that these conditions were not being met, the World Bank pulled out in 2008. 'The project's outcome is disastrous,' a coalition of human rights and environmental groups said at the time. 'In the name of fighting poverty, it has rather contributed to impoverishing Chad's people and adding a new member to the petro-dictators' club.' Oil reserves in Chad are only expected to last around three decades and the failure of this so-called test case is seen as a huge blow to its citizens.

Calls for a new framework
In the wake of the current global economic crisis, Prime Minister Gordon Brown, as well as other European leaders and various international organisations, have been calling for a reform of the Bretton Woods system and the institutions it established. 'It is true that at a difficult time during the Second

World War far-sighted leaders like Roosevelt and Churchill were already thinking about the framework that would be needed for the future, whilst in the heat of battle they were taking steps to forge the reconstruction and peace that was to come,' said Gordon Brown in October 2008. 'It is with the same courage and foresight of these founders that we must now reform and renew the international financial system and we should do it around the agreed principles that are shared by every country of transparency, integrity, responsibility, good housekeeping and co-operation across borders.'

'If the economic relationships between nations are not, by one means or another, brought fairly close to balance, then there is no set of financial arrangements that can rescue the world from the impoverishing results of chaos.'

GEOFFREY CROWTHER, *editor of* The Economist, *1948*

Zimbabwe

Where is it?

The Republic of Zimbabwe is a landlocked country in Southern Africa bordered by Botswana, Mozambique, South Africa and Zambia. It is home to plentiful mineral resources, rare wildlife and around 11.5 million people, whose average life expectancy is the lowest in the world (34 for women, 37 for men). The Victoria Falls, one of the natural wonders of the world, straddles the border of Zimbabwe and Zambia.

Cecil the colonialist

Cecil Rhodes – a businessman and arch-imperialist who founded the diamond company De Beers – formed the British South Africa Company (BSAC) after obtaining a Royal Charter in 1889. The charter effectively granted BSAC the authority to govern a huge swathe of Africa, and included the right to establish a police force, distribute land and make treaties. The controlled territory was named 'Rhodesia' in 1895, after the colonialist, who once said: 'We must find new lands from which we can easily obtain raw materials and at the same time exploit the cheap slave labour that is available from the natives of the colonies.' In 1898 the area south of the Zambezi River (now Zimbabwe) was officially named Southern Rhodesia while the territory north of the river was later called Northern Rhodesia (now Zambia). Southern Rhodesia became a self-governing colony in 1923.

How did Zimbabwe gain its independence?

By the early 1960s the colonial grip on Africa had weakened and many countries gained their independence. In 1965 Ian Smith, who had become prime minister of Southern Rhodesia the previous year, announced independence from Britain with the Unilateral Declaration of Independence. This received strong criticism from Britain, which was only ready to accept independence on the condition of the introduction of majority rule (where the black majority of the population had a fair share of power), which Smith refused to introduce.

During the 1970s there was a civil war with the Zimbabwe African National Union (ZANU) and the Zimbabwe African People's Union (ZAPU), led by Robert Mugabe and Joshua Nkomo respectively, conducting guerrilla war campaigns against Smith's government. In 1979 a ceasefire was declared as part of the Lancaster House Agreement, an internationally recognised agreement for an independent and democratically governed country.

Elections in 1980 saw Mugabe become prime minister of the newly created Republic of Zimbabwe. Mugabe, seen by many as a hero at the time, has dominated Zimbabwean politics for nearly three decades and driven the country into a mire of economic stagnation, corruption, violence, unemployment and disease.

Land reform

As part of the Lancaster House agreement a 'willing buyer, willing seller' idea was introduced after independence to reform the ownership of land – 70% of it at this point was owned by Zimbabwean whites who constituted less than 1% of the population. The government would buy land from willing white farmers with money provided by the British government and redistribute it to members of the poor black population. Throughout the 1980s, however, many white farmers were unwilling to sell their land, and not enough money was provided for compensation. In 1992, therefore, the government introduced a new Land Acquisition Act, which forced white farmers to sell land. Since then, many of the farms have ended up in the hands of senior government officials and businessmen instead of benefiting the landless poor. There have been reports of white farmers being beaten and even killed, and Mugabe has continued to seize land and encourage squatters to occupy farms. In spite of coming up against the Zimbabwean Supreme Court – which ruled the programme illegal in 2000 before changing their minds a year later – and international outcry, those with political muscle have benefited from the reform, while the majority it purported to help have been ignored. The programme has been blamed by many for acting as a catalyst to the economic crisis and the alarming food shortages.

A nation crippled

As well as food shortages, the people of Zimbabwe have continued to suffer further crises under the rule of Mugabe, who changed the constitution to become executive president in 1987. Zimbabwe has the world's highest inflation rate and its currency is virtually meaningless. The policy of consistently printing more and more money has been blamed for its plummeting value. One way of dealing with these extreme economic woes has been to allow rich tourists to shoot big game, which has had a devastating effect on the country's wildlife. Zimbabwe has not yet recovered from a devastating HIV/AIDS epidemic which peaked in the late 1990s, infecting a quarter of the population, and has also suffered a recent cholera outbreak: between August 2008 and March 2009 over 4,000 people died and more than 91,000 cases were reported. Mugabe and his ministers blamed the British, avoiding responsibility for the poor sanitation and lack of clean water in the country.

Information Minister Sikhanyiso Ndlovu said that the epidemic is a 'genocidal onslaught on the people of Zimbabwe by the British'.

Hope for change?

In 1999 the Movement for Democratic Change was formed and narrowly lost the elections against Mugabe's ZANU-PF in 2000. Over the next few years the party's leader, Morgan Tsvangirai, was repeatedly charged with treason, once for allegedly plotting to assassinate Mugabe, and was also badly beaten up in 2007. But in early 2008 his party won the parliamentary election and he won the first round of the presidential poll. Despite this, Mugabe clung on to power, and later that year Tsvangirai pulled out of the run-off election, saying there was no way it could be conducted under free and fair conditions. After tense negotiations a power-sharing deal was struck, with Mugabe remaining president and Tsvangirai becoming prime minister. In spite of this agreement there are concerns over Mugabe's willingness truly to relinquish any of his power, and in May 2009 Tsvangirai accused Mugabe of 'flagrant disregard to the commitments and agreements' of the power-sharing deal.

'It may be necessary to use methods other than constitutional ones.'

'We don't mind having sanctions banning us from Europe. We are not Europeans.'

'Cricket civilises people and creates good gentlemen. I want everyone to play cricket in Zimbabwe; I want ours to be a nation of gentlemen.'

ROBERT MUGABE